FORMULA ONE 2020

Written by Claire Millins

Picture Research by Cameron Prentice

Designed by Paul Galbraith and John Anderson

A Pillar Box Red Publication

© 2019. Published by Pillar Box Red Publishing Limited, in association with the Daily Mirror. Printed in the EU.

Images © PA Images.

ISBN 978-1-912456-29-1

CONTENTS

Thank You Charlie

CHARLIE WHITING (1952 – 2019)

This annual is dedicated to the memory of FIA Technical Director, Charlie Whiting, who sadly died just before the Australian Grand Prix 2019.

Danke Niki

NIKI LAUDA (1949 – 2019)

This annual is also dedicated to the memory of 3 x F1 World Champion, Niki Lauda, who we sadly lost just before the Monaco Grand Prix 2019.

FAST FACTS

F1 TRIVIA TO AMAZE YOUR FRIENDS

32 COUNTRIES HAVE HELD AN F1 RACE SINCE 1950.

ITALY HOLDS THE RECORD FOR THE MOST RACES WITH 96, WHILST MOROCCO HAS HELD ONLY ONE.

THERE HAVE BEEN

3 WORLD DRIVER CHAMPIONS WITH THE SURNAME 'HILL':

Phil (1961), Graham (1962, 1968) and his son Damon (1996).

372.6km per hour

WAS THE FASTEST OUTRIGHT SPEED RECORDED IN A GRAND PRIX RACE

by Juan Pablo Montoya (Colombia) in a McLaren-Mercedes at Monza in the Italian Grand Prix on 4 September 2005. Montoya started the race in pole position, and led from start to finish to win.

JUAN MANUEL FANGIO WAS 46

when he won his fifth and final World Drivers' Championship, making him the oldest champion to date.

BRITISH DRIVER, JOHNNY HERBERT ENTERED

16 RACES WITHOUT GETTING A POLE POSITION.

1600 LIGHTING PROJECTORS

ARE FITTED ALONG THE MARINA BAY CIRCUIT FOR THE F1 NIGHT RACE IN SINGAPORE.

Each projector consists of internal reflectors that project the light beams at different angles to prevent it from blinding the drivers. As a result, the track is four times more brightly lit than a stadium.

WOMEN DRIVERS HAVE ENTERED A FORMULA ONE GRAND PRIX SINCE 1950, COMPARED TO 822 MEN.

The most successful was Lella Lombardi, an Italian racing driver who raced between 1974 and 1976. She entered 17 races, started 12, finished seven and scored 0.5 points at the 1975 Spanish Grand Prix where she finished in sixth place.

1.88 SECONDS

IS THE **FASTEST PIT STOP** EVER RECORDED

It was achieved by Red Bull Racing at the 2019 German Grand Prix.

THE BASIC ENTRY FEE THAT EACH FORMULA ONE TEAM HAD TO PAY TO ENTER THE CHAMPIONSHIP IN 2019 IS

$546,133 (£422,736)

On top of this they each paid an extra amount depending on where they finished in 2018. As constructor champions Mercedes had to pay $6,553 (£5,072) per point scored, whilst the others teams paid $5,459 (£4,225) per point.

-4.98g

is the amount of G-force that acts on an F1 driver during maximum deceleration at turn seven of the Marina Bay Street Circuit, Singapore.

*ALL CORRECT AS OF 31 JULY 2019.

Flag Spotting Guide

ALL FORMS OF MOTORSPORT USE FLAGS FOR THE RACE OFFICIALS TO COMMUNICATE DIRECTLY WITH THE DRIVERS.

In Formula One, although some flags have been replaced by signal lights their meaning remains the same and learning their meaning is the first thing any driver has to do.

Chequered Flag

The chequered flag is waved at the end of every session and the race.

Yellow Flag

Yellow flags mean danger ahead and all drivers must slow down. A single yellow flag indicates danger ahead such as crash debris. Overtaking is not allowed unless a driver is being lapped, or the driver you overtake is retiring. Double waved yellows mean great danger and drivers should be prepared to stop. Again no overtaking is allowed unless a driver is being lapped. Yellow flags PLUS a large white board with the letters 'SC' on mean the safety car has been deployed. Drivers are not allowed to overtake and should be prepared to leave the 'racing line' or stop as a hazard is blocking some, or all, of the track.

Red Flag

A red flag means the session has been stopped. This could be due to weather conditions being dangerous for racing to be safe, or an accident where the car, or pieces of the car, are lying in a dangerous position. All flags around the circuit will show red flags and drivers have to proceed to the pit lane and stop. If the safety car has been deployed, drivers should follow it to the pit lane and wait there until the race director indicates whether the session or race will be resumed or abandoned.

Blue Flag

Blue flags indicate to drivers that faster cars are approaching from behind. During the race, blue flags are warnings that drivers are about to be lapped by a faster car and they must move aside and not intentionally block the faster car's progress. If the lapped driver ignores three successive blue flags they may incur a penalty.

Green Flag

Green means go and green flags mean the track is now clear and drivers can proceed at racing speed and overtake.

White Flag

A white flag warns of a slow-moving vehicle on track. This could be the safety car, a tow truck or a retiring car. It instructs drivers to slow down.

Black Flag

A black flag is waved when a driver has been disqualified. The driver must return to the pits immediately and report to the clerk of the course.

Black & White Flag

This black and white flag is shown if a driver's behaviour has been deemed unsporting. A sign with the driver's number will always accompany this flag.

Black Flag with Orange Circle

When this flag is shown, along with the driver's number, it indicates the car is damaged and/or has a mechanical fault. The driver in question must return to the pits immediately.

Red & Yellow Striped Flag

Slippery when wet. This flag warns drivers that the track surface ahead is slippery due to oil, water or loose debris.

SPOT THE DIFFERENCE

Can you spot the six differences in the pitstops?

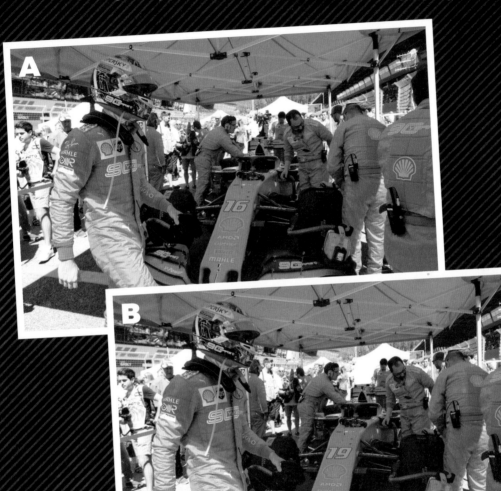

ANAGRAMS

I'M A SHOW LENTIL	BARB JAM HACK	SH MUCH ACHE CLAIMER
A UFO IN A JUNGLE MAN	SET JAW RACEKIT	ANNE'S NOTARY
A LOANS TRIP	UNDIAL KIA	
EVIE'S BATTLE TANS	QUILT NOSE PEN	

ANSWERS ON PAGE 60.

GOOD MORNING
VIETNAM

★ ★ ★ ★ ★ ★ ★ ★ ★ ★ ★ ★ ★ ★ ★

JOINING CHINA, JAPAN AND SINGAPORE, IN 2020 FORMULA ONE WILL VISIT THE STREETS OF THE VIETNAMESE CAPITAL, HANOI, FOR THE FIRST TIME.

But how will the new stop on the F1 calendar fare? Alongside what is known about the new circuit and the city, we take a look at some of the other Asian circuits that didn't fare so well.

★ HISTORY

Former F1 Chief Executive, Bernie Ecclestone first explored the idea of a race in Vietnam. However these plans were abandoned due partly to the failures of the Korean and Indian Grands Prix and partly because there were already four races in Asia: China, Japan, Singapore and Malaysia.

Following Liberty Media's buyout of the Formula One Group in January 2017, the idea of a grand prix in Vietnam was revisited.

Following negotiations, the Vietnamese Grand Prix was announced in November 2018 and is scheduled to take place in April 2020 as part of a multi-year contract.

★ THE TRACK

The Vietnamese Grand Prix will be held on a temporary street circuit around the streets of Hanoi, the capital of Vietnam.

The Hanoi Street Circuit joins the exclusive club of street circuits which includes Monaco, Singapore and Azerbaijan.

Hermann Tilke, in collaboration with the City of Hanoi authorities, has been in charge of designing the anti-clockwise, 5.5km, semi-permanent circuit in the vicinity of the My Dinh National Stadium on the western side of Hanoi.

A permanent pit and paddock area will be constructed before the first race in 2020 and the circuit will initially feature a hybrid of public roads and a purpose-built section which will later be opened to the public.

★ TRACK DESIGN

The Hanoi Street Circuit will be 5.565km long with 22 turns.

Tilke has taken inspiration from other F1 circuits such as Monaco, Malaysia, Japan and the Nurburgring and the new circuit incorporates long straights, slow-speed turns and flowing sections.

So what can the drivers expect from the new circuit:

• There is a long 1.5km straight where drivers will be able to reach speeds of up to 335kph

• Turns 1 and 2 take inspiration from the Nurburgring (which was last on the F1 calendar in 2013)

• Turns 12-15 have been designed with Monaco's first section as a guide

• Turns 16-19 imitate the 'Esses' at Suzuka

• The final few corners take inspiration from Sepang (last on the F1 calendar in 2017)

HERMANN TILKE

Hermann Tilke is one of four designers recognised by the FIA but has predominantly been the only one to be commissioned to design Formula One tracks.

Tilke was instrumental in overhauling Hockenheimring (Germany), Circuit de Catalunya (Spain), Nürburgring (Germany) and the Fuji Speedway (Japan).

Tilke has designed the following circuits from scratch:

• **Sepang International Circuit** (Malaysia)
• **Bahrain International Circuit**
• **Shanghai International Circuit** (China)
• **Istanbul Park Racing Circuit** (Turkey)
• **Valencia Street Circuit** (Spain)
• **Marina Bay Street Circuit** (Singapore)
• **Yas Marina Circuit** (Abu Dhabi)
• **Korea International Circuit**
• **Buddh International Circuit** (India)
• **Circuit of the Americas** (USA)
• **Sochi Autodrom** (Russia)

★★★★★★★★★★

MALAYSIA

Hosted F1 between 1999 and 2017.

LENGTH: 5.543km (3.445 miles)

TURNS: 15

LAP RECORD:
1:34.080 (Sebastian Vettel, Ferrari, 2017)

DRIVER WITH MOST WINS:
Sebastian Vettel (2010, 2011, 2013, 2015)

CONSTRUCTOR WITH MOST WINS:
Ferrari (1999, 2000, 2001, 2004, 2008, 2012, 2015)

MOST (IN)FAMOUS MOMENT:
Remember 'multi 21'? It was at the 2013 Malaysian Grand Prix that team orders fell on deaf ears when Vettel ignored them to pass his Red Bull team-mate, Mark Webber.

INDIA

Hosted F1 between 2011 and 2013.

LENGTH: 5.125km (3.185 miles)

TURNS: 16

LAP RECORD:
1:27.249 (Sebastian Vettel, Red Bull Racing, 2011)

DRIVER WITH MOST WINS:
Sebastian Vettel (2011, 2012, 2013)

CONSTRUCTOR WITH MOST WINS:
Red Bull-Renault (2011, 2012, 2013)

MOST FAMOUS MOMENT:
Sebastian Vettel won the 2013 Indian Grand Prix and that victory sealed his championship for the fourth time, becoming only the fourth driver to achieve that, after Michael Schumacher, Juan Manuel Fangio and Alain Prost.

TURKEY

Hosted F1 between 2005 and 2011.

LENGTH: 5.338km (3.317 miles)

TURNS: 14

LAP RECORD:
1:24.770 (Juan Pablo Montoya, McLaren Mercedes, 2005)

DRIVER WITH MOST WINS:
Felipe Massa (2006, 2007, 2008)

CONSTRUCTOR WITH MOST WINS:
Ferrari (2006, 2007, 2008)

MOST (IN)FAMOUS MOMENT: 2006 podium controversy when winner Felipe Massa received the trophy from Mehmet Ali Talat, who was referred to as the "President of the Turkish Republic of Northern Cyprus". This breakaway area of the island of Cyprus is only recognised by Turkey. The government of the Republic of Cyprus filed an official complaint with the FIA. After investigating the incident, the FIA fined the organizers of the Grand Prix $5 million.

KOREA

Hosted F1 between 2010 and 2013.

LENGTH: 5.615km (3.489 miles)

TURNS: 18

LAP RECORD:
1:39.605 (Sebastian Vettel, Red Bull Racing, 2011)

DRIVER WITH MOST WINS:
Sebastian Vettel (2011, 2012, 2013)

CONSTRUCTOR WITH MOST WINS:
Red Bull-Renault (2011, 2012, 2013)

MOST FAMOUS MOMENT:
2012 when everyone was 'Gangnam Style' crazy.

AERODYNAMICS

Aerodynamics is the study of the properties of moving air and the interaction between the air and solid bodies moving through it. The main focus for aerodynamics in F1 is how the air flows over, around and through the car therefore producing downforce and controlling drag.

APEX

The **apex** is where the racing line meets the centre of the turn. In general, by 'hitting the apex', drivers can take the straightest line through that corner, whilst at the same time driving at the fastest possible speed through it. However, if the corner is part of a complex sequence, such as turns 1 and 2 in China, hitting the apex isn't the best approach. Another exception is double apex corners which tend to be very long turns and the racing line takes cars in-out-in to maintain maximum speed, a good example of a double apex corner is 'Pouhon'.

APPEAL

An **appeal** is when a team appeals against the steward's decision following a penalty, if they feel that the driver has been penalised unfairly.

BACKMARKER

A **backmarker** is a term used to describe a driver usually towards the back of the field that is encountered by the race leaders. Backmarkers have to move out of the way of race leaders not race them, and are made aware that they are going to be lapped by the waving of blue flags.

BLISTERING

When the tyre, or part of the tyre on an F1 car overheats it will start to **blister**. This extra heat causes the tyre rubber to soften and break away in chunks. Blistering can be caused by selecting the wrong tyre compound, an improperly set up car or too high tyre pressure.

BRAKING POINT

As the name suggests this is the point which F1 drivers start **braking** as they approach a corner. The braking point is usually found between 50m and 150m from the corner itself depending on the corner type.

CHICANE

A **chicane** is a sequence of corners, usually located after a long straight bit of track to slow cars down. They are, generally, one of the best spots for overtaking. There are two common types of chicane: S-type and bus-stop.

CLEAN AIR

Clean air is air that isn't turbulent, that is, air that is undisturbed by other cars on the track. When drivers are on an empty track or have no cars around them they're racing in clean air. Clean air offers the best aerodynamic conditions for an F1 car.

DEBRIEF

The **debrief** is a team meeting which happens after an on-track session, usually between a team's drivers and engineers. In the debrief they discuss car set-up, performance and strategy. The 'after-race' debrief meetings usually involve more people from various departments and discussions centre around what went right, what went wrong, what lessons can be learned, where improvements can be made and what is coming up next.

DRIVE THROUGH PENALTY

This is an in-race penalty against a driver or team, handed out by the stewards whilst the race is still running. It must be taken before the chequered flag. To serve this penalty, the driver must leave the track and drive through the pit lane at the reduced pit lane speed before re-joining the track.

FIA

The Federation Internationale De L'Automobile (**FIA**) is the governing body for world motorsport and the federation of the world's leading motoring organisations including Formula One. It is a non-profit organisation, founded in 1904 and has its headquarters in Paris.

FLAT SPOT

If a driver locks his brakes, causing the tyre to be dragged along the track without spinning, a **flat spot** can form. The flat spot itself will normally be no larger than the size of a small coin, but can ruin the car's handling, cause huge vibrations and may force the driver to pit for another set of tyres.

FORMATION LAP

The **formation lap** is when the cars complete one full lap of the track from their grid spot. Following the formation lap, the light sequence starts only when all cars are back on their grid. A marshal walks across the back of the grid waving a green flag signalling to the 'person who presses the button' that all is safe to proceed. The formation lap also allows all the team personnel to get themselves and their kit from the starting grid back to the pit lane.

G-FORCE

G-force is a physical force equivalent to one unit of gravity that is multiplied during rapid changes of direction or velocity. Every day humans experience G-force stronger than 1 g, for example a cough can produce a momentary g-force of 3.5 g and a sneeze, 2 g. F1 drivers, however, experience severe G-forces every time they corner, accelerate or brake.

In 1977, F1 driver David Purley survived an estimated 179.8 g when he decelerated from 108mph (173 km/h) to 0mph in a distance of 26 inches (66cm) after his throttle got stuck wide open and he hit a wall during practice for that year's British Grand Prix at Silverstone.

GRAINING

Graining typically occurs when the car slides causing little bits of rubber to break off and then immediately stick back onto the tyre's hot surface. This very slightly separates the tyre from the track surface creating an uneven, irregular surface to drive on. This makes braking and cornering difficult and reduces grip and traction. It is often a short-term problem and with careful driving can go away as the tyre wears and becomes uniform again.

GRAVEL TRAP

A **gravel trap** is one-type of run-off area situated on the outside of a corner. They were designed to reduce the speed of a car which leaves the track and bringing it safely to a halt.

HALO

The **halo** is a driver crash protection system which was made mandatory in 2018 and it looks like the top of a flip flop. The halo system consists of a bracket that surrounds the driver's head and is connected at three points to the car's frame. The frame is made of titanium and the frame and mountings can weigh up to 15kg. The halo is capable of holding the weight of a London double decker bus, that's the equivalent of 12 tonnes balancing on a 9kg metal frame!

INSTALLATION LAP

An **installation lap** is just one lap at medium speed and the cars return to the pit lane at the end. This lap is done early in the free practice (or testing sessions) so the teams and drivers can check that the key parameters of the car are working properly: engine, throttle and brake performance.

>> THE A-Z >> OF F1 >>

LOCK UP

If an F1 car **locks up** it generally means the driver has braked sharply (applied too much force) and one or more tyres has locked, that is stopped turning, whilst the others continue to turn. Tyre smoke and flat spots are common side effects. A lock up also loses you time on that lap.

MARBLES

Marbles is the term used for the small pieces of rubber that wear off the tyre during a session on track. They build up at the side of the track, off the racing line, and are very slippery when driven on. Drivers liken it to driving on marbles, hence the name and is one of the reasons why overtaking off the racing line is difficult. If you go to a grand prix, after the race you are allowed on the track and can pick up marbles as a souvenir.

MARSHAL

A **marshal** is a course official, normally a volunteer, who has many jobs to ensure the safe running of the race. You can spot them easily as they all wear orange overalls. Marshals fulfil many roles including giving flag signals, helping to remove stranded cars/drivers from the track, clearing debris from the track, reporting the facts of an accident and observing spectators to ensure they do not endanger themselves or the competitors.

OUTBRAKE

When a driver **outbrakes** it means they have either braked too late or too softly and as a result have overrun the corner. This could also result in a lock-up. Outbraking is a common mistake made when overtaking.

OVERSTEER

When you **oversteer** into a corner, it means that the car steers more than the driver intended. As a result the car's rear end will try and overtake the front end because the rear wheels have lost grip. To correct oversteer, the driver needs to use opposite-lock to turn the front wheels into the skid.

PIT STOP

A **pit stop** during any session is when the driver brings the car into the pit lane for the mechanics to work on it. During the race, a standard pit stop will see the mechanics change the tyres. They might also adjust the angle of the front wing, clean the driver's visor and the car's rear wing. A good pit stop is one where the car is stopped for less than three seconds. The fastest recorded pit stop is 1.88 seconds. [See 'Fast Facts' on page 8]

PIT WALL

Each team has their own individual **pit wall**. It is the structure opposite the teams' garages, literally on the pit wall, that is the small wall barrier that separates the pit lane from the start-finish straight on the race track. It is where the team principals, managers and engineers spend the race. Effectively it is the team's own 'Mission Control' where all tactical and strategic calls are made from.

RACING LINE

The **racing line** is the best line to take around a corner on the racetrack. Generally, the racing line starts at the braking point and will make use of the entire width of the track from that point through the turning point into the apex and out at the corner's exit. All drivers aim for the best racing line because it helps improve their lap times.

SAFETY CAR

The **safety car** is a high performance road car, in 2019 it was the Mercedes AMG GT S. The safety car is normally deployed during a race to allow marshals and officials to clear the track of debris, recover a crashed vehicle and/or attend a driver. It can also be used to keep speed safe during bad weather, whilst allowing the race to continue. When deployed, the safety car will join the track immediately and from that point no overtaking is allowed. The safety car will then allow cars to pass it until the race leader is immediately behind it. A safety car board is also displayed to drivers as they cross the start-finish line, and the information will also be relayed over radios from the pit lane.

SCRUTINEERING

This is the technical checking of cars and drivers' equipment to check they are safe and compliant with the technical regulations. During the grand prix weekend every car is first scrutinised on the Thursday (Wednesday at Monaco). A car cannot compete until it has passed this initial scrutineering. The scrutineers may subsequently check the eligibility of a car or competitor at any time during the event. If a car is damaged or has significant work done on it after the initial scrutineering, it must be re-scrutineered before it can be used on track again.

STEWARDS

At every grand prix there are four **stewards**. The stewards are changed regularly during the course of the season. Three of the stewards are appointed by the FIA, and one of these three must be an experienced former driver. The fourth steward is a national of the host nation and a member of the local FIA organisation. All stewards must each hold an FIA Super Licence. Once chosen, the stewards elect a chairman. Stewards are asked to pass judgement on issues that arise over the grand prix weekend. This can be anything from a technical infringement of the car to incidents that happen on track. The stewards look at all the evidence and cast a vote to determine their final decision regarding any penalties. And just like Strictly Come Dancing, in the event of a split in voting the chairman has the final say.

STOP-AND-GO PENALTY

This is the second **in-race penalty** against a driver or team that can be handed out by the stewards whilst the race is still running and is more severe than the drive-through penalty. And again, it must be taken before the chequered flag. To serve this penalty, the driver must leave the track, enter the pit lane and stop at his pit for 10 seconds before leaving. During this time team mechanics are forbidden to work on the car during the 10 seconds. Usually, if this penalty is applied, drivers will serve it as part of their pit stop with mechanics waiting the 10 seconds before changing the tyres.

SUPER LICENCE

The **Super Licence** is the race driving licence level that all drivers must hold to be eligible to race in F1. The Super Licence was first issued in the 1990s and required a driver to demonstrate their abilities to drive an F1 car through personal achievement or "outstanding ability in single-seater formula cars". Since 2015, however, potential Super Licence holders have been required to satisfy more stringent criteria including accumulating a minimum of 40 points, within a three-year period, across a range of other single-seater championships. A driver pays a minimum fee to obtain their licence and then pays an annual renewal fee which is based on points scored in F1 on top of a flat fee. The majority of F1 drivers pay a six-figure sum for their licence.

TYRE COMPOUNDS

The type of rubber mix used in the construction of a tyre, produce different **tyre compounds** ranging from soft through medium to hard. Each compound offers a different performance and wear characteristic. For the 2019 season teams had three different coloured tyres to choose from for races: 'soft' (red), 'medium' (yellow) and 'hard' (white). Tyre manufacturer, Pirelli had the final say of the hardness of those tyres from a selection of five. In case of rain there are also 'intermediate' (green) and 'full wets' (blue) tyre compounds available.

UNDERSTEER

Understeering is the opposite of oversteering. This is where the front end of the car doesn't want to turn into the corner and slides wide as the driver tries to turn in to the apex.

WAKE

Wake is the disturbance left behind by an object moving through a fluid. Think of the wake left behind by a boat on water. In racing, as the air passes over an F1 car's surface it produces a 'wake' of turbulent air. This is nicknamed 'dirty air'. The 'wake' can benefit the car behind (see 'slipstream') but does hamper the efficiency of the following car's own aerodynamic surface; reducing downforce, making it slower in the corners and limiting the effectiveness of the cooling system.

MURRAY WALKER
CRYPTOGRAMS

#1: DIFFICULT

ENCRYPTION TABLE

A	B	C	D	E	F	G	H	I	J	K	L	M	N	O	P	Q	R
				12	16			26									

S	T	U	V	W	X	Y	Z

ENCRYPTED SENTENCE

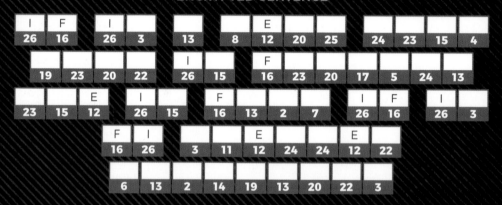

I	F		I					E								
26	16		26	3		13		8	12	20	25		24	23	15	4

					I			F					
19	23	20	22		26	15		16	23	20	17	5	24	13

		E		I			F					I	F		I	
23	15	12		26	15		16	13	2	7		26	16		26	3

F	I			E			E	
16	26		3	11	12	24	24	12	22

6	13	2	14	19	13	20	22	3

#2: EASY

ENCRYPTION TABLE

A	B	C	D	E	F	G	H	I	J	K	L	M	N	O	P	Q	R
7				12				17						10			

S	T	U	V	W	X	Y	Z
		11					

ENCRYPTED SENTENCE

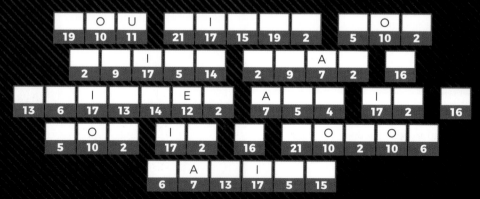

	O	U		I						O		
19	10	11		21	17	15	19	2		5	10	2

		I						A			
2	9	17	5	14		2	9	7	2		16

	I			E				A			I			
13	6	17	13	14	12	2		7	5	4		17	2		16

	O			I					O		O	
5	10	2		17	2		16		21	10	2	10	6

		A		I	
6	7	13	17	5	15

ANSWERS ON PAGE 60.

GREATEST COMEBACKS IN F1 ↩

ROBERT KUBICA

Polish driver Robert Kubica has returned to the F1 scene following a break of eight years.

Between 2006 and 2009 Kubica drove for Sauber, taking his maiden F1 victory at the 2008 Canadian Grand Prix and finishing that season in fourth place.

In 2010 he moved to Renault and was set to drive for them again in 2011.

However, just after pre-season testing in February 2011, Kubica was involved in a serious accident whilst taking part in the Ronde di Andora Rally. He was driving a Super 2000 specification Škoda Fabia, and during the first stage in Testico, his car left the road and hit a crash barrier at high speed.

He was trapped in the car for more than an hour before he was freed, then he was flown to Santa Corona Hospital in Pietra Ligure where doctors confirmed he had suffered a partial amputation of his forearm, compound fractures to his right elbow, shoulder and leg, as well as significant blood loss. The injuries sustained were mainly due to the crash barrier penetrating the car's cockpit and hitting Kubica. His co-driver was unscathed in the accident.

Kubica underwent a seven-hour operation and then two more lengthy operations a few days later to repair the fractures to his leg, shoulder and arm.

The condition of his hand was not clear and he missed the 2011 season, being replaced at Renault by his old Sauber team-mate Nick Heidfeld.

In November 2011, it was confirmed that Kubica would not be ready for the 2012 F1 season either.

As bad luck would have it, in January 2012, Kubica slipped on the ice near his home and re-broke his right leg. This put him out of competitive racing for most of 2012 as well.

In 2013, Kubica returned to motorsport, focusing on rallying, driving for Citroen in the European and World Rally-2 Championships. He continued in rallying until 2016.

In June 2017, Kubica took part in a test, organised by Renault, of their 2012 car at the Circuit de Valencia. This was his first F1 event since his accident.

In July 2017, he took part in the in-season testing, after the Hungarian Grand Prix where Renault could fully assess his capabilities and the likelihood of whether it would be possible

for him to return to F1. Kubica completed 142 laps and finished fourth fastest.

Kubica was in the running to take Felipe Massa's Williams seat for 2018, following Massa's retirement announcement. In the end, he was announced as Williams' reserve driver for the year. His F1 return put on hold... for now.

In November 2018, just before the final grand prix of the season, Williams announced that Kubica would return to full-time racing in F1, as one of their 2019 drivers.

NIKI LAUDA

The most famous comeback in F1 history belongs to Austrian driver, Niki Lauda.

If you've ever seen the movie "Rush", you'll know the story of how, despite all odds, Lauda was back behind the wheel of his Ferrari and fighting for the 1976 World Championship.

On 1 August 1976, cars lined up on the starting grid at the Nurburgring in Germany. Lauda, at the time was currently first in the drivers' standing and was concerned with the safety conditions of the track and the weather conditions. He attempted to get the other drivers to boycott the race, but following a vote he lost by one and the race went ahead.

British driver James Hunt, Niki's championship rival, took pole and Lauda himself qualified in second.

The race did start in the wet, but after the first lap it cleared up and all drivers, including Lauda, were trying to make up for the time lost on lap one.

As Lauda approach the 150mph bend halfway round the course, at Bergwerk, his Ferrari twitched left and then veered off the road before bouncing back onto the track in flames. (The impact having caused the car's fuel tanks to rupture).

Drivers Harald Ertl and Brett Lunger both hit the Ferrari. Unlike Lauda, they managed to get out of their cars. Arturo Merzario and Guy Edwards next arrived on the scene. And all four drivers stopped and started trying to save Lauda from the burning car. If it wasn't for them Lauda would surely have perished that day.

IF IT WASN'T FOR THEM LAUDA WOULD SURELY HAVE PERISHED THAT DAY.

Lauda had suffered not only severe burns to his face, but had also inhaled toxic smoke from the fumes. He was rushed by helicopter from the track to the Bundeswehr Hospital in Koblenz, then to the Trauma Clinic in Ludwigshafen, Germany's most advanced burn ward. There he literally fought for his life, his lungs were vacuumed and he was even administered the last rites.

Amazingly though, Lauda stepped back into his Ferrari just six weeks after the accident. With his burns still bandaged, Lauda had to wear a specially adapted crash helmet. Lauda only managed one lap during the Friday running, but then on the Saturday he decided to take his time and build up his speed gradually. He managed to qualify fifth, beating both his team-mates and ended up finishing fourth in the race.

Not bad for someone who had been given the last rites just six weeks earlier!

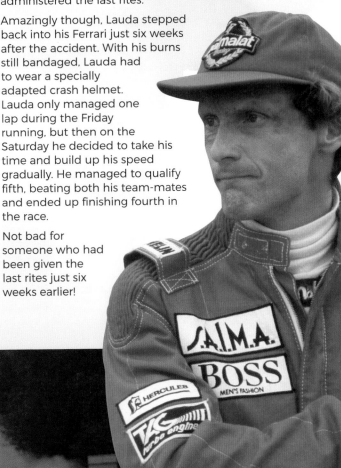

MIKA HAKKINEN

On 12 November 1995, during qualifying for the final grand prix of the season in Australia, Hakkinen suffered a tyre failure.

This sent Hakkinen and his McLaren flying into the concrete wall, at the high speed Brewery Bend between Jones and Brabham Straights, at 120mph.

Hakkinen was knocked unconscious, his head rolling like a rag doll and his face started turning blue, due to an airway blockage. The trackside medical team, which included doctors from the nearby Royal Adelaide Hospital, saved Hakkinen's life by performing an emergency tracheotomy at the trackside, before he was transported to hospital.

He suffered a skull fracture, damage to his inner ear and minor brain injuries and remained in a critical condition for two months.

Just three months later, in February 1996, Hakkinen felt strong enough to drive

again. McLaren arranged a private test of the 1996 car at Paul Ricard Circuit and, only 87 days after his accident, Hakkinen managed 63 laps of the circuit. His fastest lap was over half a second quicker than that of Michael Schumacher, who had tested in his new Ferrari the previous day!

Hakkinen was declared fit for the 1996 season and finished fifth in the season opener in Melbourne.

FELIPE MASSA

A freak accident in the last seconds of the second qualifying session for the Hungarian Grand Prix 2009 happened to Brazilian driver Felipe Massa.

As he was travelling at 162 mph, debris hit his helmet just above his left eye.

The impact of the debris knocked Massa unconscious and his car continued travelling towards the grass verge and tyre wall, which it hit at 62 mph. The engine was still revving which indicated Massa still had his foot on the accelerator and was unconscious. On-board video footage, released afterwards showed that Massa did indeed have his feet on both the accelerator and brake pedals.

MASSA SUFFERED A FRACTURED SKULL AND, AFTER EMERGENCY SURGERY, HE WAS PLACED IN A COMA.

The debris turned out to be a spring off the car in front of Massa, the Brawn of Ruebens Barichello, which had come loose from the rear suspension.

Massa suffered a

fractured skull and, after emergency surgery, in the area around his left eye, he was placed in a coma. His condition was initially life-threatening, however he improved rapidly. A week later he was flown back home to Brazil where a steel plate was inserted into his skull.

HIS CONDITION WAS INITIALLY LIFE-THREATENING, HOWEVER HE IMPROVED RAPIDLY

Following a lengthy spell of rehabilitation, Massa successfully completed a series of neurological examinations, co-ordinated by the FIA's medical delegate. On 12 October 2009, Ferrari announced that they had arranged for Massa to test a 2007 Ferrari on GP2 tyres at Ferrari's private racetrack, Fiorano to continue his re-acclimatisation to racing.

Massa started the 2010 season by qualifying and finishing in second place at the Bahrain Grand Prix.

JOHNNY HERBERT

Johnny Herbert almost had his F1 career finished before it had even begun.

In the mid-1980s, after significant success in junior championships, winning the 1985 British Formula Ford Festival and 1987 British Formula Three title, he was regarded as the 'next big thing' in F1, and was on the radar of Ferrari, Williams and Benetton.

But in 1988 he suffered a horrendous crash during the Formula 3000 race at Brands Hatch.

Following a collision with his rival Gregor Foitek, Herbert's car crashed into a concrete bridge

support before ricocheting back across the track and ending up in the Armco barriers.

The front of Herbert's car had been ripped off upon impact with the concrete bridge support, leaving his legs to take the impact of the Armco barrier.

Both of his feet and ankles were shattered and although he avoided amputation, he was told he would never walk again.

That did not stop Herbert though. Following many operations and months of painful rehabilitation, Herbert got to the point where he could drive.

In 1989 he was signed to drive for Benetton, and just seven months after his accident he drove in his first F1 grand prix, finishing fourth. This was despite him still being on crutches, in incredible pain and having to be lifted into the car.

His form dropped off over the course of the year and he was eventually replaced.

From 1990 to 2000 Herbert raced successfully in F1, making 161 starts and collecting three wins and seven podiums.

He also won the Le Mans 24 Hours, driving as part of the Mazda team in 1991.

THE BIG

PUT YOUR F1 KNOWLEDGE TO

Fifty questions from 1950 to 2019. Award yourself one point for a correct answer – some do carry bonus points.

01 The 1000th Grand Prix took place in 2019, but which race was it?

02 What year did the first Grand Prix take place?

03 And where was the first race held?

04 Who was the youngest driver on the F1 grid in 2019?

05 Who was the oldest driver on the F1 grid in 2019?

06 How many rookies were there in the 2019 season?

07 Who won the Australian GP 2019?

08 When asked by Mark Webber what he had for breakfast, what was his reply?

09 What was it that caused damage to George Russell's car during first practice at the Azerbaijan GP in 2019, causing the session to be cancelled?

10 Who were the Toro Rosso drivers at the start of the 2019 season? [2pts]

11 Who won the 2018 F1 Driver's Championship?

F1 QUIZ

THE TEST IN OUR FIENDISH QUIZ

12 Which race did he win it at?

13 Who crashed under the safety car at the Azerbaijan GP in 2018?

14 Who did he try and blame?

15 What, now famous, radio message did Valtteri Bottas receive during the German GP in 2018?

16 Fernando Alonso out-qualified his McLaren teammate, Stoffel Vandoorne, at every Grand Prix in 2018, but what year was the last time that happened?

17 Who were those teammates?

18 Of the 20 drivers competing in 2018, how many of them scored points?

19 In which 2018 race did Mercedes have their only double DNF?

20 How many points are awarded to the race winner at each Grand Prix?

21 What year did Jenson Button win the F1 World Championship?

22 Which current F1 team, formed in 2007, is based at Silverstone?

23 Who did Lewis Hamilton pass to win the 2008 F1 World Championship?

24 Who were the Scuderia Ferrari drivers for the 2004 season? [2pts]

25 In 1997, which team didn't make it past the first race due to financial difficulties?

THE BIG F1 QUIZ

26 Who were the three drivers who drove for Ligier in 1995? [3pts]

27 Who secured Ferrari's only win in 1994 at the German Grand Prix?

28 In 1992, which future World Champion made his debut for the Brabham-Judd team?

29 Which Brit won the British Grand Prix in 1995?

30 Who was the 1998 F1 World Champion?

31 How many US circuits were used during the 1980s?

32 Can you name them? [6pts]

33 In 1982, who became the first F1 World Champion to win the title with only one race win since John Surtees in 1964?

34 1986 Lotus driver, Johnny Dumfries was a painter and decorator, but he also had a royal occupation. What was it?

35 Who was his teammate?

36 Who did Nelson Piquet fight with at the 1982 German Grand Prix for crashing into him?

37 How many races did Swedish driver, Ronnie Peterson win from 1970 to 1979?

38 James Hunt celebrated his first win at the 1975 Dutch Grand Prix. What team was he driving for?

THE BIG F1 QUIZ

39 Which engine manufacturer returned to F1 in 1976 with Brabham?

40 Who secured Williams F1's first ever Grand Prix win at the British Grand Prix?

41 John Surtees left Ferrari halfway through 1966 to join which team?

42 Which famous race disappeared from the F1 calendar after 1960?

43 Who won the Argentinian Grand Prix in 1960?

44 Which three top drivers created their own teams during the 1960s? [3pts]

45 The Pedralbes circuit, hosted two Grand Prix in 1951 and 1954, but which Spanish city is it near?

46 In 1958 the Cooper and Lotus teams did not use their own engines. Which British engine did they use?

47 In 1956 which British driver sacrificed his chance to win the World Championship so that Fangio could win his fourth?

48 Where was the 1955 British Grand Prix held?

49 What team dominated the very first F1 season in 1950?

50 Who was the very first F1 World Champion?

TOTAL AVAILABLE POINTS: 61

29

MONACO

Baby!

MONACO! IT'S THE ONE GRAND PRIX MOST PEOPLE KNOW ABOUT AND POSSIBLY THE ONE THAT EVERYONE WOULD LOVE TO GO TO.

It's a street circuit based around the narrow streets in the Principality, so how has the track evolved over the years and just what does go in to setting up the most famous race on the F1 calendar?

BACKGROUND

The **F1 Monaco Grand Prix** is widely regarded as one of the most prestigious motorsport events in the world, with a reputation as illustrious as that of the **Indianapolis 500**, **Le Mans 24 Hours** and **Rallye Monte-Carlo**, affectionately nicknamed 'the Monte'.

Since its creation back in 1929, drivers and teams alike have always relished the challenge of competing around such a narrow circuit through the undulating streets of the glamorous Principality, with countless changes of elevation, tight corners and the famous tunnel. It is beyond doubt one of the most demanding and punishing circuits on the **Formula 1 World Championship** calendar – and the grand prix that drivers and teams want to conquer more than any other!

The race weekend schedule is atypical in that the first two free practice sessions take place on the Thursday, with the circuit open to the public on the Friday afternoon and each evening. The **Monaco Grand Prix** attracts some 200,000 spectators over the course of the weekend, and is considered by fans to be one of the unmissable events on the Formula 1 sporting calendar.

Maintaining, developing and improving all of these events requires on-going and unrelenting hard work.

This means that, having already undergone substantial modifications such as the new pits area and the **Chicane du Port**, the circuit continues to be regularly evaluated with a view to enhancing its safety and the sustainability of the race

CIRCUIT HISTORY AND DEVELOPMENT

Since its creation in 1929 the circuit itself remained unchanged until 1952 when modifications were made to the **Sainte Devote bend**.

In 1973, the circuit was extended by a further 135m with a new track along the port. This section of track joined the track at the **Swimming Pool** and ended at **La Rascasse**.

As the length of each lap increased, the grand prix was shortened to 78 laps, which is still the same today.

In 1976 two more chicanes were added: **Sainte Devote** and **La Rascasse**.

In 1986 a further chicane was added at the foot of the **Boulevard Louis II** descent (just after the tunnel exit) due to the road, **Quai des Etats Uni** being widened.

In 1997, the first 'S' at the **Swimming Pool** was redrawn and the corner renamed **Virage Louis Chiron** in honour of the 1931 grand prix winner and long-time clerk of the course.

Between 2000 and 2003, some 5,000 square metres of land was reclaimed from the sea on the southern side of the harbour, to create a platform along with a 150m long quayside wall on the old front.

After an incident-filled 2011 **Monaco Grand Prix**, **Automobile Club de Monaco** directors met with

NEW PLATFORM

Quayside wall was made by stacking 400 concrete blocks each weighing approximately 10 tonnes.

It serves as retaining wall for 5,000m² platform.

25,000m³ of calibrated backfill was used for reclaiming the land.

3km of trenches laid within the platform to supply the area with drinking water, electricity, telephone, television and sewage.

The circuit between the second part of the swimming pool section and La Rascasse was completely redesigned and moved 10 metres towards the waterfront.

There are 36 concrete supports on the platform for assembling the metal scaffolding for the spectator boxes.

2011 CHANGES

Pit lane exit widened to 20m.

Road surface from tunnel to the Nouvelle Chicane was planed by up to 20cm which removed a bump and corrected some banking.

Impact point of the Nouvelle Chicane was pushed back by 14.6m.

Tracks surface at the exit of the Nouvelle Chicane and Mirabeau escape lanes replaced with an abrasive braking surface.

Pit lane protection completely refurbished. Metal safety gratings replaced windows.

Tyre barriers at Sainte Devote and Swimming Pool S-Bend replaced with TecPro barriers.

Charlie Whiting, F1 World Championship Race Director and Safety Delegate to discuss and implement changes to the track to optimise safety.

In 2013 **TecPro** barriers also replaced tyre barriers in and on the **Mirabeau Superior** bend escape lane.

In 2014 a new pit wall was built, consisting of 90 steel blocks filled with concrete, each weighing 2.7 tonnes. A gateway was also created along the pit wall, in the middle of the pit lane to allow persons working on the starting grid to get back to the pits safely.

Small changes were made to the **Tabac corner** for 2015, where the track was moved 2.5m closer to the harbour, forcing a slightly earlier turn in. The realignment continues up to the **Swimming Pool** complex which slightly changes the entry apex. The changes happened following the 2013 crash between **Pastor Maldonado** and **Max Chilton**, where a section of TecPro barrier was dislodged, blocking the track and forcing the race to be stopped.

Following the introduction of a new race control building, 2016, and the **Royal Box**, 2017, new high-tech pits were installed in 2018. This was to maintain a coherent style and harmony which fitted with the whole location.

HOW IS THE CIRCUIT SET UP FOR THE GRAND PRIX?

The circuit itself is part of the public roads around the **Principality**, so are in constant use. And, unlike other street circuits such as **Singapore** the track is opened back up to the public every evening during the race weekend.

It's the stands and pit lanes that require assembling and dismantling each year.

The fundamental requirements of a temporary street circuit is it has to have the ability to be built and pulled down quickly.

Monaco is set up in seven weeks and pulled down in three!

HIGH-TECH PITS

Available space increased by a third due to the introduction of a second floor.

All 12 pits can be constructed in two weeks.

Each pit has a total floor space of 450m2, comprising three floors of 150m2 each:

Ground floor – **mechanical equipment.**

1st floor – **IT infrastructure, track monitors, meeting rooms, engineers' offices.**

2nd floor – **drivers' rest rooms, hospitality for sponsors and VIP guests.**

Front of the building, pit lane side, are two sloping columns of mirrored glass.

CROSSWORD

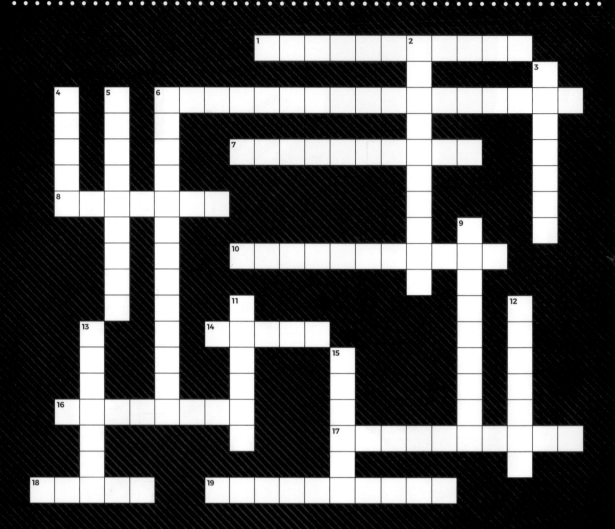

ACROSS

1. New team name of Force India (6,5)
6. German seven-time Championship winner (7,10)
7. Haas F1 'energy drink' sponsor for 2019 (4,6)
8. Nationality of Alfa Romeo's Antonio Giovanazzi (7)
10. Which rookie is the youngest driver on the 2019 grid (5,6)
14. Home to the Italian Grand Prix (5)
16. Team known as the 'Silver Arrows' (8)
17. Venue of the Australian Grand Prix (6,4)
18. Which 2019 grand prix was the 1000th F1 race (5)
19. Max, Red Bull Racing - Honda driver (10)

DOWN

2. Circuit where the French Grand Prix is held (4,6)
3. Oldest racing team on the grid (7)
4. City that will host the 2020 Vietnam Grand Prix (5)
5. First name of Toro Rosso driver, Albon (9)
6. TV pundit famed for his 'grid walk' (6,7)
9. ...and away we go! What David Croft says at the start of every race (6,3)
11. Nationality of Williams' driver Robert Kubica (6)
12. Nationality of Sergio Perez (7)
13. 2019 tyre manufacturer (7)
15. Which 2019 grand prix did Vettel receive an 'infamous' penalty (6)

WORDSEARCH
····· F1 CAR COMPONENTS ·······

Find the words in the grid. Words can go horizontally, vertically and diagonally in all eight directions.

T	E	B	M	A	D	G	S	A	B	R	D	R	T	D	N
A	K	T	U	R	B	O	C	H	A	R	G	E	R	B	M
P	A	M	S	R	E	K	K	T	A	L	P	S	C	D	O
A	T	S	U	T	V	I	U	O	E	R	S	J	G	O	A
D	O	W	H	E	E	L	B	A	S	E	G	E	A	P	E
D	A	Q	C	Z	N	E	Y	J	O	I	G	T	V	B	R
L	I	M	O	I	G	A	R	S	I	D	E	P	O	D	O
E	R	A	S	R	I	B	P	R	O	K	A	C	E	L	T
S	B	J	A	K	N	L	E	F	H	B	R	N	N	I	S
X	O	B	R	H	E	S	E	K	A	R	B	E	D	T	Y
J	X	U	S	T	U	E	A	N	L	A	O	M	P	Y	G
A	E	R	C	F	G	B	N	T	O	P	X	U	L	G	R
V	A	Y	F	I	R	C	X	Y	L	L	H	O	A	T	E
E	A	I	A	G	B	N	P	R	O	A	U	T	T	O	N
G	D	O	Y	A	R	T	R	E	D	N	U	I	E	M	E
B	N	C	H	A	S	S	I	S	I	S	O	K	T	E	V	I	P

AIRBOX
BARGEBOARD
BRAKES
CHASSIS
DIFFUSER
DRS
ENDPLATE

ENERGY STORE
ENGINE
GEARBOX
HALO
KERS
PADDLES
PLANK

SIDEPOD
TURBO CHARGER
TYRES
UNDERTRAY
WHEELBASE

ANSWERS ON PAGE 60.

HISTORY

1950

13 May
1st F1 championship race,
British Grand Prix,
Silverstone

1953

18 January
1st F1 race in South America,
Buenos Aires, Argentina

1958

Championship for
Constructors introduced

1985

3 November
1st GP in Oceania
– Australian Grand Prix,
Adelaide street circuit

1984

19 August
400th grand Prix
– Austrian Grand Prix,
Spielberg

1978

Medical car
introduced

1990

4 November
500th grand prix
– Australian Grand Prix,
Adelaide street circuit

1993

Safety car officially
introduced

1994

1 May
Ayrton Senna and Roland
Ratzenburger die in separate
incidents at San Marino
Grand Prix

2019

14 April
1000th grand prix
– Chinese Grand Prix,
Shanghai International
Circuit

OF F1

1958
19 October
1st F1 race in Africa,
Casablanca, Morocco

1961
6 August
100th grand prix - German
Grand Prix, Nurburgring
Nordschleife

1967
6 August
First grand prix to be
televised in colour
– German Grand Prix,
Nurburgring Nordschliefe

1978
4 March
300th grand prix
– South African Grand Prix,
Kyalami

1973
23 September
Safety car introduced,
yellow Porsche 914
– Canadian Grand Prix

1971
23 May
200th grand prix
– Monaco Grand Prix

1997
13 April
600th grand prix
– Argentine Grand Prix,
Buenos Aires

2003
6 April
700th grand prix
– Brazilian Grand Prix,
Interlagos

2004
Michael
Schumacher
wins his 7th
World Drivers'
Championship
(his 5th in a row)

2014
6 April
900th grand prix
– Bahrain Grand Prix, Bahrain

2008
28 September
800th grand prix
– Singapore Grand Prix,

2008
29 July
Formula One Teams
Association (FOTA) formed

F1
At
1000

THE 2019 CHINESE GRAND PRIX WAS THE 1000TH FORMULA ONE (F1) RACE SINCE THE WORLD CHAMPIONSHIP'S INCEPTION IN 1950.
So when and where have all the other 'milestone' races taken place?

The very first F1 race was the British Grand Prix, held at Silverstone on 13 May 1950. It was to be the first of seven in that opening season of the World Championship.

Giuseppe Farina, one of four Alfa Romeo drivers, was fastest in qualifying.

22 cars took their place on the starting grid.

Farina and the three other Alfa Romeo drivers, Fagioli, Fangio and Parnell, made up the front row.

The second row consisted of Prince Bira of Siam (also known as B. Bira) in a Maserati and the two factory Talbot-Lago cars driven by French drivers Giraud-Cabantou and Martin.

In accordance with the standard at the time, the rest of the grid consisted of rows of four and three alternating, up to the sixth row.

The three Alfa Romeo cars of Farina, Fagioli and Parnell came first, second and third respectively.

Future five-time world champion Fangio retired on lap 62 with an oil leak.

RACE 200

The 1971 Monaco Grand Prix was the setting for the 200th F1 race.

This was also the last race on the original Monaco circuit before the dedicated pit lane along the harbour before Tabac corner was built for the 1972 grand prix.

In 1971 11 races made up the season.

Of the 23 cars entered for the 400th race at Monaco, only 18 qualified to start.

British driver Jackie Stewart qualified on pole in his Tyrell-Ford.

Only 10 cars actually finished the race, with the winner being Jackie Stewart.

INTERESTING FACT:
The Who used part of the grand prix and Jackie Stewart in the music video for their song 'Baba O'Riley'.

RACE 100

The 100th race was the German Grand Prix held on 6 August 1961 at the Nürburgring-Nordschleife.

There were eight grand prix that year.

26 cars lined up on the starting grid and 17 finished the race, although the Cooper-Climax car driven by Bernard Collomb was not classified as finishing because he had not completed 75% of the race.

America driver Phil Hill, took pole position in his Ferrari.

The race was won by British driver Stirling Moss, who drove a Lotus 18/21 for a privately owned team, the Rob Walker Racing Team.

Race 100 was Stirling Moss's 16th and final grand prix victory.

RACE 300

On the 4 March 1978, the 300th grand prix took place at the Kyalami Racing Circuit in South Africa.

In 1978, 16 races were on the calendar.

1977 World Champion Niki Lauda, in his first season with Brabham, took pole position but he retired from the race on lap 52 with an engine failure.

The 'Super Swede', Ronnie Peterson, in his Lotus-Ford won the race following a battle on the last lap with the Tyrrell driven by Patrick Depailler.

The 300th race was also the F1 race debut of future world champion Keke Rosberg.

RACE 400

Only six years later, on the 19 August 1984, the 400th grand prix was run, this time at the Österreichring, the permanent racing facility in Spielberg, Austria.

There were 16 races on the calendar in 1984.

1983 World Champion Nelson Piquet took pole position in his Brabham.

Of the 26 cars that qualified only 12 finished, with every car from fifth position down having been lapped.

A problem with the starting lights caused chaos among the drivers. Niki Lauda claimed that he saw "Red, green, yellow then red again", this caused 3rd fastest qualifier Elio de Angelis to hesitate badly off the line and his Lotus-Renault was almost hit from behind by several cars.

On the formation lap for the re-start, pole sitter Piquet, who had seen the McLarens change tyres on the grid, angered the other drivers when he led the field on an extremely slow lap in an effort to not allow Prost or Lauda to scrub in their new Michelin rubber.

The race was eventually won by Niki Lauda in his McLaren-TAG, who would go on to win that year's world championship and his third title.

RACE 500

The sixth Australian Grand Prix to be held at the Adelaide Street Circuit on 4 November 1990 was the 500th F1 race and the last of the 16 races that season.

The 1990 championship had already been secured by Ayrton Senna at the previous race in Japan.

Ayrton Senna took pole position with a lap time of 1:15.671. This was the fastest-ever recorded lap time of the circuit.

Of the 30 cars who qualified, only 13 finished.

The winner was Nelson Piquet in his Benetton-Ford.

This was also a race marred with controversy before it had even run. During a post-qualifying interview with Ayrton Senna, former triple World Champion, Jackie Stewart claimed that for a racer of his ability, Senna (also a triple world champion then) was part of too many race accidents. Senna was visibly annoyed and said that he couldn't believe that Stewart, with his background and experience, would say something like that and challenged him to check his facts.

RACE 600

The 600th race was the 1997 Argentine Grand Prix held at the Autodromo Oscar Alfredo Galvez on 13 April 1997.

This was the third race of that year's championship.

Of the 22 cars that qualified, only 10 crossed the finishing line.

Jacques Villeneuve, in the Williams' car, took pole position and the race and would eventually go on to win the 1997 championship making him the second son of a former F1 World Champion to win. The first father-son championship pairing being Graham and Damon Hill.

The Tyrrell team caused a stir at the grand prix as their car had four new wings, two on the nose cone and the other two alongside the drivers head. They resembled x-wings and this became their nickname.

RACE 700

The Brazilian Grand Prix on 6 April 2003 at Interlagos was the 700th F1 race.

20 cars qualified but only 10 finished the very wet race, where only 56 of the 71 scheduled laps were completed. New regulations in 2003, aimed at cost cutting, meant teams were only allowed to bring one wet-weather tyre.

Due to torrential conditions the race start was delayed by 10 minutes and then started under the safety car.

There was confusion about the timing of the final red flag that halted the race and the win was initially awarded to Kimi Räikkönen of McLaren, with Giancarlo Fisichella of Jordan in second, and Fernando Alonso of Renault in third. The Jordan team appealed and on 11 April 2003 an FIA court in Paris concluded that Fisichella was leading and he was awarded the win.

Since the Brazilian podium ceremony had been conducted with none of the podium steps occupied by the correct driver, Alonso had missed it due to receiving medical attention, an unofficial ceremony took place at the next race in Imola, where McLaren and Räikkönen handed over the winner's and constructor's trophies to Fisichella and Jordan. This win was Fisichella's first but the last for Jordan Racing.

RACE 800

The 800th grand prix was the very first night race to take place at the newly built Marina Bay Circuit in Singapore on 28 September 2008.

Of the 20 cars that qualified, 15 crossed the finish line.

Ferrari's Felipe Massa took pole, but it was the Renault driven by Fernando Alonso that ended up on the top step of the podium.

This race went down in history, not for the being the first race, but for being the scene of 'Crashgate'...

Nelson Piquet Junior crashed, which at the time was attributed to a simple mistake. His team-mate Alonso, was in the pits being refuelled at the time of the crash, and he eventually

went on to win the race.

Fast forward to August 2009 after Piquet Junior had left Renault, and allegations emerged that he had crashed deliberately to give Alonso an advantage.

Following an FIA investigation, Piquet Junior stated he had been asked to crash by Flavio Briatore, Renault Team Principal, and engineer Pat Symonds.

On 4 September 2009 Renault were charged with conspiracy and race fixing.

The Renault team were given a suspended disqualification from F1 for two years, pending any further rules infringements.

Briatore was banned from all FIA-

sanctioned events for life and Symonds banned for five years.

However, Briatore and Symonds successfully sued the FIA through the French courts and on 5 January 2010 the Tribunal de Grande Instance overturned their bans.

RACE 900

Race 900 took place on 6 April 2014 at the Bahrain International Circuit.

In the new hybrid era, it was the Mercedes of Nico Rosberg that qualified on pole, but his team-mate Lewis Hamilton that took the win.

Of the 22 drivers that lined up on the grid, 17 passed the chequered flag.

On lap 22, a crash between Esteban Gutiérrez and Pastor Maldonado brought out the safety car.

Maldonado was handed a 10-second stop-go penalty on lap 49, and following a steward's investigation after the race was handed a 5-place grid drop penalty for the next race and 3 penalty points on his super licence.

RACE 1000

Fast forward to 14 April 2019 and the 1000th race took place at the Shanghai International Circuit in China.

With so much build-up to the race, it turned out not to be the most thrilling of races...

Valtteri Bottas from Mercedes took pole position, but after a bad start it was his team-mate, Lewis Hamilton that took the win.

Of the 20 cars that started, 18 crossed the finish line.

MERCEDES-AMG PETRONAS MOTORSPORT

· DRIVER LINE-UP ·

VALTTERI BOTTAS

DATE OF BIRTH: 28 August 1989	
BORN: Finland	
CAR NUMBER: 77	
NUMBER OF WINS: 5	
NUMBER OF PODIUMS: 36	
2018 CHAMPIONSHIP POSITION: 5th (247 points)	
BEST CHAMPIONSHIP POSITION: 3rd (2017)	
OTHER F1 TEAMS: Williams (2013-2016)	

Valtteri Bottas was test driver for Williams for three years before securing a seat for the 2013 season.

In 2010 he competed in and won the Masters of Formula Three, driving for ART Grand Prix and in 2011 won the GP3 Series, racing for Lotus ART.

2012 saw Bottas as Williams' test driver where he took part in 15 free practice sessions over the course of the season, before being signed in November 2012 as one of Williams' F1 drivers for 2013. His team-mate for the 2013 season was Pastor Maldonado.

In his first season, he finished 17th, ahead of Maldonado's 18th in the championship. For the next three years, Bottas's team-mate was Felipe Massa.

*All stats correct as of June 2019.

● **Mercedes-AMG Petronas Motorsport** is the name of the F1 team run by Mercedes-Benz through its subsidiary company 'Mercedes-Benz Grand Prix Limited'.

● The team is based in **Brackley, Northamptonshire** and run under a German licence.

● Mercedes-Benz made its debut in F1 in **1954** and ran a team for two years.

● In 1954 and 1955, Mercedes-Benz driver, **Juan Manuel Fangio**, won the World Drivers' Championships.

● Mercedes did not return to F1 until **1994**, when they re-joined as an engine supplier to Ilmor, which Mercedes later bought out.

● 1995 saw Mercedes enter into a successful 20-year engine-supplier partnership with **McLaren**, which ended in 2015.

● In 2009, Mercedes supplied **Force India** and the **Brawn F1** team, who went on to win both the Constructors' and Drivers' Championships that year.

● Mercedes bought out **Brawn F1** at the end of 2009 and for 2010 the team was renamed Mercedes GP.

· DRIVER LINE-UP ·

- Mercedes supplied **Lotus F1** with engines in 2015 and Manor in 2016.

- As an engine supplier alone, Mercedes have collected over **170 wins**, making it the 2nd most successful supplier in F1 history. (The most successful being Ferrari).

- **Seven Constructors'** and **11 Drivers' Championships** have been won with Mercedes-Benz engines.

- **Mercedes-AMG Petronas Motorsport** is the most successful team in recent history, following the introduction of hybrid engines in 2014, having won the Constructors' and Drivers' Championships since that date.

- Three drivers have won all seven **Mercedes Drivers' Championships**. Two of them five-time champions:

Juan Manuel Fangio
(1954, 1955)
Nico Rosberg (2016)
Lewis Hamilton (2014, 2015, 2017, 2018)

LEWIS HAMILTON

DATE OF BIRTH: 7 January 1985	
BORN: Stevenage, England	
NUMBER OF WINS: 78	
NUMBER OF PODIUMS: 141	
2018 CHAMPIONSHIP POSITION:	
1st World Champion (408 points)	
BEST CHAMPIONSHIP POSITION:	
1st (World Champion 2008, 2014, 2015, 2017, 2018)	
OTHER F1 TEAMS: McLaren (2007-2012)	

Five-time champion, **Lewis Hamilton**, is one of only three drivers to achieve all seven Mercedes Drivers' Championships, the others being Michael Schumacher and Juan Manuel Fangio.

Hamilton was signed to McLaren's 'Young Driver Support Programme', in 1998 when he was just 13 years old. He won the British Formula Renault UK Championship in 2003, the Bahrain SuperPrix in 2004, the Formula 3 Euro Series and the Masters of Formula 3 Championships on 2004 and finally the GP2 title in 2006, before securing his first full-time F1 seat in 2007.

When he burst on to the F1 stage in 2007, he stood on the podium for the first nine races of the season. At the start of the final race of the 2007 season, Hamilton, the rookie, led the championship from his team-mate, two-time world champion, Fernando Alonso and Ferrari's Kimi Räikkönen. In the end it was Räikkönen who was victorious that year, the first time since 1950 that the person in third at the last race went on to win the championship.

During his rookie season, Hamilton set numerous records including: Most Consecutive Podium Finishes from Debut (9); the Joint Most Wins in a Debut Season (4), and Most Points in a Debut Season (109).

His first world championship came in 2008, fighting all season with Ferrari's Felipe Massa, Hamilton won in dramatic fashion; on the last corner of the last lap of the last race of the season. Clinching his first title, he became the youngest F1 World Champion in history, until Sebastian Vettel in 2010.

Between 2009 and 2012 Hamilton's McLaren car became less and less competitive and a second title seemingly further away than ever.

In 2013 he signed for Mercedes, a move which many viewed as a step backwards. However, Hamilton said that he wasn't expecting to win many races in 2013, but when the new regulations were introduced in 2014, Mercedes would prove to be a competitive car.

And so it did, from 2014 to 2018 Mercedes won every Constructors' Championship with Hamilton winning four out of the five Drivers' Championships, losing out to his team-mate, Nico Rosberg in 2016.

Away from the track, Hamilton has many interests including music and fashion, as well the loves of his life, his two British Bulldogs; Roscoe and Coco, who can often be seen around various paddocks.

In 2018 he launched a clothing line, 'TOMMYXLEWIS' in collaboration with American designer, Tommy Hilfiger.

However, none of this distracts him from his goals; title number six, maybe even seven or eight and being known as the best F1 driver ever.

*All stats correct as of June 2019.

SCUDERIA FERRARI MISSION WINNOW

· DRIVER LINE-UP ·

CHARLES LECLERC

DATE OF BIRTH:	16 October 1997
BORN:	Monte Carlo, Monaco
CAR NUMBER:	16
NUMBER OF WINS:	0
NUMBER OF PODIUMS:	2
2018 CHAMPIONSHIP POSITION:	13th (39 points)
BEST CHAMPIONSHIP POSITION:	13th (2018)
OTHER F1 TEAMS:	Sauber (2018)

Having only joined the Ferrari Driver Academy in 2016, it's been a short but impressive run to a full-time F1 Ferrari seat for Monegasque-born **Leclerc**, who signed a four-year deal with the Scuderia in September 2018.

2016 saw him acting as development driver for both HaasF1 and Scuderia Ferrari, where he took part in the first practice for Haas at the 2016 British Grand Prix. That year also saw him driving with ART Grand Prix in the GP3 Series Championship, which he won.

In 2017 Leclerc signed for Prema Racing to compete in the FIA Formula 2 Championship. He won the championship in the penultimate round of the season at Jerez and became the youngest-ever champion of the main support series for Formula 1 at 19 years and 356 days old. He also became the first driver since Nico Hülkenberg in 2009 to win the championship in their rookie season (a feat which only Nico Rosberg and Lewis Hamilton have previously accomplished) and is also the only driver to claim a championship with the Dallara GP2/11 chassis in their rookie season.

Leclerc was signed by Alfa Romeo Sauber F1 as one of their F1 drivers for the 2018 season. This was the first time a Monegasque F1 driver had been on the grid since Olivier Beretta in 1994. A sixth place finish at the Azerbaijan Grand Prix meant he was only the second Monegasque to score points in F1 since Louis Chiron at the 1950 Monaco Grand Prix.

*All stats correct as of June 2019.

● **Ferrari** are the oldest surviving and most successful F1 team, having competed in every race since the very first grand prix in 1950.

● Founded in 1929 by **Enzo Ferrari**, the company initially became the racing team for **Alfa Romeo**, both building and racing cars under the Alfa banner, but by 1947 Ferrari were building and racing under their own name: **Scuderia Ferrari**.

● **Scuderia** is Italian for a stable reserved for racing horses and is a term commonly applied to Italian motor racing teams.

● Ferrari's logo is a 'prancing horse' which was also the symbol on the fighter plane of the fallen Italian World War I pilot, **Francesco Baracca**. His parents were close acquaintances of Enzo Ferrari and suggested that Ferrari use the symbol as the logo of the Scuderia, telling him it would bring him good luck.

● The '**tifosi**' is the term used to describe the passionate Ferrari fan base.

- The Italian team has its headquarters at **Maranello**, a town in the region of Emilia-Romagna in Northern Italy.

- They also own and operate the **Fiorano Circuit**, a test track on the same site built in 1972 which is used for testing road and race cars.

- In terms of success, Ferrari have a win record: **16 Constructors' Championships** and **15 Drivers' Championships**.

- Their last win was in 2008, and their most successful period was when **Michael Schumacher** was their driver.

- They won the **Constructors' Championship** in: 1961, 1964, 1975, 1976, 1977, 1979, 1982, 1983, 1999, 2000, 2001, 2002, 2003, 2004, 2007 and 2008.

- Nine drivers have won **Ferrari's** 15 Drivers' Championships:

Albert Ascari (1952,1953)
Juan Manuel Fangio (1956)
Mike Hawthorn (1958)
Phil Hill (1961)
John Surtees (1964)
Niki Lauda (1975,1977)
Jody Scheckter (1979)
Michael Schumacher (2000, 2001, 2002, 2003, 2004)
Kimi Raikkonen (2007)

SEBASTIAN VETTEL

DATE OF BIRTH:	3 July 1987
BORN:	Heppenheim, Germany
CAR NUMBER:	5
NUMBER OF WINS:	52
NUMBER OF PODIUMS:	115
2018 CHAMPIONSHIP POSITION:	2nd
BEST CHAMPIONSHIP POSITION: World Champion 2010, 2011, 2012, 2013	
OTHER F1 TEAMS: BMW Sauber (2006); Toro Rosso (2007, 2008), Red Bull Racing (2009-2014)	

Four-time world champion **Sebastian Vettel** signed for the Scuderia in 2015. In the Mercedes-dominant hybrid era however, Vettel's quest for another world championship and, more importantly, a world championship with Ferrari has been elusive.

2015 and 2016 saw Ferrari struggle for speed. Since 2017 however, the Ferrari pace has improved and Vettel has been fighting for wins and the championship once more. Both times though, Vettel saw the crown go to Lewis Hamilton before the end of the season.

The 2018 season was labelled "The Fight for Five" as the two four-time champions, Vettel and Hamilton, squared up against each other to become only the third F1 driver, after Michael Schumacher and Juan Manuel Fangio, to become a five-time world champion. And the first half of the season was indeed a terrific tussle as the championship lead see-sawed from one driver to the other. But a disastrous second-half of the season followed which saw Vettel lose out to Hamilton at the Mexican Grand Prix.

Vettel is clearly still as determined as ever to win another championship, especially one with Ferrari, and no one would be surprised if he did.

On top of holding the record of being the youngest-ever four-time world champion, Vettel holds many other F1 records, including:

- **Most podium finishes** in a season (17 in 2011)
- **Most wins** in a season (13 in 2013)
- **Most pole positions** in a season (15 in 2011)
- **Most laps led** in a season (739 in 2011)
- **Most consecutive wins** (9, Belgium to Brazil, 2013)
- **Most consecutive grand slams** (2, Singapore and South Korea, 2013)
- **Most wins from pole** in a season (9 in 2011)
- **Youngest grand prix pole sitter** (21 years and 72 days at Italian Grand Prix, 2008)
- **Youngest driver to score a double** (21 years and 73 days at Italian Grand Prix, 2008)
- **Youngest driver to score a hat-trick** (21 years and 353 days at British Grand Prix, 2009)
- **Youngest driver to score a grand slam** (24 years and 119 days at Indian Grand Prix, 2011)
- **Youngest F1 World Drivers' Champion** (23 years and 135 days, 2010)
- **Youngest F1 World Drivers' Championship runner-up** (22 years and 121 days, 2009)
- **Driver with the shortest time** in his F1 career before gaining a penalty (6 seconds for speeding in the pit lane at the 2006 Turkish Grand Prix)

*All stats correct as of June 2019.

MAX VERSTAPPEN

DATE OF BIRTH:	30 September 1997
BORN:	Hasselt, Belgium
CAR NUMBER:	33
NUMBER OF WINS:	4
NUMBER OF PODIUMS:	4
2018 CHAMPIONSHIP POSITION:	4th (249 points)
BEST CHAMPIONSHIP POSITION:	4th (2018)
OTHER F1 TEAMS:	Toro Rosso (2014-2016); Red Bull (2016 – present)

Max is son to former F1 driver Jos Verstappen. He made his Formula 1 debut in 2015 with Scuderia Toro Rosso, and made history as the youngest ever driver to compete in F1 at 17. He only got his road drivers licence on his 18th birthday, 6 months after starting!

In 2016, he only drove for Scuderia Toro Rosso for the first four races of the season, before replacing Daniil Kvyat at Red Bull Racing. In his first eight races with his new team, he achieved six top-five finishes and four podiums.

Max has achieved a number of records since joining F1 including: Youngest Driver to Compete in F1; Youngest Driver to Lead a Lap; Youngest Driver to Set a Fastest Lap; Youngest Driver to Score Points; Youngest Driver to Secure a Podium; Youngest Winner; Youngest Multiple Grand Prix Winner; Youngest to Win the Same Grand Prix Multiple Times, and Youngest to Win the Same Grand Prix in Successive Years.

*All stats correct as of June 2019.

PIERRE GASLY

DATE OF BIRTH:	7 February 1996
BORN:	Rouen, France
CAR NUMBER:	10
NUMBER OF WINS:	0
NUMBER OF PODIUMS:	0
2018 CHAMPIONSHIP POSITION:	15th (29 points)
BEST CHAMPIONSHIP POSITION:	15th (2018)
OTHER F1 TEAMS:	Toro Rosso (2017-2018)

Pierre Gasly was part of the Red Bull Junior Team and signed with Arden in 2014 to compete in the Formula Renault 3.5 Series. He finished as runner-up.

He drove for DAMS in the GP2 Series in 2015 moving to PREMA Racing in 2016 where he finished the season as GP2 champion.

He made his F1 debut at the Malaysian Grand Prix in 2017, replacing Danill Kvyat for a number of races. He permanently replaced Kvyat at Toro Rosso for the remainder of the 2017 season from Mexico and became their full-time driver for the 2018 season.

Following Daniel Ricciardo's move to Renault, Gasly was signed to the senior Red Bull Team for the 2019 season.

*All stats correct as of June 2019.

Team Profiles •

ASTON MARTIN RED BULL RACING

- **Red Bull Racing** came into existence in 2004 and started racing in F1 in 2005.

- They are based in **Milton Keynes**, England.

- For the 2005 and 2006 season they raced under an English licence, but since 2007 have raced under an Austrian licence.

- Red Bull have used three engine manufacturers: **Cosworth** (2005-2006), **Renault** (2007-2018) and **Honda** (2019-present).

- Following a breakdown in the **Red Bull-Renault** relationship during 2016-2018 seasons, the Renault engine was re-badged as '**TAG Heuer**'.

- They won four consecutive Constructors' and Drivers' Championships between 2010 and 2013. **Sebastian Vettel** won all four championships.

Team Profiles
RENAULT

- **Renault** has been associated with F1 since 1977.

- The French team has a factory in **Enstone**, Oxfordshire, where the chassis is developed and manufactured. The engine is developed at the Renault factory in **Viry-Chatillon**, France.

- In **1977** Renault entered F1 as a constructor and introduced the **turbo engine** to F1.

- By **1983**, they were supplying engines to other teams.

- As a constructor they left F1 in 1985, returning in 2000 when they bought out **Benetton**.

- In 2002 they rebranded as **Renault F1** and won both the Drivers' and Constructors' Championships in 2005 and 2006.

- Between 2011 and 2015 they raced as **Lotus**, only retaining the Renault name for the 2011 season.

- In **2016** they returned to being a works manufacturer.

- During their time in F1, Renault has supplied engines to other manufacturers including: **Red Bull** (2007-2015), **Benetton Formula** (1995-1997, 2001) and **Williams** (1989-1997, 2012-2013).

- As an engine supplier, Renault has contributed to nine other World Drivers' Championships and clocked up over **160** wins.

DANIEL RICCIARDO

DATE OF BIRTH:	1 July 1989
BORN:	Perth, Western Australia
CAR NUMBER:	3
NUMBER OF WINS:	7
NUMBER OF PODIUMS:	29
2018 CHAMPIONSHIP POSITION:	6th (170 points)
BEST CHAMPIONSHIP POSITION:	3rd (2014, 2016)
OTHER F1 TEAMS:	HRT (2011), Toro Rosso (2012-2013), Red Bull (2014-2018)

Also known as 'The Honey Badger', **Daniel Ricciardo** has been on the F1 scene since 2011.

For the 2011 season, he was Toro Rosso's test and reserve driver, until being contracted to HRT by Red Bull Racing, to replace Narain Karthikeyan mid-season. He made his F1 debut at the 2011 British Grand Prix, where he qualified 24th (last place) and finished 19th (last place).

Two seasons at Toro Rosso followed, before he was signed to Red Bull in 2014 where he replaced fellow countryman Mark Webber. In his first season with the team he beat his team-mate, four-time world champion, Sebastian Vettel, and clocked up three wins in the process. Fast with a knack of pulling off fantastic overtakes, 2015-218 saw Ricciardo clocking up more wins and podiums as well as introducing the F1 world to the now famous 'shoey'.

*All stats correct as of June 2019.

NICO HÜLKENBERG

DATE OF BIRTH:	19 August 1987
BORN:	Emmerich am Rhein, Germany
CAR NUMBER:	27
NUMBER OF WINS:	0
NUMBER OF PODIUMS:	0
2018 CHAMPIONSHIP POSITION:	7th (69 points)
BEST CHAMPIONSHIP POSITION:	7th (2018)
OTHER F1 TEAMS:	Williams (2010), Sahara Force India (2011-2012), Sauber (2013), Sahara Force India (2014-2016)

Nico 'Hulk' Hülkenberg made his F1 debut in 2010 racing for Williams and grabbed his first and, to date, only pole position at the Brazilian Grand Prix.

A year as test and reserve driver for Force India followed in 2011. In 2012, he was signed as a full-time driver for Force India, where he finished the year 17 points ahead of his teammate Paul di Resta and he out-qualified him 12 times, to di Resta's eight. 2013 saw him drive for Sauber, before he returned to Force India for the 2014 season. 2019 is his third season with Renault.

Although Hülkenberg holds the record for the most grand prix starts without a podium finish, he did however compete in two rounds of the World Endurance Championship in 2015 and won Le Mans at his first attempt.

*All stats correct as of June 2019.

• DRIVER LINE-UP •

ROMAIN GROSJEAN

DATE OF BIRTH: 17 April 1986	
BORN: Geneva, Switzerland	
CAR NUMBER: 8	
NUMBER OF WINS: 0	
NUMBER OF PODIUMS: 10	
2018 CHAMPIONSHIP POSITION: 14th (37 points)	
BEST CHAMPIONSHIP POSITION: 7th (2013)	
OTHER F1 TEAMS: ING Renault (2009), Lotus Renault (2011), Lotus F1 (2012-2015)	

Romain Grosjean was made Renault test driver in 2008, a role he continued in 2009 and graduated to the Renault seat mid-season, following Nelson Piquet Jr's departure in the wake of 'Crashgate'. Without a seat for 2010, Grosjean took part in the FIA GT1 World Championship, Le Mans 24 Hours and Auto GP. A further year out of F1 followed in 2011, where Grosjean returned to GP2 and won the championship.
He was signed to Lotus F1 in 2012. He started the season well, but was given a race-ban after causing a multi-car pile-up at the start of the Belgian Grand Prix. This was the first race ban to be given since Michael Schumacher in 1994. He was involved in another two incidents in two more races that season, and his actions were condemned by many drivers in the paddock. He signed for the newly formed Haas F1 in September 2015.

All stats correct as of June 2019.

KEVIN MAGNUSSEN

DATE OF BIRTH: 5 October 1992	
BORN: Roskilde, Denmark	
CAR NUMBER: 20	
NUMBER OF WINS: 0	
NUMBER OF PODIUMS: 1	
2018 CHAMPIONSHIP POSITION: 9th (56 points)	
BEST CHAMPIONSHIP POSITION: 9th (2018)	
OTHER F1 TEAMS: McLaren (2014), Renault (2016)	

Kevin is son of former F1 driver, **Jan Magnussen**. He was part of McLaren's Young Driver Programme and made his debut in F1 in 2014, when he replaced Sergio Perez at McLaren.
On his debut race at the Australian Grand Prix, he qualified in fourth and finished in third, taking his first and only podium to date. This made him only the second Danish driver to score points in F1, the other being his father, and the first F1 debutant since Lewis Hamilton in 2007 to take a podium in his first grand prix.
A year out as McLaren's test and reserve driver in 2015 followed, before Magnussen was signed to Renault for 2016. He spent a year at Renault before signing for Haas F1 in November 2016.

All stats correct as of June 2019.

HAAS F1

● **Haas F1** team made its F1 debut in 2016.

● The team was established in 2014 by NASCAR Monster Energy Cup Series co-owner **Gene Haas** and is based in **Kannapolis**, North Carolina where it shares facilities with its sister team, NASCAR Stewart-Haas Racing.

● The team also has a UK base in **Banbury**.

● It is the first American team to compete in F1 since the **Haas Lola** team in 1985/86 – Haas Lola was a team owned by Teddy Mayer and Carl Haas (no relation to Gene Haas).

● Haas have pioneered a low-cost model towards F1 as they use a **Ferrari** power unit with Italian manufacturer, **Dallara**, building the chassis.

● At the 2016 Australian Grand Prix, Haas F1 became the first American constructor, and the first team since **Toyota Racing** in 2002, to score points in its first race.

● In their first two seasons Haas finished eighth in the **Constructors' Championship**.

● In **2018** they finished fifth.

● In February 2019 they rebranded as **Rich Energy Haas F1**, as part of a multi-year sponsorship deal with British energy drink company, Rich Energy.

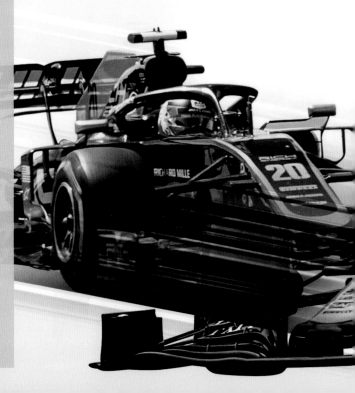

MCLAREN TEAM

- The British team is based at the **McLaren Technology Centre** in Woking, Berkshire.

- The team was founded in 1963 by **Bruce McLaren**, a New Zealand race car designer, driver, engineer and inventor.

- The first F1 race McLaren entered was the **1966 Monaco Grand Prix**. Bruce McLaren retired from the race after nine laps due to an oil leak.

- **McLaren F1 Team** is the 2nd oldest active F1 team on the grid after Ferrari.

- They are also the 2nd most successful team having won 182 races, **12 Drivers' Championships** and **eight Constructors' Championships**.

- McLaren also dominated the **Canadian-American Challenge Cup (CanAm)** winning 56 races and five **Constructors' Championships** and have won three Indianapolis 500 races, as well as the 24 Hours of Le Mans and 12 Hours of Sebring.

- **Seven drivers** have won a total of 12 Drivers' Championships with McLaren:

Emerson Fittipaldi (1974)
James Hunt (1976)
Niki Lauda (1984)
Alain Prost (1985, 1986, 1989)
Ayrton Senna (1988, 1990, 1991)
Mika Hakkinen (1998, 1999)
Lewis Hamilton (2008)

· DRIVER LINE-UP ·

CARLOS SAINZ JR

DATE OF BIRTH:	1 September 1994
BORN:	Madrid, Spain
CAR NUMBER:	55
NUMBER OF WINS:	0
NUMBER OF PODIUMS:	0
2018 CHAMPIONSHIP POSITION:	10th (53 points)
BEST CHAMPIONSHIP POSITION:	9th (2017)
OTHER F1 TEAMS:	Toro Rosso (2015-2017); Renault (2017-2018)

Carlos Sainz Jr is the son of former two-time World Rally Champion Carlos Sainz.

He made his Formula 1 debut in 2015, partnering another F1 rookie that year, Max Verstappen. During the 2017 season, it was announced he would be driving for Renault from 2018. However, Renault decided to drop British driver Jolyon Palmer early and Sainz replaced him at Renault for the US Grand Prix, with Kvyat replacing him at Toro Rosso for the remainder of the season.

Sainz signed for McLaren for the 2019 season, replacing fellow Spaniard Fernando Alonso.

*All stats correct as of June 2019.

LANDO NORRIS

DATE OF BIRTH:	13 November 1999
BORN:	Bristol, England
CAR NUMBER:	4
NUMBER OF WINS:	0
NUMBER OF PODIUMS:	0
2018 CHAMPIONSHIP POSITION:	N/A (Rookie Season)
BEST CHAMPIONSHIP POSITION:	N/A
OTHER F1 TEAMS:	N/A

F1 rookie, **Lando Norris**, signed as a McLaren junior driver in 2017. That year he raced full-time for Carlin in the European Formula 3 Championship, where he won the title. He also tested for McLaren in a scheduled mid-season test.

In 2018, Norris became the official McLaren test and reserve driver, and also raced for Carlin in the FIA Formula 2 Championship, where he came runner-up behind fellow F1 rookie, George Russell.

Norris was announced as McLaren's F1 driver in November 2018.

*All stats correct as of June 2019.

SPORTPESA RACING POINT F1

SERGIO PÉREZ

DATE OF BIRTH:	26 January 1990
BORN:	Guadalajara, Mexico
CAR NUMBER:	11
NUMBER OF WINS:	0
NUMBER OF PODIUMS:	8
2018 CHAMPIONSHIP POSITION:	8th (62 points)
BEST CHAMPIONSHIP POSITION:	7th (2016, 2017)
OTHER F1 TEAMS:	Sauber (2011-2012), McLaren (2013), Force India (2014-2018)

Sergio Pérez became a member of the Ferrari Driver Academy in October 2010. That same month he was signed to Sauber for the 2011 season. In 2012 he took his first podium at the Malaysian Grand Prix, a drive which fuelled speculation of a move to Ferrari.

This wasn't to be however, as in September 2012 Pérez was announced as Lewis Hamilton's replacement at McLaren for the 2013 season. This move saw him released from the Ferrari Driver Academy.

He lasted one year at McLaren and signed for Force India for the 2013 season.

Since 2014 he has appeared on the podium a further five times, and achieved his best championship finishes in 2016 and 2017.

*All stats correct as of June 2019.

● 2019 is **SportPesa Racing Point**'s first F1 season, although it is 'The Team Formerly Known as Force India Racing Point'.

● The team's leading sponsor is **SportPesa**, a sports betting company from Kenya.

● The team is based at **Silverstone** and races under a British licence.

● It is owned by **Racing Point UK**, a company set up in August 2018 to buy the assets of Force India which had gone into administration.

● The team competed from the **Belgian Grand Prix 2018**, and for the rest of the season as the Racing Point F1 Team.

● Although a new name, the team itself can be traced back to the **Jordan Grand Prix** team which entered F1 in 1991.

LANCE STROLL

DATE OF BIRTH:	29 October 1998
BORN:	Quebec, Canada
CAR NUMBER:	18
NUMBER OF WINS:	0
NUMBER OF PODIUMS:	1
2018 CHAMPIONSHIP POSITION:	18th (6 points)
BEST CHAMPIONSHIP POSITION:	12th (2017)
OTHER F1 TEAMS:	Williams (2017-2018)

Canadian **Stroll** was part of the Ferrari Driver Academy from 2010-2015. He had championship wins in Italian F4 (2014), Toyota Racing Series (2015) and European Formula 3 (2016) before making his debut for Williams in 2017.

His debut season has been his best to date as he finished 12th in the championship standings that year, also securing his first podium at the eventful Azerbaijan Grand Prix. That appearance made him the Youngest Rookie Driver to stand on the podium, aged 18. He also became the Youngest Driver to start on the front row at the Italian Grand Prix that year when grid penalties for both Red Bull drivers saw Stroll promoted to 2nd on the starting grid.

He was signed to Racing Point in November 2018.

*All stats correct as of June 2019.

Team Profiles

RED BULL TORO ROSSO

- **Red Bull Toro Rosso** is the second, and junior team, owned by Austrian drinks company Red Bull.

- As the junior team to Red Bull, one of its aims is to develop the skills of promising young drivers for the senior team.

- The team was established at the end of 2005 when Red Bull owner, **Dietrich Mateschitz** bought Paul Stoddart's remaining shares in the **Minardi F1** team.

- Red Bull Toro Rosso made its F1 debut in 2006, and gained full independence from **Red Bull Racing** in 2010.

- From 2007 to 2013 they ran Ferrari engines, switching to **Renault** for 2014 and 2015, switching back to Ferrari in 2016, then back to Renault for 2017 before moving to **Honda** engines for 2018 .

- Toro Rosso's only pole, podium and win came in 2008 at the Italian Grand Prix courtesy of **Sebastian Vettel**.

• DRIVER LINE-UP •

DANIIL KVYAT

DATE OF BIRTH: 26 April 1994	
BORN: Ufa, Russia	
CAR NUMBER: 26	
NUMBER OF WINS: 0	
NUMBER OF PODIUMS: 2	
2018 CHAMPIONSHIP POSITION: 14th (37 points)	
BEST CHAMPIONSHIP POSITION: 7th (2015)	
OTHER F1 TEAMS: Red Bull Racing (2015-2016 (part))	

With wins in the Formula Renault 2.0 Alps and GP3 Series, Kvyat moved to F1 in 2014, driving for Toro Rosso, moving to the senior Red Bull team in 2015 as a replacement for Sebastian Vettel.

Kvyat achieved his best championship result place of seventh in the 2015 F1 season.

He started the 2016 season for Red Bull, but following a collision with Ferrari's Sebastian Vettel at the Russian Grand Prix, Red Bull management decided to demote Kvyat back to Toro Rosso, and promote Max Verstappen.

Sitting the 2018 season out, as test driver for Ferrari, Kvyat was resigned back to Toro Rosso for the 2019 season.

*All stats correct as of June 2019.

ALEXANDER ALBON

DATE OF BIRTH: 23 March 1996	
BORN: London, England	
CAR NUMBER: 23	
NUMBER OF WINS: 0	
NUMBER OF PODIUMS: 0	
2018 CHAMPIONSHIP POSITION: N/A (Rookie)	
BEST CHAMPIONSHIP POSITION: N/A (Rookie)	
OTHER F1 TEAMS: N/A (Rookie)	

The first Thai driver to compete in F1 since Prince Bira in 1954, Thai-British racer Alexander Albon became part of the Red Bull Junior Team in 2012.

He raced in Eurocup Formula Renault 2.0, European Formula 2, GP3 and Formula 2 before making his F1 debut in 2019.

In the first seven races of the 2019 season, Albon has notched up seven points, only three less than his more experience team-mate..

*All stats correct as of June 2019.

· DRIVER LINE-UP ·

ROKIT WILLIAMS

ROBERT KUBICA

DATE OF BIRTH:	7 December 1984
BORN:	Poland
CAR NUMBER:	88
NUMBER OF WINS:	1 (Canada 2008)
NUMBER OF PODIUMS:	12 (2006-2010)
2018 CHAMPIONSHIP POSITION:	N/A (not racing)
BEST CHAMPIONSHIP POSITION:	4th (2008)
OTHER F1 TEAMS:	BMW Sauber (2006-2009); Renault (2010)

Robert Kubica is the first, and only, Polish racing driver to compete in F1. 2019 marks a return to the grid after a nine-year absence, following a serious accident Kubica had whilst rally driving in 2011.

In his heyday, Kubica had the speed and potential to become a world champion, taking his first win at the Canadian Grand Prix in 2008. He led the championship at one stage during the 2008 season, but eventually finished fourth. After a long road of recovery, Kubica was signed as Williams' driver for the 2019 season, partnering rookie driver, George Russell.

*All stats correct as of June 2019.

GEORGE RUSSELL

DATE OF BIRTH:	15 February 1998
BORN:	King's Lynn, Norfolk, England
CAR NUMBER:	63
NUMBER OF WINS:	0
NUMBER OF PODIUMS:	0
2018 CHAMPIONSHIP POSITION:	N/A (Rookie Season)
BEST CHAMPIONSHIP POSITION:	N/A
OTHER F1 TEAMS:	N/A

F1 rookie, **George Russell** is the 2018 FIA Formula 2 Champion and 2017 GP3 Series Champion.

In 2017, he took four wins, three positions and five podiums and sealed his championship win with a race still to run.

In 2018, Russell was signed as Mercedes-AMG Petronas F1 reserve driver, where he shared duties with Pascal Wehrlein. He was also signed to ART Grand Prix, along with Jack Aitken, to race in the FIA Formula 2 Championship. Following a season-long fight with fellow 2019 F1 rookie, Lando Norris, Russell won the championship in the feature race at Abu Dhabi, the last stop on the calendar.

Russell was announced as Williams' F1 driver in October 2018.

*All stats correct as of June 2019.

● The British team, racing in 2019 as **ROKiT Williams Racing**, is based at Grove, Oxfordshire.

● It was founded in 1977 by **Sir Frank Williams** and engineer, **Patrick Head**. Both men are still involved with the company.

● **All Williams cars' chassis** are 'FW' followed by a number. In 2019 the car is known as 'FW42', with the number being the number of years since 1977.

● The first F1 race for Williams was the **1977 Spanish Grand Prix**, for which they used a March chassis.

● Their first F1 race as a constructor was the **1978 Argentine Grand Prix**.

● Williams' first win was at the **1979 British Grand Prix**, courtesy of Swiss driver Clay Regazzoni.

● To date, Williams have won 114 races, seven **Drivers' Championships** and nine **Constructors' Championships**.

● Williams' most successful engine partnership to date is with **Renault**, with whom they won five of their nine Constructors' Championships.

● Williams are one of only five teams that won every **Drivers' Championship** between 1984 and 2008 and every **Constructors' Championships'** between 1979 and 2008. The other teams being: Ferrari, McLaren, Benetton and Renault.

● The following drivers won F1 Drivers' Championships with Williams:

Alan Jones (1980), **Keke Rosberg** (1982), **Nelson Piquet** (1987), **Nigel Mansell** (1992), **Alain Prost** (1993), **Damon Hill** (1996), **Jacques Villeneuve** (1997)

ALFA ROMEO RACING

- **Alfa Romeo** has been involved with F1 many times over the years, first as a constructor and engine supplier sporadically between 1950 and 1987, then as a commercial partner since 2015.

- The Alfa Romeo works team won the very first two World Drivers' Championships; **Nino Farina** (1950), **Juan Manuel Fangio** (1951).

- During the 1960s Alfa Romeo was not officially in F1, although several teams used independently developed Alfa Romeo engines.

- Following the success of Alfa Romeo's flat-12 engine, designed by **Carlo Chiti**, by taking the 1975 World Sportscar Championship, Bernie Ecclestone (Brabham team owner at the time) persuaded Alfa Romeo to supply the same engine, for free, for the 1976 F1 season.

- The 1976 Brabham-Alfa Romeo season was moderately successful, it was the 1977 and 1978 seasons that saw the most success with cars taking 14 podium finishes, including two race victories for **Niki Lauda**.

- Alfa Romeo returned to F1 between 1979 and 1985 but in that time the works drivers never won a race, and the team never placed higher than 6th in the Constructors' Championship.

- The Alfa Romeo name returned to F1 in 2015 when their logo appeared on the **Ferrari** car.

- They became the title sponsors for **Sauber** in 2016.

· DRIVER LINE-UP ·

KIMI RAIKKÖNEN

DATE OF BIRTH: 17 October 1979	
BORN: Espoo, Finland	
CAR NUMBER: 7	
NUMBER OF WINS: 21	
NUMBER OF PODIUMS: 103	
2018 CHAMPIONSHIP POSITION: 3rd (251 points)	
BEST CHAMPIONSHIP POSITION: World Champion (2007)	
OTHER F1 TEAMS: Sauber (2001), McLaren (2002-2006), Ferrari (2007-2009), Lotus (2012-2013), Ferrari (2014-2018)	

The Iceman made his debut in F1 driving for Sauber, having only driven in 23 other races, albeit winning 13 of them. In his first F1 season he achieved points in four races and eight finishes in the top eight and helped Sauber to their then-best result of fourth in the Constructors' Championship.

Five years at McLaren followed where **Räikkönen** finished second in the Drivers' Championship in both 2003 and 2005. Moving to Ferrari for the 2007 season, Räikkönen took pole, fastest lap and the win at the season-opener in Australia. The 2007 season finished with Räikkönen as World Drivers' Champion, by one point ahead of both McLaren drivers, Hamilton and Alonso.

After a stint at Lotus, he returned to Ferrari in 2014 until he signed for Alfa Romeo Racing in September 2018. Although Räikkönen appeared on the podium many times, it wasn't until the US Grand Prix in October 2018 that he made it to the top step again.

*All stats correct as of June 2019.

ANTONIO GIOVANAZZI

DATE OF BIRTH: 14 December 1993	
BORN: Martina Franca, Italy	
CAR NUMBER: 99	
NUMBER OF WINS: 0	
NUMBER OF PODIUMS: 0	
2018 CHAMPIONSHIP POSITION: N/A (Rookie)	
BEST CHAMPIONSHIP POSITION: N/A (Rookie)	
OTHER F1 TEAMS: N/A (Rookie)	

As Ferrari's third reserve driver, **Giovanazzi** actually made his F1 debut at the Australian Grand Prix in 2017 for Sauber, when he replaced the injured Pascal Wehrlein. As Wehrlein continued his recovery Giovanazzi drove again at the second 2017 race in China.

Prior to F1, Giovanazzi was runner-up in the 2016 GP2 series, losing out on the last race of the season to Pierre Gasly. He also raced in Masters of Formula 3, British Formula 3, FIA Formula 3 European Championship and Formula Pilota China.

*All stats correct as of June 2019.

MAKE YOUR OWN 2D ORIGAMI CAR!

WHY NOT HAVE A GO AT MAKING THIS SIMPLE ORIGAMI CAR?

ALL YOU NEED IS A PIECE OF SQUARE PAPER.

INSTRUCTIONS

1

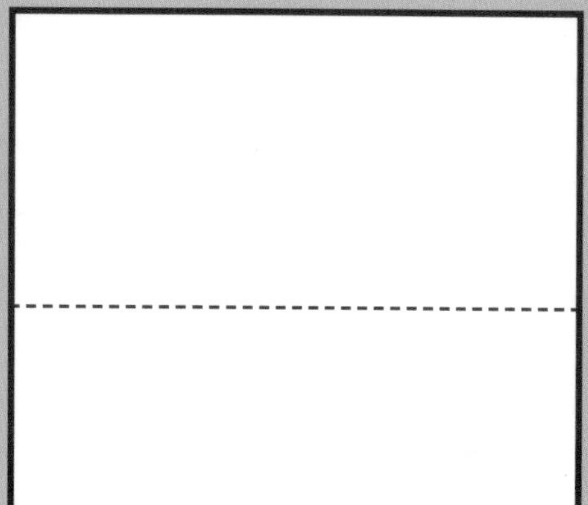

Take a square piece of paper and put it on the table. (If it's a coloured piece of paper, place it coloured side down).

Fold the paper in half and unfold.

2

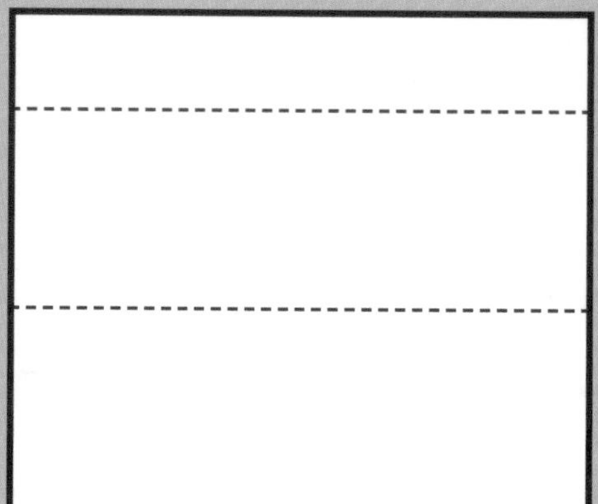

Make a fold on the top half of the paper – about 1/3 of the way from the top.

3

Repeat on the bottom half of the paper.

4

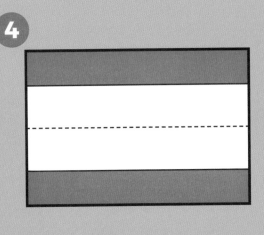

Your paper should now look like the above.

5

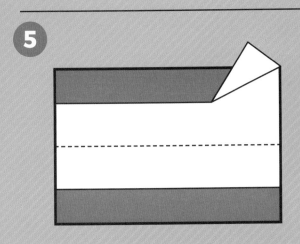

Next make a fold on the top right corner flap – start from 1/3 way from the edge.

6

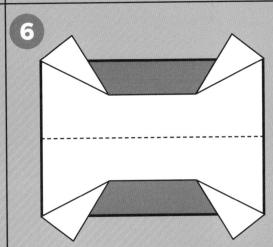

Repeat for the remaining three corners.

Fold the very tips of each corner down.

7

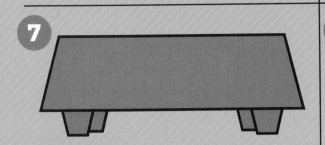

Using the fold you made in step 2, fold the car over.

8

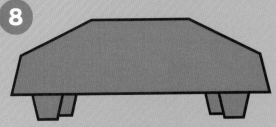

Finally, do an 'inside reverse fold' to make the windscreen and back window. To do this simply fold the paper inwards.

DECORATE YOUR CAR!

INFOGRAPHIC

DISTANCE DRIVEN

If you add all the laps at all the tracks together, each driver drove a maximum of 6400.732km throughout the 2019 season.

That's the same as going (as the crow flies) from:

LONDON TO MONACO 6 TIMES
(or there and back 3 times)

LONDON TO CASABLANCA 3 TIMES
(or doing a round trip and then driving back to Casablanca)

LONDON TO NUUK
(capital of Greenland) and back once

LONDON TO NAPERVILLE,
Indiana in the United States

LENGTH OF F1 CAR

The 2019 F1 car was 5656mm long (5.656m).
That's the same as:

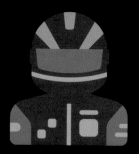

31½
F1 drivers
(average height of 2019 drivers is 178.5cm)

8½
Pirelli tyres
(each tyre is 670mm wide)

1
Male giraffe
(height approx. 5500mm)

INFORMATION

TYRES

At every race, each driver is allocated 13 tyres AND four intermediate tyres and three wet tyres... just in case. Over the course of the 2019 season that means each driver is allocated 273 tyres. That means Pirelli supplied a total of 5460 tyres. Each tyre is 670mm wide which means that if you put all the tyres used in 2019 side by side they would stretch for 3,658,200mm (3658.2m).

That's the same as:

121
blue whales

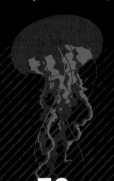

50
Lionsmane jellyfish
(wingspan)

4.4
Burj Khalifa's
(tallest building
in the world)

WEIGHT OF AN F1 CAR

The minimum weight of an F1 car, excluding driver and fuel is 733kg.

That's the same as the weight as:

14,660,000
drops of water

5,311.5
iPhones

4,889
bananas

1,295
basketballs

0.5
Porsche Carrera

0.02
of the first computer
built in 1945

Roll Of Honour
DRIVERS' CHAMPIONSHIP WINNERS

YEAR	NATIONALITY	DRIVER	CONSTRUCTOR	YEAR	NATIONALITY	DRIVER	CONSTRUCTOR
1950		Giuseppe Farina [1]	Alfa Romeo	1984		Niki Lauda [14]	McLaren
1951		Juan Manuel Fangio [2]	Alfa Romeo	1985		Alain Prost [21]	McLaren
1952		Alberto Ascari [3]	Ferrari	1986		Alain Prost [21]	McLaren
1953		Alberto Ascari [3]	Ferrari	1987		Nelson Piquet [19]	Williams
1954		Juan Manuel Fangio [2]	Maserati Mercedes	1988		Ayrton Senna [22]	McLaren
1955		Juan Manuel Fangio [2]	Mercedes	1990		Ayrton Senna [22]	McLaren
1956		Juan Manuel Fangio [2]	Ferrari	1991		Ayrton Senna [22]	McLaren
1957		Juan Manuel Fangio [2]	Maserati	1992		Nigel Mansell [23]	Williams
1958		Mike Hawthorn [4]	Ferrari	1993		Alain Prost [21]	Williams
1959		Jack Brabham [5]	Cooper	1994		Michael Schumacher [24]	Benetton
1960		Jack Brabham [5]	Cooper	1995		Michael Schumacher [24]	Benetton
1961		Phil Hill [6]	Ferrari	1996		Damon Hill [25]	Williams
1962		Graham Hill [7]	BRM	1997		Jacques Villeneuve [26]	Williams
1963		Jim Clark [8]	Lotus	1998		Mika Häkkinen [27]	McLaren
1964		John Surtees [9]	Ferrari	1999		Mika Häkkinen [27]	McLaren
1965		Jim Clark [8]	Lotus	2000		Michael Schumacher [24]	Ferrari
1966		Jack Brabham [5]	Brabham	2001		Michael Schumacher [24]	Ferrari
1967		Denny Hulme [10]	Brabham	2002		Michael Schumacher [24]	Ferrari
1968		Graham Hill [7]	Lotus	2003		Michael Schumacher [24]	Ferrari
1969		Jackie Stewart [11]	Matra	2004		Michael Schumacher [24]	Ferrari
1970		Jochen Rindt [12]	Lotus	2005		Fernando Alonso [28]	Renault
1971		Jackie Stewart [11]	Tyrrell	2006		Fernando Alonso [28]	Renault
1972		Emerson Fittipaldi [13]	Lotus	2007		Kimi Räikkönen [29]	Ferrari
1973		Jackie Stewart [11]	Tyrrell	2008		Lewis Hamilton [30]	McLaren
1974		Emerson Fittipaldi [13]	McLaren	2009		Jenson Button [31]	Brawn
1975		Niki Lauda [14]	Ferrari	2010		Sebastian Vettel [32]	Red Bull
1976		James Hunt [15]	McLaren	2011		Sebastian Vettel [32]	Red Bull
1977		Niki Lauda [14]	Ferrari	2012		Sebastian Vettel [32]	Red Bull
1978		Mario Andretti [16]	Lotus	2013		Sebastian Vettel [32]	Red Bull
1979		Jody Scheckter [17]	Ferrari	2014		Lewis Hamilton [30]	Mercedes
1980		Alan Jones [18]	Williams	2015		Lewis Hamilton [30]	Mercedes
1981		Nelson Piquet [19]	Brabham	2016		Nico Rosberg [33]	Mercedes
1982		Keke Rosberg [20]	Williams	2017		Lewis Hamilton [30]	Mercedes
1983		Nelson Piquet [19]	Brabham	2018		Lewis Hamilton [30]	Mercedes

YEAR	CONSTRUCTOR	DRIVERS	YEAR	CONSTRUCTOR	DRIVERS
1958	Vanwall	Stirling Moss, Tony Brooks	1988	Williams	Alain Prost, Ayrton Senna
1959	Cooper	Jack Brabham, Stirling Moss, Bruce McLaren	1989	McLaren	Ayrton Senna, Alain Prost
			1990	McLaren	Ayrton Senna, Gerhard Berger
1960	Cooper	Jack Brabham, Bruce McLaren,	1991	McLaren	Ayrton Senna, Gerhard Berger
1961	Ferrari	Phil Hill, Wolfgang von Trips	1992	Williams	Nigel Mansell, Riccardo Patrese, Alain Prost
1962	BRM	Graham Hill			
1963	Lotus	Jim Clark	1994	Williams	Damon Hill , Ayrton Senna, David Coulthard, Nigel Mansell
1964	Ferrari	John Surtees, Lorenzo Bandini,			
1965	Lotus	Jim Clark	1995	Benetton	Michael Schumacher, Johnny Herbert
1966	Brabham	Jack Brabham			
1967	Brabham	Denny Hulme, Jack Brabham,	1996	Williams	Damon Hill, Jacques Villeneuve
1968	Lotus	Graham Hill, Jo Siffert, Jim Clark, Jackie Oliver	1997	Williams	Jacques Villeneuve, Heinz-Harald Frentzen
			1998	McLaren	David Coulthard, Mika Häkkinen
1969	Matra	Jackie Stewart, Jean-Pierre Beltoise	1999	Ferrari	Michael Schumacher, Eddie Irvine, Mika Salo
1970	Lotus	Jochen Rindt, Emerson Fittipaldi, Graham Hill, John Miles	2000	Ferrari	Michael Schumacher, Rubens Barrichello
1971	Tyrrell	Jackie Stewart, François Cevert	2001	Ferrari	Michael Schumacher, Rubens Barrichello
1972	Lotus	Emerson Fittipaldi	2002	Ferrari	Michael Schumacher, Rubens Barrichello
1973	Lotus	Emerson Fittipaldi, Ronnie Peterson	2003	Ferrari	Michael Schumacher, Rubens Barrichello
1974	McLaren	Emerson Fittipaldi, Denny Hulme, Mike Hailwood, David Hobbs, Jochen Mass	2004	Ferrari	Michael Schumacher, Rubens Barrichello
			2005	Renault	Fernando Alonso, Giancarlo Fisichella
1975	Ferrari	Clay Regazzoni, Niki Lauda	2006	Renault	Fernando Alonso, Giancarlo Fisichella
1976	Ferrari	Niki Lauda, Clay Regazzoni			
1977	Ferrari	Niki Lauda, Carlos Reutemann	2007	Ferrari	Felipe Massa, Kimi Räikkönen
1978	Lotus	Mario Andretti, Ronnie Peterson	2008	Ferrari	Kimi Räikkönen, Felipe Massa
1979	Ferrari	Jody Scheckter, Gilles Villeneuve	2009	Brawn	Jenson Button, Rubens Barrichello
1980	Williams	Alan Jones, Carlos Reutemann	2010	Red Bull	Sebastian Vettel, Mark Webber
1981	Williams	Alan Jones, Carlos Reutemann	2011	Red Bull	Sebastian Vettel, Mark Webber
1982	Ferrari	Gilles Villeneuve, Didier Pironi, Patrick Tambay, Mario Andretti	2012	Red Bull	Sebastian Vettel, Mark Webber
			2013	Red Bull	Sebastian Vettel, Mark Webber
1983	Ferrari	Patrick Tambay, René Arnoux	2014	Mercedes	Lewis Hamilton, Nico Rosberg
1984	McLaren	Alain Prost, Niki Lauda	2015	Mercedes	Lewis Hamilton, Nico Rosberg
1985	McLaren	Niki Lauda, Alain Prost, John Watson	2016	Mercedes	Lewis Hamilton, Nico Rosberg
1986	Williams	Nigel Mansell, Nelson Piquet	2017	Mercedes	Lewis Hamilton, Valterri Bottas
1987	Williams	Nigel Mansell, Nelson Piquet, Ayrton Senna	2018	Mercedes	Lewis Hamilton, Valterri Bottas

ANSWERS

ANAGRAMS (P11)

I'M A SHOW LENTIL
LEWIS HAMILTON

A UFO IN A JUNGLE MAN
JUAN MANUEL FANGIO

SH MUCH ACHE CLAIMER
MICHAEL SCHUMACHER

A LOANS TRIP
ALAIN PROST

EVIE'S BATTLE TANS
SEBASTIAN VETTEL

BARB JAM HACK
JACK BRABHAM

SET JAW RACEKIT
JACKIE STEWART

UNDIAL KIA
NIKI LAUDA

QUILT NOSE PEN
NELSON PIQUET

ANNE'S NOTARY
AYRTON SENNA

SPOT THE DIFFERENCE (P11)

THE BIG F1 QUIZ (P26)

1. Chinese Grand Prix
2. 1950
3. Silverstone
4. Lando Norris
5. Kimi Räikkönen
6. Four
7. Valtteri Bottas
8. Porridge
9. A loose drain cover
10. Daniil Kvyat and Alexander Albon
11. Lewis Hamilton
12. Mexico Grand Prix
13. Romain Grosjean
14. Marcus Ericsson
15. "Valtteri, it's James, please hold position" –
    1 point for the entire quote, ½ point for partial
16. 2008
17. Fernando Alonso and Nelson Piquet Jr.
18. 20
19. Austrian GP
20. 25
21. 2009
22. 1 point for either Force India or Racing Point
23. Timo Glock
24. Michael Schumacher and Ruebens Barrichello
25. Lola
26. Martin Brundle, Olivier Panis and Aguri Suzuki
27. Gerhard Berger
28. Damon Hill
29. Johnny Herbert
30. Mika Häkkinen
31. Six
32. Long Beach, Watkins Glen, Las Vegas,
    Detroit, Dallas and Phoenix
33. Keke Rosberg
34. The Marquis of Bute
35. Ayrton Senna
36. Eliseo Salazar
37. 10
38. Hesketh
39. Alfa Romeo
40. Clay Regazzoni
41. Cooper Maserati
42. The Indianapolis 500
43. Bruce McLaren
44. Dan Gurney, Jack Brabham and Bruce McLaren
45. Barcelona
46. Climax
47. Peter Collins
48. Aintree
49. Alfa Romeo
50. Juan Manuel Fangio

MURRAY WALKER CRYPTOGRAMS (P20)

EASY ANSWER:
"YOU MIGHT NOT THINK THAT'S CRICKET, AND IT'S NOT, IT'S MOTOR RACING"

DIFFICULT ANSWER:
"IF IS A VERY LONG WORD IN FORMULA ONE; FACT IF IS FI SPELLED BACKWARDS"

CROSSWORD (P34)

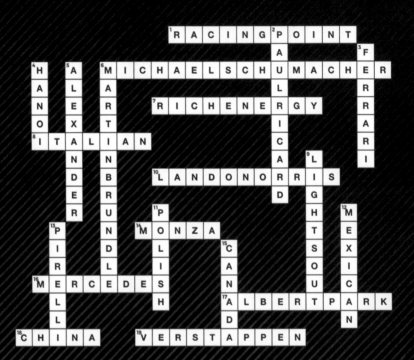

WORDSEARCH (P35)

SPOT THE DRIVERS

Can you spot Bottas, Hamilton and Verstappen hiding in the crowd at the 2019 German Grand Prix?

SHOCK TO THE SYSTEM

The Illustrated Biography by Mark Putterford.

OMNIBUS PRESS

LONDON · NEW YORK · SYDNEY

Edited by Chris Charlesworth.
Picture research by David Brolan.

ISBN 0.7119.2823.1
Order No.OP 46671

Exclusive distributors:
Book Sales Limited
8/9 Frith Street, London W1V 5TZ, UK.
Music Sales Corporation
225 Park Avenue South, New York, NY 10003, USA.
Music Sales Pty Limited
120 Rothschild Avenue, Rosebery, NSW 2018, Australia.

To the Music Trade only:
Music Sales Limited
8/9 Frith Street, London W1V 5TZ, UK.

Photo credits: Glenn A. Baker Archives: 15, 20, 21, 22, 46b;
Dick Barnett/Redferns: 26, 28, 29, 30, 31; Ross Barnett/Retna: front cover;
George Bodnar: 74b, 75 78, 80b; George Bodnar/Idols: 79; George Bodnar/Relay: 70;
Larry Busacca/Retna: 5b, 6, 8, back cover x 2; Fin Costello/Redferns: 54/55, 57;
Erica Eschenberg/Redferns: 65; Ken Friedman/Retna: 90; Bob King/Redferns: 87;
LFI: 7, 9, 11, 12, 24, 32t&b, 42b, 43, 45b, 46t, 56b, 60, 63, 64, 66, 71, 72t, 82, 83,
85t&b, 86, 88; Janet Macoska/Retna: 4, 44, 45t; Ulf Magnusson/Idols: 93;
Pictorial Press: 13, 14, 16, 17, 25, 33, 35, 36, 62, 67, 77, 80t;
Barry Plummer: 10, 18, 27, 40, 41, 48, 50, 56t, 58, 72b, 92; Relay: 42t, 47, 51, 56c,
59t&b, 68, 73, 74t, 81, 89; 76; Jodi Summers/Retna: 76; David Willis/Idols: 5t.

Printed in the United Kingdom by
Ebenezer Baylis & Son Limited, Worcester.

ACKNOWLEDGEMENTS:

As always, every effort has been made to ensure that the factual content of this book
is accurate but not everyone approached for help had the decency to co-operate and
provide relevant information. The author would like to stress his gratitude to those who
helped with the project.

They include Malcolm Dome, Tony Mottram, Mary Hooton, Steve Payne, Sharon and Ozzy
Osbourne, J-M Litton, Robert Ellis, Wendy Dio, Phil Alexander, Debs
and Mark Gutterres, Sylvie Simmons, Xavier Russell, Jerry Ewing, Shonadh French,
Part Rock Management, Chris Charlesworth, Mark Evans, Michael Browning, Dave Dee,
Tony Platt, Simon Wright and Pete Way.

Love to Rocky, Rosie and especially Lynn, to whom this whole thing is dedicated.

For those about to read... I salute you!

Mark Putterford, November 1991.

Chapter I

For Those About To Rock (...He's Behind You!)

n the chill of the night, mystery tightens an air of suspense. Beneath the giant cathedral of webbed-scaffolding and towering speaker cabinets, the heads of the faithful twitch and turn in synchronised bewilderment, a seething carpet glowing in the colours of raining spotlight beams. The music, testosterone with a beat, pumps unperturbed...

Where did he go? Where is he? Up there...? Over there...? Here...? Where...?

The music pumps on. Eyes catch other eyes, faces flash over shoulders, necks strain.

Minutes pass. Then...

A roar! There he is, on the screen, on three screens in fact... but where exactly IS he?

The beat quickens, fingers jab in triumph... look, HE'S BEHIND YOU!

Angus Young, the most energetic termite in rock history, stripped to the waist and scrabbling frantically with his predicament, stands on a hydraulic platform high above his disciples shaking like a fresh-born infant, still attached to the womb of the stage by some strange, invisible umbilical powerchord. Not a note is dropped, not a facial grimace sacrificed.

The stunt is familiar but the gesture no less genuine: this bizarre man-child, an iconic symbol of teenage angst suspended in eternal adolescence, a real working class hero-in-half-pants, at one with his punters. The band drive on like they always did, hammering out their time-honoured tattoo with débutant-enthusiasm. Angus, ever the outraged troll, thrashes in a nervous hysteria, clinging to the life-support of his guitar in rock's most well-rehearsed routine of spontaneity. And, champing at the bit of their own loyalty, the throng remains the same.

This is supposed to be the kind of thing that leads to frenzied suicides. This is supposed to be the music of the devil. This is what parents everywhere are worried witless about. In reality, it's just a good old pantomime, only louder.

Rock-atheists would no doubt giggle into their Evian. And granted, the notion of 72,500 presumably sane people paying £22.50 to stand in a Leicestershire field for 12 bone-chilling hours to watch a 36-year-old Australian 'duck-walk' around a stage dressed as a schoolboy does sound marginally unbelievable.

But then the reality of AC/DC defies logic like the perennial popularity of 'the devil's music' defies its detractors: never... in the field of musical accomplishment... has so much been achieved... for so many fans... by so few chords.

Some 17 years after they first struggled through the toilets of Sydney - in the days when appalling 'soaps', kid-next-door pop stars and the rest of the current stomach-turning cultural infestation from Oz was just a nightmare-in-waiting - AC/DC are true Monsters Of Rock. Headlining Castle Donington's namesake festival on August 17, 1991, for a record third time in ten years, underlined that very fact.

The festival itself has become the highlight of the rock cognoscenti calendar; a spectacular AGM of the self-appointed Great Unwashed, a celebration of isolation from trendy society, a homage to a dinosaur tradition undiminished by derision and persecution.

Comfortingly, the press hate it; snooty sideswipes from The Independent, The Daily Telegraph, The Daily Mail and others littered the media prior to AC/DC's third Donington campaign. But all tickets for the event were snapped up within days of going on sale, proving once again that years of wet weekends in the mud at Reading or Knebworth haven't dampened the rock fan's enthusiasm for a festival.

They're big business too. The original

idea of an open-air pop festival, popularised in the late '60s by Hyde Park, Woodstock, the Isle Of Wight and others, may have been about simply congregating in a spare field with a few thousand kindred spirits and absorbing the vibes until you came round, but these days - especially in the wake of Live Aid - each show costs a fortune to stage and requires an enormous amount of organisation.

The Donington circus itself involved a stage constructed of 250 tonnes of steel, plus another 250 tonnes of production equipment, requiring 34 huge articulated trucks to ferry the whole lot around. Hundreds of crew - 116 production workers contracted to AC/DC alone - toil for over a week to prepare the site, and millions of pounds change hands in the business that the event generates. According to The Daily Telegraph, '... taking into account their cut of the all-important merchandising at Castle Donington, AC/DC can expect to come away with more than £1 million...'.

Yet strip away all the inevitable trimm-

ings and AC/DC are still a club band. Paradoxically in a medium typified by outrageous attire and ostentatious, egotistical presentation, AC/DC come dressed in the same jeans and T-shirts they've worn onstage for six years. Angus is the one element of theatre in a show otherwise purged of affectation. There's no between-song banter, no introductions, no make-up, no hairspray, no backslapping, no ballads, no covers, no medleys, no drum solos, no keyboards, no tapes and very little movement from anyone except the inexhaustible Angus. In short, AC/DC even go against the grain of rock's own little trends.

Yet contradictions are very much integral to the AC/DC subconscience. At odds with the sexual ambiguity of their name, AC/DC's lyrics have remained lasciviously heterosexual. And hints at diabolism ('Hell Ain't A Bad Place To Be', 'Highway To Hell', 'Hell's Bells', etc) which have caused controversy and consternation around the so-called civilised world, could scarcely be further from the truth.

The band themselves, one of the hardest working live acts in the world

today, also keep one of the lowest profiles offstage. And the very concept of Angus - a little white boy playing old black men's blues - may still test the bounds of reason for some.

On a more poignant note, perhaps the biggest irony of AC/DC's career came in 1980 when, just months after the death of the band's universally-loved singer and widely-acknowledged spiritual leader Bon Scott, AC/DC finally realised their commercial potential, after years of hard slog, with the multi-platinum chart-topping 'Back In Black'. It was a bitter-sweet moment which stirs the emotions in the AC/DC camp even today.

Today, though Brian Johnson - looking more like a docker than a rocker - is the focal-point of AC/DC, the irrepressible personification of Tyneside Working Men's Clubs, Newcastle Brown Ale and 40 tabs a day. With Cliff Williams clocking up his fourteenth year on bass and bald beat-master Chris Slade making his first tour with the band seem like his tenth, AC/DC are as solid as ever.

They hit the Donington stage at 8.20pm with 'Thunderstruck', tiny figures beneath a tumbling sky making one full metal racket. Angus, the

evergreen *enfant terrible* hops, skips and scampers around the boards like a six-year-old in a playground, hair wet with sweat before the second verse, impossibly little legs a pale, bony blur beneath his giant SG. The pilgrims, many of whom must've witnessed this ritual a dozen times or more, greet each signature with the customary clenched-fist salute. For them, AC/DC are the sweetest form of déjà-vu.

Unabashed, 'Shoot To Thrill' and 'Back In Black' are next, testing the double-glazing of neighbouring housing estates while the huge seven-section, state-of-the-art lighting rig ripples rainbows from above. Then 'Hell Ain't A Bad Place To Be' comes accompanied by a monstrous inflatable Angus dummy which threatens to smother Chris Slade as it balloons

from nowhere to bob in the breeze. Set to the primitive throb of bastardised blues, these very '90s gimmicks help foster another contradictory thread through AC/DC.

'Heatseeker' is next as the velvet canopy of night lowers itself over the Leicestershire countryside, then we get 'Fire Your Guns', 'Jailbreak', 'The Jack', 'Dirty Deeds Done Dirt Cheap', 'Money Talks', 'Hell's Bells', 'Whole Lotta Rosie', 'TNT' and 'Let There Be Rock', complete with Angus's essential hide-and-seek nonsense. At the usual points in between there's also a shower of fake dollar bills, a one-and-a-half ton bell and two more inflatable beasts to behold.

To cap the lot though, first-encore 'Highway To Hell' is followed by 'For Those About To Rock', wherein no less

than 21 cannons perched across the top of the cliff-like stage sound the appropriate salute in spectacular fashion. The flashes can be seen some four miles away from the southbound carriageway of the M1 by those sensible enough to get a headstart on the chaotic post-festival exodus.

It's an infallible show, safe as houses. In many ways it sums up AC/DC, sticking so close to the formula as to actually BE the formula itself. But there's no parody; AC/DC's virtual superhuman capacity for rejuvenated repetition sees to that.

Anyone doubting it before Donington 1991 must've sobered up the next day to agree with the fact that AC/DC are one of the most unique acts in rock today... and very possibly, tomorrow.

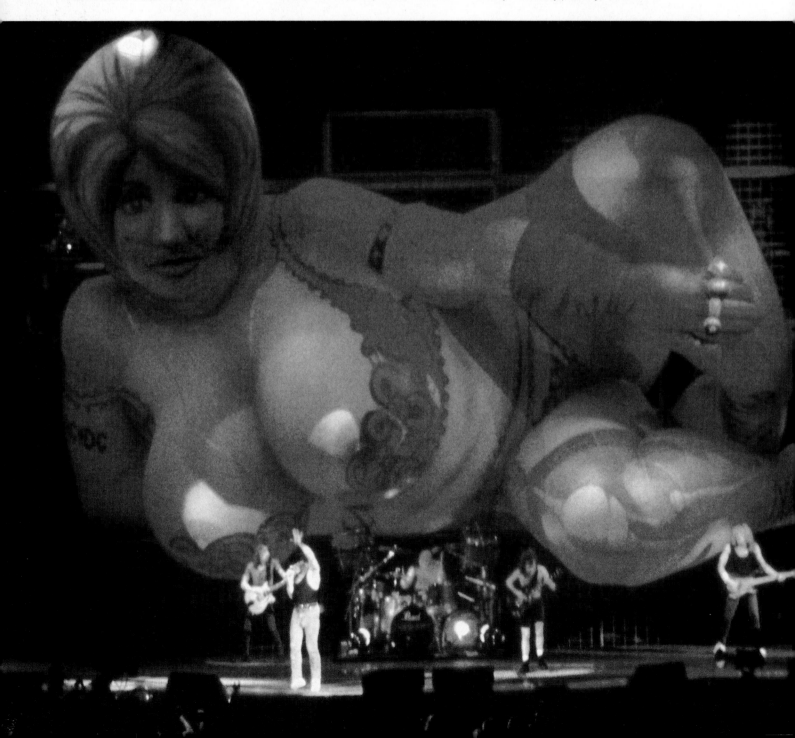

Chapter II

In The Beginning
(...Back In 1955)

When Malcolm Young was born on January 6, 1953, it was a well-rehearsed routine for the Young family. They already had five kids running amok in their modest Glasgow home but the baby born that new year would turn out to be the most exceptional of all their children.

Other, older members of the clan would certainly offer crucial qualities to the development of the Young dynasty, and a brother yet to be born was destined to be the centrepiece of it all, but to Malcolm fell the role of prime mover and foundation of the rock band on which the fortunes of the Young family would prosper until they became the most powerful family in the history of Australian music.

All of which aches for a 'rags-to-riches' cliché (so there you go). A large working class family getting by in one of Britain's toughest cities, the Youngs survived on whatever their father – an unskilled labourer who "did a bit of paint-spraying" – could bring home each week; no easy way of life, even in the post-war atmosphere of relative prosperity. On March 31, 1955, yet another son, Angus McKinnon, swelled the family to nine. Life in the concrete confines of the clustered Strathclyde city was no picnic and the Youngs realised their days in Scotland were numbered. "All I remember of Glasgow was being hit by a car and playing football in the streets near the housing estate where we lived," Angus recalled later.

Angus was eight and Malcolm was ten when, like many families in search of a bright new future in the hazy Utopia of a far-flung continent, The Young Ones uprooted their Glaswegian anchor to chase the potentially more exotic climes of Australia. They settled in the south eastern city of Sydney in New South Wales – discovered in 1788 by Captain Arthur Phillips, 18 years after the historic explorations of Captain James Cook, and popularly known as 'the birthplace of Australia' – and found themselves at the heart of an explosive boomtown in the southern hemisphere.

Post-war optimism and the end of the depression had given a sharp fillip to Australian nationalism. The Sixties became a period of steady economic expansion, indexed to a rise in self-confidence and perhaps the first truly great period of cultural growth since the 1890s.

Moreover, mass immigration from Europe was rapidly diminishing the country's previous isolation, and suddenly the vast, lonely territory once dubbed 'Terra Australia Incognita' – the

unknown southern land – and designated as the last and most desolate and therefore most suitable place on earth for the penal destination of convicts, was hurtling towards the standards of sophistication set in Europe and America.

By the time the Youngs relocated in 1963, the settlement built on a landscape littered with human bones less than 200 years before, had become a modern metropolitan complex covering 700 square miles. Housing now spread from the rim of the Blue Mountains in the west to the beaches and bays of 152 miles of shoreland on the Pacific coast in the east. And foreign influences were permeating 'Oz' society with new fangled notions from women's lib to student protests, hippies to pizzas… and even something called rock'n'roll.

The greatest manifestation of the upsurge in rock'n'roll in Australia occurred when The Beatles turned the country on its head in June of 1964. Then at the peak of their global popularity, The Beatles created scenes of unprecedented uproar in several cities with crowds of 100,000 or more turning out to welcome the group at airports, to line the routes to their hotels or simply to stand and stare in the streets below balconies in the hope that the quartet would show themselves. Reliable eye witness reports indicate that of all the countries The Beatles visited during the heady days of Beatlemania, no country gave them a greater reception than Australia. It was a liberating experience and Australia was never quite the same again after their visit.

The Youngs had already made a passing acquaintance with this rock'n' roll thing. All of the elder children

discovered music back in Glasgow, with Alex taking up the trombone and saxophone (and following a professional career under the name of George Alexander), George hankering after the electric guitar, and sister Margaret also picking up rock'n'roll and r&b imports from America by such artists as Bill Haley, Elvis Presley, Little Richard, Buddy Holly and, most crucially in the eyes of her younger brother, Charles 'Chuck' Berry.

In the midst of this revolutionary musical explosion, there is ample justification that the opening line of 'Let There Be Rock' – from whence the title of this chapter comes – is chronologically correct. In 1955 Bill Haley and his energetic Comets made their big breakthrough, galvanising a generation with 'Rock Around The Clock', one of the biggest-selling singles of all time; Elvis Presley made his first local chart entry in the US; and Chuck Berry met fellow blues player Muddy Waters, signed his first record deal and reached No.5 on the Billboard charts with his début single, 'Maybelline'.

More than anyone, Berry proved a powerful influence on Malcolm and Angus. From the infectious, insistent simplicity of his chugging guitar style to the goofy 'duck-walk' which would remain as much a part of Angus' act as the infamous school uniform, Berry made such an impression on the brothers that some 30 years later Angus would still cite him as one of his favourite artists.

"My friends would come around and talk about Eric Clapton," said Angus in

1991, recalling his formative years, "and my brothers would go, 'What's this Eric Clapton crap? The guy is Chuck Berry!' And they'd talk about him, so they got me thinking, 'Why do they like Chuck Berry?' When you see the guy play, then you realise..."

Berry's style, honed on that very first single in July '55, was an uptempo blues-based 12-bar rhythm spiked with country rockabilly licks and played with maximum emphasis on the off beat. In addition, Berry wrote some of the wittiest lyrics of his era, sharp teenage anthems delivered with clarity and precision which brought a discipline to his recordings that continues to influence rock guitarists and lyricists across two continents to the present day.

Born in 1926, in San Jose, California, Berry nurtured this electric new slant on the blues during the early Fifties when he clubbed around the St. Louis circuit with a primitive guitar-piano-drums trio. Then, after running into Muddy Waters in Chicago, he was recommended to the pioneering Chess Records label. 'Roll Over Beethoven' hit the US Top 30 in June 1956, 'School Day' proved a million seller in May '57, and after a string of other successes like 'Oh Baby Doll', 'Rock And Roll Music' and 'Sweet Little Sixteen', a song called 'Johnny B Goode' hit the Top 30 on both sides of the Atlantic. This cryptic tale of a would-be guitar hero not only ensured Berry's legendary status, but also wrote itself into the annals of rock history by becoming one of the most popular rockers to be covered by other artists.

Berry's fortunes waxed and waned during the Sixties and Seventies. He went to jail on trumped up vice charges for a couple of years and developed a reputation as a bitter, tetchy man, the scourge of concert promoters, ever inclined to demand extra money (in immediate cash) to play an encore while an audience was baying for more and threatening the furniture. He terrorised under-rehearsed pick-up bands in the UK: when one unfortunate back-up player timidly inquired of him which songs they were to play minutes before a show, he replied... "Chuck Berry songs, you fool!" He scored with a freak UK No.1 hit in November '72 (the double entendre novelty singalong, 'My Ding-A-Ling') and went back to jail on tax evasion charges, but thousands of imitators have materialised in his wake, not least in the Young household, where even four-year-old Angus had started to fumble around with any one of his older brothers' guitars.

The first Young to make any notable progress in music, however, was George. Born on November 6, 1947, he made his mark more as a schoolboy soccer player than as a musician in Scotland, but on arriving at Villawood Migrant Youth Hostel in outer Sydney in 1963 he chanced upon a number of other European émigrés with a similar interest in the mushrooming Beatles-style pop, and plans were laid for a group which would attempt to capitalise on this very marketable sound.

The Easybeats timed their approach on the ripe Antipodean teen audience with exacting precision. Featuring 'Little' Stevie Wright on vocals, George Young and Harry Wandan (né Vanda) on guitars, Dick Diamonde on bass and Gordon 'Snowy' Fleet on drums, they became the resident group at Sydney's Beatle Village Club in 1964, attracting the interest of producer Ted Albert who subsequently signed them to Australian Parlophone.

The following year The Easybeats hit the top of the Australian charts with 'She's So Fine', the first of five hits in Oz during a period of popularity which was inevitably dubbed 'Easyfever'. Then, mindful of the limitations of the domestic pop scene, they decided to chance their arm abroad, returning 'home' to Britain during 1966 and quickly scoring with the fondly remembered Vanda/Young composition 'Friday On My Mind', which reached No.6 in the charts during December and is still regularly featured as a golden oldie on nostalgia shows.

Given the mercurial mid-Sixties climate of short lifespans in pop and the standard of competition at the time, the failure of The Easybeats to sustain their brief success wasn't surprising, and despite a minor UK hit with 'Hello, How Are You?' in May '68, they were destined to disintegrate by the end of the decade. Young and co-writer Harry Vanda eventually returned to Australia to work within the Albert Studios complex in Sydney's King Street, writing and producing acts for their old friend Ted Albert under the umbrella of Albert Productions, while the other members of the group headed for the yawning orifice of obscurity.

For the pubescent Australian pop scene this was something of a body blow. While Britain and America were busy churning out stars at will in the Sixties, the best Australia could offer was Johnny O'Keefe (who started out,

Angus' hero Chuck Berry in classic duck-walking position.

like Cliff Richard, as an Elvis clone), Frank Ifield (a country & western/MOR-style singer with a penchant for yodelling), chuntering cartoonist Rolf Harris, The Bee Gees and The Seekers. And even that's stretching a point: both Ifield and The Bee Gees originated from Britain (Coventry and Manchester respectively), while children's entertainer Harris only really made his name after moving to Britain, achieving his biggest success with the classic under-fives tear-jerker 'Two Little Boys' in 1969.

This cultural retardation of contemporary Australian music (and the arts in general) was mainly the result of the stifling apathy, ingrained bigotry and crusty conservatism of the country's media and various pompous guardians of morality and law and order. Anything more progressive than jazz was commonly frowned upon until the mid-Sixties when the overwhelming momentum of change in Europe and America snapped the Australian establishment out of its backward daze. The irony was that during this period of social and cultural emancipation, the subversive and sexually-liberating journalism of excommunicated Aussies Richard Neville and Germaine Greer respectively, was having as much of an impact as anything on the periphery of European psychedelia.

Nevertheless, back in Sydney the seeds of an entirely different future for Oz music had been planted by the imported sounds of Fifties r&b and the closer-to-home success of The Easybeats. Reared as they were on old rock'n'roll records, Malcolm and Angus suddenly saw at first hand the benefits of having your own band when big brother (and national heart throb) George broke into 'the big time'. At the peak of 'Easyfever' the Youngs' family home in the Sydney district of Burwood came under siege from frenzied schoolgirls when the address was mischievously leaked by the local media. The incident caused much consternation among the more senior members of the family but for Angus the adoring attention of frenzied teenage girls seemed like an incredibly good idea.

"One day George was a 16-year-old kid sitting on his bed playing guitar," Angus reflected, "and the next day he was worshipped by the whole country. I was going to school at the time – or rather trying not to go to school – and I was very impressed. He (George) was getting all the girls. That's why I always said

It's the truth!"

Malcolm picked up the guitar first, graduating quickly from acoustic to electric and picking up tips from his older brother whenever The Easybeats returned from a tour. At Ashfield Boys High School he often found himself scorned because of his connection with the Easybeat madness and his tendency to get into scraps meant that by the time Angus started school some two years later, "I was caned on the first day just to make sure I didn't get any of his ideas."

Angus messed around with his older brothers' guitars for years before his mother finally bought him his own... "a cheap little acoustic, a kind of Woolies job". Then, while Malcolm worked as an apprentice fitter and eventually a machine maintenance man for Berlei Bras and bought more professional models, Angus would get his brothers' hand-downs. By the time he was 11 he had flirted with a tutorial course, but he preferred DIY and most of his musical education was pure trial and error.

Eventually Malcolm put a few small bands together, knocking around with school friends in the humblest traditions

with Australia's own Velvet Underground (no relation to the legendary US version), who'd relocated to Sydney from Newcastle, New South Wales, looking for their big break. Ironically, they featured a singer called Brian Johnson (not the later AC/DC singer) but he was short-lived and the band entered 1972 with both Andy Imlah and Ted Mulry contributing vocals, joining bassist Steve Crothers, drummer Herm Kovak and guitarist Les Hall. Like all minor league outfits, their fortunes were rarely affected by the changes in personnel.

Nevertheless Angus, now a fast learning 17-year-old, was hugely impressed by the progress of his closest brother, and duly laid plans for his own band, appropriately called Tantrum. Occasionally the two brothers would fool around together at home, with Angus later admitting that "most of what I learned about guitar I picked up from Malcolm", but for the time being they were pacing along different paths. Angus, for a start, had only just left school.

13

admits. "If I could get out of going to school – if anyone could think of a way – it was me. I done all the tricks: paint spots on my face, climb out of the bedroom window before my mother woke me..."

Not surprisingly, Angus left school at 15, the moment he was legally able to do so. His only real academic interest was art which allowed him some freedom of expression ("I once made a six-foot long fly out of papier mâché which scared the shit out of everyone on the bus home"), so at the first opportunity he cut loose from Ashfield ("The third worst school in the state," he boasted with some degree of perverted pride later) and, for a while, earned his upkeep in printing, working on a soft-porn mag called Ribald.

"...But at the time what I was doing was dying off as a trade," he recalls. "Computers were coming in and even the people I worked with would say 'You're wasting your time in here, kid. Go and do something else'."

His ambitions lay elsewhere anyway, and for a year prior to leaving school he'd been practising guitar almost constantly, jamming around with friends

Angus would come home from school, snatch his guitar and dash out again, before he could be roped into any chores. This meant he'd turn up for practise sessions still decked out in his school uniform, presenting an unlikely spectacle which a year or so later his sister Margaret would suggest might be used deliberately to make him the focal point of a band. It would prove one of Angus's most profitable accidents, a fluke of design which was to cultivate a unique and lasting image in contemporary popular music.

For the time being, though, Angus was still looking for direction, practising his bar-chord Chuck Berry licks and getting off on the likes of The Who, The Rolling Stones, The Yardbirds (the spacey guitar sound on 'I'm A Man' made a big impression on him), and anything else he'd find in his brothers' record collections. That was until Malcolm decided he needed a second guitar player – and not a pianist as someone tried to suggest – for the band he was putting together in the wake of Velvet Underground's demise, and turned to Angus for help. "He said he needed to fill the sound out with two guitars,"

joined the band to beef things up a bit. I wasn't really doing much at the time, so I thought, 'What the hell...'."

It was 1973, the year glam rock followed in the wake of a hard rock onslaught spearheaded by Led Zeppelin, Deep Purple and Black Sabbath. It was the post-psychedelic era, and young Australians were finally beginning to shake off the shackles of claustrophobic convention. Malcolm's vision for his new band was a hard-edged boogie sound married to the in-vogue image of long hair and stack-heeled boots. Angus was to provide the novelty angle – a virtual babe-in-arms who played guitar like a maniacal demon.

For experience, Malcolm called on the services of drummer Colin Burgess, who'd previously played in Untamed (from 1966-67), The Haze (1967-68), The Master Apprentices (1968-72) and the George Hatcher Band (no relation to the UK namesake which emerged during the mid-Seventies). The line-up was completed by bassist Larry Van Knedt and singer David Evans, two struggling

Malcolm Young (sitting) with his pre-AC/DC band Velvet Underground, circa 1972.

else. Early rehearsals consisted of reworkings of old blues and r'n'b standards and discussions on what to call the fledgling creation.

"In the end," explained Angus, "my sister (Margaret) suggested something she'd seen on the back of her vacuum cleaner: AC/DC. It had something to do with electricity, so it seemed to fit..."

The abbreviation stands for alternating current/direct current in electrical parlance, a reference to the contrasting flow of two separate transmissions of power through a conductor. However, in their naïvety the Youngs were ignorant of the term's bisexual connotations, and the band were to spend the next few years vehemently insisting on their heterosexuality. Indeed, on their very first tour of Australia they found themselves opening for bisexual ex-Velvet Underground (the 'real' one) star Lou Reed on a few occasions, an unfortunate situation which seemed to confirm their bisexuality to every gay venue in the country which subsequently tried to book them. It became a running joke.

Back in the winter of 1973 though, the fledgling AC/DC were booked to play at a New Year's Eve party at Sydney's Chequers nightclub. It was their début gig and their set of rock'n'roll standards spilled over into 1974. While it would be all too easy to romanticise about the roaring success of that night, it was the kick-start to nearly 20 years of almost solid live work and AC/DC never looked back. Throughout the Seventies the band's reputation would snowball into obese proportions while the Young family and their offspring wormed their way into subsections of the Oz music scene like the tentacles of some giant monster squid.

George, along with his partner Harry Vanda, worked on various projects at Albert Studios in the early Seventies. Probably the most significant was the Marcus Hook Roll Band, whose early recording sessions for their eponymous 1973 début LP featured not only George and Harry, but Malcolm and Angus in their first ever recorded work. The Vanda/Young team then masterminded AC/DC's rise to the top, signing them to Albert Productions, producing them and moulding them along the way. Later they produced two solo albums for former Easybeats singer Stevie Wright ('Hard Road' and 'Black Eyed Bruiser' respectively, the former featuring the Vanda/Young-penned hit single 'Evie'), and they also wrote and produced a number of less memorable acts for

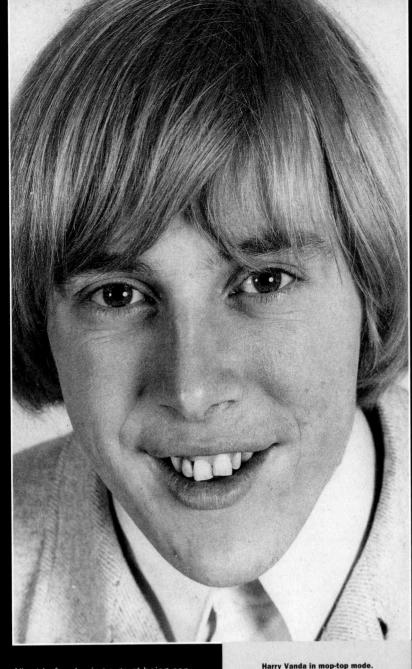

Harry Vanda in mop-top mode.

Albert before having a go at being pop stars again themselves. During the rest of the Seventies and even in the early Eighties, they had varied success as the Band Of Hope, Paintbox and Flash & The Pan, their biggest single success coming in June '83 when, as Flash & The Pan they hit No.7 in the UK with 'Waiting For A Train'. Two subsequent albums failed to create any kind of impact, however.

Another of George and Harry's production successes was John Paul Young's hit single 'Love Is In The Air' in the mid-Seventies, while Alex Young also joined up with Albert Productions, eventually running the company's Hamburg office. While working in Germany he too turned his hand to the art of songwriting, penning the title track of Teutonic metal outfit Accept's second album, 'I'm A Rebel'.

Margaret would marry Easybeats tour manager Sam Horsburgh, who went on to mix Rose Tattoo's 'Assault And Battery' LP in 1981. Their son, Sammy

Horsburgh Junior (also known as Sammy Young), ended up engineering Rose Tattoo's follow-up album, 'Scarred For Life', during a promising career at – where else? – Albert Studios.

Later in the Eighties another nephew of the Young brothers, Stevie Young, would fill in for Malcolm during a break from touring commitments, before returning to push his own band, Little Big Horn (managed, of course, by AC/DC's management – Stewart 'no relation' Young!). While yet another nephew, James Young, would crop up in B.B. Steal, a Def Leppard-style Aussie outfit signed to PolyGram Australia and produced by Leppard guitarist Phil Collen.

From the early Seventies, it seemed, the Australian music scene was destined to remain Young at heart.

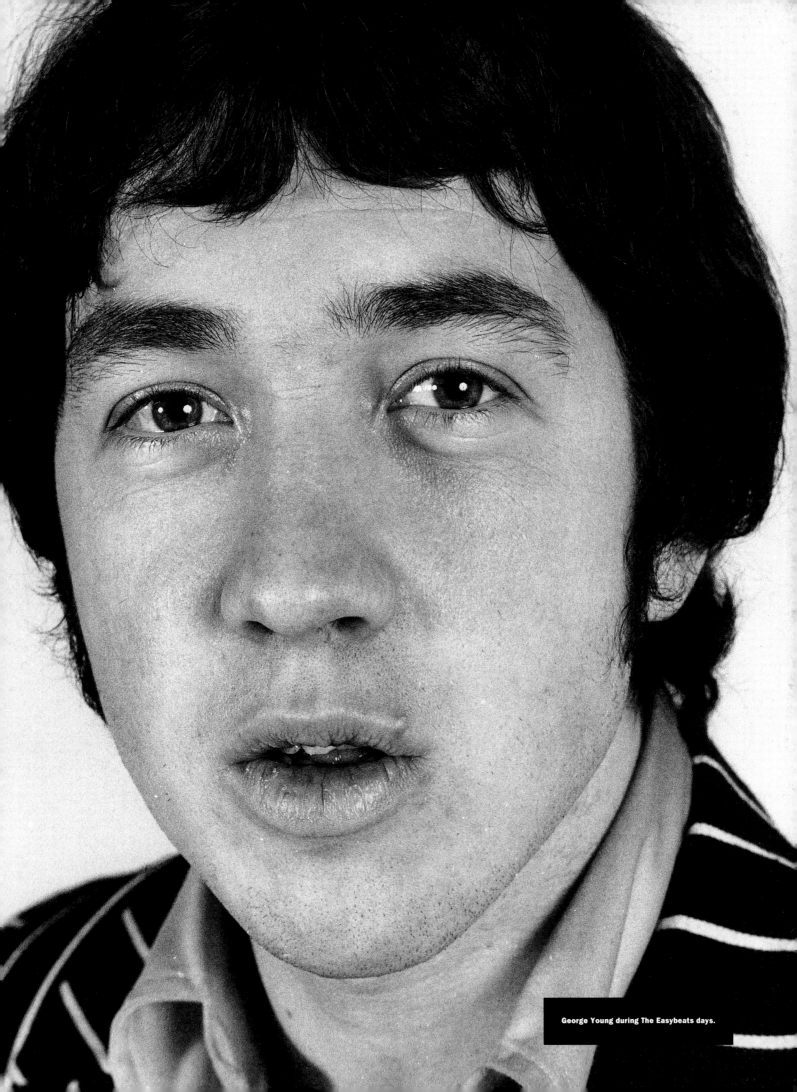

George Young during The Easybeats days.

Chapter III

T.N.T.
(...The Nightclub Trail)

During the months that followed AC/DC's first tentative steps on the yellow brick road to recognition and acclaim, Malcolm and Angus Young frequently shuffled the line-up of the band in their quest for the right chemistry.

First to go was Colin Burgess, bound for His Majesty (and eventually to reform The Master Apprentices in 1988), and out too went Larry Van Knedt. Ron Carpenter and Rob Bailey (ex-Natural Gas) filled the vacancies respectively. Neither of these replacements lasted long enough to make an impression; Carpenter swiftly made way for Russell Coleman (who himself handed the drum-stool to Peter Clack within weeks), and Bailey also found his days numbered by the end of the summer of 1974.

Singer Dave Evans, meanwhile, developed a Rod Stewart/Gary Glitter fixation, which naturally didn't sit well with the Young brothers, but with genuine talent hard to come by in the rock'n'roll outback that was early Seventies Sydney, Malcolm and Angus had to make do with the best of a bad bunch for the time being.

The embryonic AC/DC did, however, manage to break out on to vinyl. During June 1974 the Young-Young-Evans-Bailey-Clack line-up were whisked into Albert Studios in Sydney to record a single, 'Can I Sit Next To You Girl'/ 'Rockin' In The Parlour', which surfaced in Australia in July on Albert Records and in New Zealand on Polydor. Master-minded by the Vanda/Young production team, it was a minor hit in Perth and Adelaide, and is now a rarity buried in AC/DC's archives. Certainly anyone still in possession of the record, or even footage of the band playing the song live which appeared on Australian TV at the time, has a real collectors' item.

Essentially, the brothers were still very much finding their feet at this point, scrabbling around for the right formula in every department. The earliest AC/DC gigs found 19-year-old Angus in an assortment of wacky costumes and disguises – as a gorilla, as the masked swordsman Zorro and even as his own version of Superman – 'Super-Ang'! The Youngs felt they needed a visual novelty, something memorably outrageous, to compete with the powerful allure of the amber nectar at the bars and clubs in which they played. Something more than an incessant boogie stomp was needed to catch people's attention, and once they'd managed to get the razzled roughnecks to lift their eyes from the bottom of their glasses, they'd need to make a lasting impression if they

AC/DC circa summer '74 -
30 inch satin flares just out of shot.

were to secure further bookings.

That's when Margaret made her suggestion. Initially, Angus had tried the schoolboy get-up in one of his previous bands, and he later talked about his concept of a nine-year-old Guitar God who would play one show before disappearing forever, thus ensuring legendary status in the process. But this time the idea was to make the image a permanent fixure...

"Of course at first I thought 'No way!'," Angus said later. "I mean, I never liked school anyway. But my brother George said to me, 'Wear this and you'll be rich' - a complete wind-up of course - and I was a sucker. When I put it on I felt such a monkey that I just had to keep moving onstage. I figured somebody's gonna hit me with a bottle, I'm such an obvious target, so I just kept going, head shaking, just went wild."

The famous Angus freak-out was well on its way, once again completely by accident. Angus had literally stumbled across the basis of his stage routine a year or so earlier when, playing at a local school dance with Tantrum, he tripped on a guitar lead and ended up butt-over-bonce on the deck. Feeling a bit of a berk, he decided he'd try to make it look like a deliberate prank, writhing around on the floor while continuing to play. When he staggered to his feet moments later to find the crowd applauding wildly, he'd discovered another piece in the jigsaw of his stage persona.

Psychologically, the image of the schoolboy with a thousand volts through his veins, also helped Angus combat the pressures of performing. In the macho bush pubs where men are men and women are... probably men too, the

slightly iffy prospect of a cheeky school-boy in dinky little shorts fronting a band with a slightly iffy name meant Angus had to hide behind some kind of wild exterior, if only to save his own skin.

"It was a bit hairy at first," he recalled, "but I used to try and come on as tough as I could. I'd put a cigarette in my mouth, walk onstage, stub it on the floor and hope nobody would call my bluff!"

Needless to say it worked. The idea transcended its original notion as a tongue-in-cheek suggestion to become a powerful performing tool, subconsciously capitalising on society's lasting fascination with the brattish yet lovable urchin-like schoolkid.

From Kipling's Stalky & Co. at the turn of the century, Thomas Hughes' Tom Brown's Schooldays, Frank Richards' Billy Bunter and Richmal Crompton's Just William tales to the frivolous antics of The Beano's Dennis The Menace and The Bash Street Kids, the vision of the scruffy, snot-faced oik with scabs on his knees and a catapult sticking out of his back pocket has been etched into the chronicles of English literature.

Music Hall too threw up its juvenile delinquent heroes, as did the small screen in the shape of TV series like Wacko!, and while the girls also got in on the act with the St. Trinians films, it was the mischievious little monkey in the baggy shorts and the slightly askew peaked cap which always seemed paradoxically appealing: infuriating yet irresistible, rude yet funny, naughty but nice; every mother's little horror, every child's hair-pulling kid brother, an angel with a dirty face (not to mention a piece of bubblegum stuck behind his ear).

Angus himself has always been the first to refute such serious analysis, of course. The schoolboy image (conceived, remember, when Angus was a genuine playground pup) is nothing more than a gag that stuck. But whatever people make of it, whatever savage, sinister or sexual undertones people might imagine, its importance in the development of the AC/DC phenomenon cannot be understated.

Nor indeed can the balance of the band behind the diminutive, demented adolescent. Angus's precocious talent, a free-spirited fretboard frenzy, called for rhythmic solidarity and unerring consistency, not to mention a lead vocal that could decapitate a kangaroo at a hundred paces. So in mid-1974, with George always at the end of a phone for advice, the brothers moved their base to Melbourne and stepped up their search for the right line-up.

In Melbourne the band became managed by Michael Browning, who owned the local Hard Rock Café and had previously managed Billy Thorpe and The Aztecs. "I first met them after they played for me at the Hard Rock with Dave Evans," he says today. "There was something I really liked about them. At that stage they had a manager who was totally useless, dealing in drugs or something. One day Malcolm and Angus came into my office and said they were going to Adelaide for a week, but that they'd like to come back to Melbourne before going home to Sydney to play my club again. The next I heard from them was a call from Malcolm saying that the band were stuck halfway between Melbourne and Adelaide because they didn't have enough money to continue their journey. So I wired them enough money to get to Adelaide and when they got back to Melbourne they came in to thank me. We got talking and I said, 'Well, if you need a manager, maybe I could have a go.' They seemed to think it was a good idea and that was it.

"Financially, the band were in a terrible position at this time, they were virtually destitute. So myself and an associate called Bill Joseph sat down and worked out a whole wage system for them to stabilise their infrastructure so they could actually exist. I think we gave them something like $45-50 a week each, bought them an old airport bus, provided them with a road crew and put them up in a house in Lansdowne Road in Melbourne. They had a deal with the Albert organisation at this time but they

had no money coming in because in those days record labels just thought about 'The Record' as a product, not 'The Band' as a bunch of human beings who needed to be able to eat, drink and sleep with a roof over their heads in order to make 'The Record'. So what I did was to sort out their financial side so they could go about the business of making music without the worry of where the next meal was coming from."

Browning would become one of the most important factors in the band's success over the next five years, taking them from the gutter to the very brink of superstardom. Among his first contributions to the development of AC/DC was hiring a van driver called Bon Scott, but no-one guessed the significance of his recruitment at the time.

Ronald Belford Scott, in retrospect, proved to be the Youngs' greatest discovery and closest ally, the missing link which focused the character of the band perfectly. At 28 he was much older than the brothers – almost old enough to be Angus's father, so the legend went – but they shared a common background as British ex-patriots, and shared the same burning desire to break out of the confines of their mundane environment. At Dave Evans' expense, destiny appeared to magnetise them.

Bon was actually born in Kirriemuir, Scotland, on July 9, 1946. His family emigrated to Melbourne in 1952 and the locals promptly nicknamed him Bonnie Scott (after 'Bonnie Scotland') which he shortened to plain Bon when he was 16 after deciding Bonnie was far "too girlie", especially for someone trying to prove himself to those who tormented him for having such a weird accent.

Within a year of settling in Australia Bon had taken his first tentative steps in music, tinkering around on the piano

at the age of seven, and picking up the accordion at eight. Moving to Fremantle, near Perth, in 1956, Bon was drafted into his father's Scottish marching band, playing bagpipes and drums in full traditional dress along with other local Scottish immigrants. But it wasn't until 1959 that the young Scott graduated to more conventional drums, bashing around on a basic four drum/two cymbal kit in his bedroom.

Over the next five years Bon worked hard on his music at school – the only subject he did take to, judging by his reports – and eventually won six theory diplomas for percussion. He also held the title of Perth Pipe Band Under-17 Drum Champion for a while, and these achievements pleased his parents who, mindful of his wayward tendencies, soon realised he was hardly university material.

Bon left school at 16 and found work as a postman, a temporary vocation he hoped would keep him ticking over financially until he became a professional musician. At one point he might have ended up as a baker, following on a family tradition from his grandfather, who owned a bakery. But Bon always claimed he was more interested in making bread than baking bread, and steered himself unerringly towards the bright lights of rock'n'roll.

With rock'n'roll came inevitable vices. A sucker for booze, birds and brawls, Bon soon got drawn off the straight and narrow and ended up doing time for assault and battery. His sentence was doubled for 'misdemeanours' committed while in jail and he was turned down by the army for being 'socially maladjusted'. Bon's reputation preceded him wherever he went and tales are told of him

The Valentines (Bon extreme right) - love beads and dangerous collars.

bowling around the streets with a pet boa constrictor around his neck, all the better to unsettle those who might risk a confrontation. In short, he was cut out to be a rock singer.

Bon's earliest bands found him doubling up on vocals and drums. In Perth during 1966 he played with The Spectors; then he moved on to The Valentines, a poppy-sounding outfit in trendy co-ordinated clothing, who asked him to cover his tattoos with talcum powder rather than blow their carefully contrived goody-goody image. Years later Bon would confide to friends that he thought the whole idea was ridiculous, but during the Summer Of Love in 1967 The Valentines prospered with a stage act that featured smoke bombs and confetti explosions.

They were signed by Clarion Records and their first single actually reached the Top Five of the local charts, but the next three flopped and they decided to move to the ostensibly trendier city of Melbourne for a change of luck. Ironically, The Valentines recorded two Easybeats songs in their time – 'She Said' and 'Peculiar Hole In The Sky' – and went on to use another Easybeats composition for their first single on Philips Records. Entitled 'My Old Man's A Groovy Old Man', it became a national hit in July 1969, and no doubt the royalties it earned its composers endeared Bon to the Young family when he entered their lives on a more permanent basis a few years later.

Shortly after 'My Old Man...' hit number 23 in the Australian charts in September 1969, The Valentines actually found themselves opening for their heroes The Easybeats at a show in Sydney. A few weeks later The Valentines were in the press for an altogether different reason: they were the first band in Australia to be arrested for dope possession and they compounded their sins by openly admitting in the media to smoking illegal substances. The ensuing scandal shattered their clean-cut image beyond repair.

Nevertheless The Valentines notched up another hit, 'Juliette' in April 1970, before the onslaught of 'bubblegum' pop suggested to Bon that it was time to move on. He'd survived three different line-up changes in The Valentines, and left behind a legacy of four Australia-only singles on Clarion Records (which C5 Records released in August 1988 along with other material under the title of 'The Early Years') and a number of other recordings on Philips (which were later released as 'Seasons Of Change').

After The Valentines Bon moved to Sydney and sank into full hippy mode with a jazzy blues-rock band called Fraternity. They all grew beards and Bon played flute and harmonica to complete the cosmic effect. Originally formed as a covers band for the bars of Sydney, by the time they moved to Adelaide in 1971 they had adopted a slightly harder boogie style, which eventually won them a contract with RCA later that year.

After two albums for RCA Australia, 'Live Stock' in 1971 and 'Sweet Peach' in 1972, Fraternity decided to try their luck in Europe. For most of 1973 they toured the Continent, principally Britain and Germany, and even supported a semi-successful 'bubblegum' band from Newcastle called Geordie on two occasions. No one knew then the cards that fate was to deal in the life of Geordie singer Brian Johnson, or realised the irony in Bon's stated opinion that Johnson was one of his two favourite vocalists, along with Steve Winwood.

Such serendipity aside, the European trip was largely fruitless for Fraternity and they returned to Oz slightly disillusioned. For Bon there was more trouble around the corner, as a near-fatal motorcycle accident left him in a

coma for three days and in hospital for several months, effectively ending his days with the group (he was eventually replaced by Jimmy Barnes, who later found fame in Cold Chisel before branching out as a successful solo artist).

After convalescing, Bon made ends meet by taking casual work in Adelaide's shipyards – a bit of painting, a bit of labouring, anything that came his way – until one day he ran into the little band from Sydney who regularly gigged around the city. Bon still needed some extra work, and he was offered the job of driving AC/DC's van.

"He was a shit driver though," Angus laughed years later, "a maniac. We were hurtling halfway down the road the first time and he says, 'I just got out of hospital after my last motorbike wreck...'. He was frightful."

Bon lost little time in telling the band he could play drums, and before long he'd successfully auditioned for Peter Clack's position in the band. He also recommended as bass player his old friend from Fraternity, Bruce

Houwe, and with his foot now firmly in the door, Bon further convinced the band that the real problem wasn't with the rhythm section but in the vocals department. He loved the idea of AC/DC – "He saw us playing in Adelaide and couldn't stop laughing at me all night," Angus remembers fondly – but he was convinced they needed a better frontman in order to find that extra punch. Cheekily, he suggested himself as the ideal replacement...

The Youngs tried him out and voted him in. Evans was out on his ear, going on to sing with Rabbit (who ironically recorded their 1976 LP 'Too Much Rock'n'Roll' for CBS at Albert Studios), Hot Cockerel and Thunder Downunder. "He (Evans) was a Gary Glitter freak," said Angus. "We used to kick him off stage and me and Malcolm would just jam on boogies and old Chuck Berry songs, and the band would go down

better without him. But we knew Bon could sing better than he could drive, so our manager at the time asked him if he wanted to join...

"Now, he knew we were just about to go to Perth for some gigs, so he said 'I'll think about it'. Perth was where he was brought up and it turned out he wasn't too keen on going back. He'd been in jail there once - I think he hit a cop - and he reckoned his mother was still waiting for him, along with several enemies. So he waited until we came back and then he said, 'I'll take that job now'."

According to Angus, Bon's induction was pure deep-end devilry. "The only rehearsal we had was just sitting around about an hour before the gig pulling out every rock'n'roll song we knew. When we got there Bon downed two bottles of Bourbon with dope, coke, speed and says, 'Right, I'm ready!'. And he was too. He was fighting fit. There was this immediate transformation and he was running round with his wife's knickers

on, yelling at the audience. It was a magic moment. He said it made him feel young again!"

Suddenly, everything fell into place. Bon's hard-nut image – all bare-chested bravado and tattooed toughness – contrasted compellingly with the sprog-in-shorts look of Angus, affording the band far more bite and dispelling any remaining question marks about their sexual stance into the bargain. "Seriously," Malcolm was to state later, "Bon was the biggest single influence on the band. When Bon came in it pulled us all together. He had that real stick-it-to-'em attitude. We all had it in us, but it took Bon to really bring it out."

With Bon in tow AC/DC settled in Melbourne, Australia's undisputed rock capital at the time, a status confirmed by the launch of Countdown, the country's influential TV pop programme which was based there. A few years earlier Melbourne's pubs had been granted a late-night (10 o'clock) closing licence, and by the end of 1971 the city's liquor laws were repealed to allow pubs the luxury of live entertainment. Rock'n'roll flourished as a result and a wealth of young bands sprang onto the circuit. AC/DC had timed their arrival on to the blossoming scene perfectly.

The members of the band piled into the Lansdowne Road house in Melbourne and had a riot. Bon's drinking sessions quickly became folklore, as did his ability to attract willing members of the opposite sex. It was all in the interests of lyrical research, of course. "All these chicks used to come around," Bon reminisced later. "They were all dropping 'mandies' or whatever, and we didn't mind because we were getting a screw! Anyway, we all got the jack because we used to pass them around. We used to get a group rate from the doctor! Those were the days..."

"I remember Bon was caught once with a brunette bird," said Angus, "they really made a big fuss of it in the papers actually. He was in this big double bed we used to have in this house when the roadie knocks on the door and shouts, 'Bon! Bon!' So Bon says, 'Oh go away, I'm having a...', when in bursts this chick's old man. He was an ex-convict and built like a wall, and he drags Bon outside and beats the shit out of him with a couple of mates!"

Michael Browning soon observed that the new look AC/DC with Bon out front drew a predominantly female audience during these formative months. "I remember some scenes at the Freeway Gardens Hotel in Melbourne (where Bon met Rosie) which quite shocked me," he says. "I've seen a lot of things in my time in the rock'n'roll business but this was full-on debauchery. There was also this circular hotel in Brisbane which we stayed at where the queues outside the boys' rooms would literally go round the corner. It was like a busy bank or something."

During this time The Aztecs (formed by Billy Thorpe and at one time featuring Lobby Lloyd), The Skyhooks (who wrote 'Women In Uniform', later to be covered by Iron Maiden) and Hush were the three biggest noises around. By the end of '74, however, AC/DC had well and truly overtaken all of them in terms of popularity, reaping a just reward for 12 months of solid club gigging (a schedule barely upset by Bon's lightning induction) in which they honed their act in front of some of the toughest audiences Australia could throw at them.

"Some of the clubs we used to play were a bit touch and go," Angus recalls,

"dodge a bottle here, dodge a fist there... I remember one time I said, 'I'm not going out there, there's a guy running around with a bloody meat cleaver!' Malcolm looked at me and he was laughing, and all of a sudden I felt a boot and I was the first one on stage!

"Sometimes we might have been booked to go on at eight o'clock, but told to get on quickly at 7.30 because there were half a dozen people about to start fighting. So we'd diffuse the tension and get the aggression out through the music."

The macho minefield wasn't the only dangerous element of The Nightclub Trail, however. "Some of the places we played were called '50-50' clubs," Angus smirks, "which meant half the audience would be gays and lesbians, and half would be 'normal' people. And they'd book us because they thought I was some sort of camp schoolboy! I had plenty of offers...

"In one place we played, Bon turned round to me halfway through the set and said, 'Do you notice something strange about the audience... they're all middle-aged women!' Then we realised they thought we were some kind of male strippers, and they were all whistling at me, expecting me to take my clothes off!"

"They were popular with the gays," says Michael Browning, "and I think they used to play up to it a bit. Bon would get out a whip at some gigs and fool around with it. It was all good clean fun though!

"The boys would also experiment with a few other ideas at this time. At some special gigs, like TV appearances or whatever, Angus would assume different personalities, before the schoolboy thing became his most recognisable identity. We'd have him busting out of a cage in his gorilla suit, we'd have a huge spider's web made out of rope at the back of the stage for when he'd get dressed up as Spiderman, and we even used to have a phone booth onstage for when he'd change into Superman. One night the door of the booth actually got stuck – just like that scene in Spinal Tap – and there was Angus in front of 5,000 people looking very embarrassed indeed!"

These elements of wacky theatre aside, the emphasis in AC/DC's set at the time remained on a relentless blues onslaught – covers of Chuck Berry, Rolling Stones songs like 'Jumping Jack Flash', a few Elvis numbers like 'Jailhouse Rock' and 'That's All Right Mama', and Van Morrison's 'Baby Please Don't Go', which would event-

ually surface on their début album.

"I mean, when you had to play from eight in the evening right through to four in the morning, you had plenty of time to pad the set out," Angus grins. "I think the biggest compliment someone ever paid me was when this guy came up to me and said, 'You couldn't tell that was a Chuck Berry song - you murdered it!'"

AC/DC as a four-piece circa early '75 with Bon proving there is a 'pee' in Scott.

The band grafted and made a name for themselves locally, but somehow the Youngs felt things still weren't right. Before long Bruce Houwe was asked to leave, and for a while George Young took over as bassist, but commitments back in Sydney meant George couldn't join the band on a full-time basis, so they reverted to a four-piece, with Malcolm playing bass. Back in Sydney brother George had been keeping tabs on the band, harbouring designs which went beyond token brotherly guidance. By the end of the year he'd devised a plan whereby Albert Productions would produce and release an AC/DC album through EMI's Australian subsidiary, thereby ensuring both personal artistic control over the direction and marketing of the band, and major distribution for the finished product.

Other bands, jealous of AC/DC's strident attempts at making a name for themselves, complained that the band were 'getting in the back door' simply because of their brother's famous name and connections, but more impartial

observers concluded that AC/DC had achieved a level of domestic status which was fully deserving of a break.

Whatever, 'High Voltage' – with George Young playing bass and Tony Kerrante, from the novelty Aussie band The '69ers, playing drums – reared its unashamedly ugly head before the Aussie public on February 17, 1975. Coincidentally, this was the same week Britain's boogie-based equivalent, Status Quo, were riding high in the UK charts with 'Down Down'.

But the music on their début suggested that AC/DC were at least a couple of years behind their counterparts in the West. There was too much filler material that recalled remnants of bubblegum, and while AC/DC never pretended they were out to blur rock'n'roll's margins in the way Led Zeppelin or Queen were doing in 1975, their basic, hard-hitting live posture came across rather tame on record. All agree now that 'High Voltage' was a disappointment.

"It was actually recorded in ten days," Angus admitted later, "in between gigs, working through the night after we came offstage and then through the day. I suppose it was fun at the time but there was no thought put into it; somebody picked up a guitar and went, 'That's a riff!' and away we'd go. There was a lot of that and a lot of magic moments came out of it. But that was youthful energy..."

'High Voltage' informed the world AC/DC were a time-bomb awaiting imminent detonation. The old Muddy Waters blues standard 'Baby Please Don't Go', which opened Side One, was typical of the material that AC/DC performed live at that time, while 'Show Business', which closed Side Two, was a bluesy 12-bar boogie stomp which boded well for the future. Sandwiched in between, the likes of 'Soul Stripper' (written by the brothers before Bon's arrival, thus the only original track not bearing the Young-Young-Scott stamp) carved the niche in which the band would slot comfortably for the foreseeable future.

Elsewhere, 'High Voltage' showed signs of wandering. 'Stick Around' pumped through a Free-ish 'All Right Now' vein, 'You Ain't Got A Hold On Me' occupied a characterless middle ground and 'Love Song' found Angus, probably for the last time, playing an acoustic guitar on what is thus far the only ballad ever recorded by AC/DC; a genuine oddity that wouldn't register on any voltage scale.

Bon was rarely slushy though, far from it. His lyrics right from the start came with a mischievous leer and a wink of the eye, seldom straying from the panty-strewn path of backstage conquests. Yet while the lilting blues of 'Little Lover' and its like suggested eligible bachelor status, Bon was actually married, dedicating not only 'Love Song' to his wife (Irene, whom he married in 1972), but also, somewhat more revealingly, 'She's Got Balls'. They were divorced shortly after the album's release.

The release of 'High Voltage' added new impetus to AC/DC's touring schedule, and the band trekked back and forth across the continent tirelessly. On March 3 'Baby Please Don't Go' (backed with 'Love Song') emerged as a single in Australia, followed in June by a new song, 'High Voltage' (b/w 'Soul Stripper'), which curiously enough didn't appear on the album of the same name.

More importantly, a stable line-up had finally been established. Auditions had uncovered a talented and experienced drummer called Phillip Hugh Rudd, and for the first time the Youngs felt they had someone who could provide them with the kind of relentless power drumming that their brattish boogie needed.

Rudd, like Bon Scott, had already enjoyed the dubious benefits of notoriety in previous bands. He'd made his name with The Colored Balls, a skinhead band formed by guitarist Lobby Lloyd (later to have solo success in Oz) and singer

Angry Anderson (who went on to form Rose Tattoo), which terrorised the club circuit during the early Seventies with a ferocious brand of yob-rock.

Two singles ('Liberate Rock' and 'Mess Of Blues') were the only recognised fruits of Rudd's time with the Balls who, in 1974, changed their name to Buster Brown and went on to record one album ('Something To Say') for the indie Mushroom Records label later that same year. But by the beginning of '75 Rudd had had enough, and hardly hesitated when AC/DC offered him the gig.

AC/DC was still a four-piece with Malcolm playing bass when Rudd joined at the beginning of 1975, but a chance meeting in March at one of their regular haunts, the Station Hotel, a famous live venue in the Trahan district of Melbourne, brought about the missing link which ultimately made them a five-piece once more.

Seventeen-year-old Mark Whitmore Evans, born and raised in the working class Trahan area, had actually been thrown out and barred from the Station Hotel for brawling the night before the AC/DC show. Unperturbed, Evans and his mates managed to get back into the bar for the gig next night, but were eventually spotted by the hotel's bouncers who threw them out once again. During the mêlée Evans quite literally bumped into an old friend of his, one of AC/DC's roadies called Steve McGrath, knocking him to the floor. McGrath was actually talking to Bon at the time and, ever ready to throw in their lot on behalf of an underdog, they immediately took Evans' side in the argument. They insisted that if Evans and his friends weren't allowed to stay there was going to be no show and the hotel's staff begrudgingly relented.

A couple of weeks later Mark Evans joined the band. Within weeks he was actually onstage playing bass at the Station Hotel with AC/DC himself, much to the bemusement of the bouncers who'd kicked him into the street before. It's a memory he cherishes to this day.

On a more serious level, Mark Evans and Phil Rudd were the final pieces of the AC/DC jigsaw and would remain the rhythm axis of the band for the next two years, forging the trademark 4/4 beat and rumbling one-fingered bass-line. It wasn't pretty, it wasn't clever, but it was what AC/DC were all about, and as such tremendously effective.

The difference could be heard on the band's second album 'TNT', which exploded in both Australia and New

The first settled AC/DC line-up (left to right: Phil Rudd, Bon Scott, Angus Young, Malcolm Young and Mark Evans).

Zealand at the end of '75. Packaged in a gatefold sleeve complete with a display of Bon's lyrical witticisms and fake police files on each member of the band, 'TNT' was a comprehensively better album than its predecessor - sharper, more cohesive and with a harder production (once again, a Vanda/Young job at Albert Studios in Sydney). The foundations of Rudd and Evans, coupled with months of hard work on the road, had clearly focused the band's aspirations. Bon's lyrics said it all: 'I'm a rocker, I'm a roller, I'm a right out of controller...' ('Rocker'); 'You can stick your nine-to-five livin' and your collar and tie/And stick your moral standards 'cause it's all a dirty lie...' ('Rock'n'Roll Singer'); 'You ask me 'bout the clothes

I wear/And you ask me why I grow my hair/And you ask me why I'm in a band/I dig doin' one night stands...' ('High Voltage').

It was mean, macho, muscles-in-yer-face stuff, but not to be taken seriously. Bon sounded like a six-foot parrot with hormonal abnormalities. And when he proclaimed 'I'm a live wire, gonna set this town on fire' ('Live Wire'), or 'I'm TNT, I'm dynamite/I'm TNT and I'll win the fight' ('TNT'), it was as though he was really speaking on behalf of pent-up teenage frustration and closet adolescent rebellion. And always with just a hint of a self-mocking smirk.

The band in England with Dave Dee (left standing). Which one's Tich?

After all, the opening track of 'TNT' revealed what Bon really thought of being in a rock band: 'Gettin' robbed/ Gettin' stoned/ Gettin' beat up/Broken boned/Gettin' had/Gettin' took/I tell you folks it's harder than it looks...'. If any track summed up early AC/DC it was 'It's A Long Way To The Top (If You Wanna Rock'n'Roll)', a devastatingly simple boogie blueprint cast in stone, complemented by a swirl of bagpipes courtesy of Bon's highland heritage. A version of Chuck Berry's 1957 standard 'School Days' at the end of the record may have been an acknowledgement of their musical education, but 'It's A Long Way...' proved they'd long since graduated.

Finally on 'TNT', the Youngs decided to include a re-recorded version of 'Can I Sit Next To You Girl' – transformed by the more authentic dirty-mac leer of Bon – before paving the way with a slow blues doodle for Bon to play the lyrical ace up his sleeve: 'The Jack'. Thinly disguised by the double entendres available in the

commentary of a poker game, Bon's tale was one of sexual disease: 'But how was I to know that she'd been shuffled before/Said she'd never had a Royal Flush/But I should have known that all the cards were coming from the bottom of the pack/And if I'd have known what she was dealing out/I'd have dealt it back... she's got The Jack'! Bon would never win the Nobel Prize for literature, but he certainly won a lot of friends.

Like 'High Voltage', 'TNT' secured encouraging returns for those who'd put their faith in AC/DC, comfortably passing the 100,000 sales mark. But success on their own doorstep was hardly the height of ambition for the band, and least of all for their manager Michael Browning, who'd been negotiating recording contracts in the far more important and lucrative territories of Britain and America for some time.

One of the labels Browning had approached was Atlantic Records, a powerful arm of the Warners group renowned for success in the rock field whose jewel in the crown was Led Zeppelin. The label manager of the

UK arm of Atlantic at the time was Dave Dee, former lead singer of one of Britain's biggest pop bands of the Sixties, Dave Dee, Dozy, Beaky, Mick And Tich.

"We were just a small outlet for the American part of Atlantic at the time," says Dave today, "and because we were such a small operation we didn't have an A&R department, because all our signings came from America. Anyway, one day Michael Browning had walked into Phil Carson's office in London (Carson was MD of Atlantic in the UK) and told him all about this band he had in Australia called AC/DC. Carson was a bit dubious, of course, but suddenly Browning produced this brief-case-like box which had a flip-top screen, and which turned out to be like a sort of portable video player. On it he had film of one of his band's Australian shows, and he proceeded to show this tape to Phil, who was quite taken aback.

"Later I returned to the office from wherever I'd been, and Phil called me over and said, 'Look, there's this band called AC/DC I've just seen a tape of and they look quite good. Their guitar player is dressed as a schoolboy, their singer is a complete nutcase and they sound great. Come on and see what you think...' So I saw the tape and really liked it. I said to Phil, 'They're great, just like a cross between Slade and Led Zeppelin... I really fancy going for it'. So Phil said, 'So do I, we've got to sort something out'."

Unfortunately the London office of Atlantic Records had no A&R budget at that time and were thus prevented from signing new acts. "We were stuck," says Dee. "Fortunately though, I was about to go to New York to do a few things, so Phil said to me, 'Look, work on Jim Delahan (who was head of A&R for Atlantic in New York) and see if you can persuade him to do something with this band'.

"So when I get to New York I'm in the office raving about this band called AC/DC to Jim when he says, 'Wait a minute, is this the band with the manager who carries around that strange box with a flip-top video screen?' And I says, 'Yeah, that's him!' And Jim goes, 'We've passed on them already'. So I thought, 'Oh shit!'.

"So after I left the office I phoned Phil Carson and told him that Browning had already tried the Atlantic office in New York and they'd passed. Phil nearly dropped the phone. We didn't know what to do next, but we didn't want to let the band go because we were convinced they had something special.

"Anyway, I came back to Britain and Phil and I sat down and tried to work out how we could get round our lack of an A&R budget. Then we thought, 'Hang on, what we have got here is a promotion and press budget, so why can't we dip into that?' So we got Michael Browning back into the office and said, 'Look, we really want to sign this band...' – we never told him about the problems in America though – '...but we haven't got a lot of money to play with, so what do you want to do?' To cut a long story short, we ended up signing the band to a ridiculously long deal for a ridiculously cheap fee, because they were just happy to get a deal of any sort in those days, and we were able to sign them without telling anybody at Atlantic where the money had come from! It was a brilliant scam."

After the contracts were signed the two London based Atlantic men invited Angus to London as a goodwill gesture. "This was the spring of 1975," recalls Dee. "I'll never forget it. I'm a big West Ham United supporter, and on the day Angus was due to land in London West Ham were in the semi-final of the FA Cup (against Ipswich), and I had some tickets for the game. So as soon as Angus arrived at Heathrow, Coral Browning (Michael's sister) put him on a Tube and dragged him up to Chelsea, because the game was being held at Chelsea's ground, Stamford Bridge. The idea was that we were going to have lunch at a restaurant in the King's Road, and would then go on to the game... but poor Angus, he was completely lost, jet-lagged out of his mind, and wasn't even interested in football! He was like a little kid who'd lost his mum, y'know...

I found him wandering up the King's Road! I felt so sorry for him that I said, 'Don't worry, we'll have a good meal and a few beers...', but later I found out that he only drank milk anyway. It was a bizarre introduction to England for him, but I think he was so excited by the simple fact that he was here, that he sort of went along with all the crap."

The rest of the band were due to arrive in Britain in October, but as with more or less everything in the music business the plans were put back a few months for one reason or another. It wouldn't be until April 1, 1976, that AC/DC finally made it to Britain, stepping straight into a barrage of abuse from a typically xenophobic rock audience who looked on them as little more than a bunch of uncouth colonials.

But as time was to prove, AC/DC were no April Fools.

Chapter IV

Dirty Deeds From Down Under
(...Whole Lotta Aussies)

Back in Australia, AC/DC's popularity and demanding schedule meant the band had to record their third album within a year of the release of their début. So, after the Christmas break, AC/DC returned to Albert Studios in January 1976 to work once again with Vanda and Young.

"The idea was to get in there and do it as fast as possible," says Mark Evans. "We didn't have any time for rehearsals – in fact, I only did two rehearsals with AC/DC all the while I was with the band – and we only had about two weeks to get the thing done, so all the songs were written in the studio, and we just whacked it straight down on tape. There was hardly time to take a piss in those days."

Australia got its first taster of the new album in June with the release of the single 'Jailbreak' (not, incidentally, the Thin Lizzy song released the same year). Backed by the curious instrumental 'Fling Thing', a traditional folk song with a strong Scottish twinge, suitably adapted by the Youngs, it came on just as you knew it would – all sweaty and mouthy, with a menacing don't-mess-with-us chorus.

The album itself, delightfully titled 'Dirty Deeds Done Dirt Cheap', came out on home territory during September, adorned with a symbolic cartoon of the band which didn't miss a trick: beer cans, pool cues, tattoos, tight jeans, half-cocked cigarettes and a two-fingered salute from Angus... you couldn't mistake the image.

Come to think of it, you couldn't mistake the music either. The title track was just like 'Jailbreak' – a back-of-the-throat chant which smelt of stale smoke and spilt blood – while 'Ain't No Fun (Waiting 'Round To Be A Millionaire)' was stuck in a 12-bar groove long enough to register nearly 40 repeats of the chorus. If that wasn't enough, 'There's Gonna Be Some Rockin' was almost a continuation of the same track, and 'R.I.P. (Rock In Peace)' wasn't far away from being a reprise of 'There's Gonna Be Some Rockin'! The "new AC/DC album", it appeared, was almost a contradiction in terms.

On the other hand, the autobiographical 'Problem Child' was a real gem. As usual, Bon was the rebel without a care, boozin' and brawlin' with the best of them, but this time the Young brothers hit on a vicious stop-start riff which rode Phil Rudd's clockwork beat with an irresistible swagger. Beside it, 'Squealer' lacked bite and sounded rather ordinary, and

Milking their welcome, AC/DC arrive in London on April 1st 1976 (left to right: Malcolm Young, Bon Scott (hidden), Ken Evans (Head of Music, Radio Luxemburg), Mark Evans, Coral Browning (sister of Michael), Angus Young, Michael Browning (manager) and Steve Payne (Atlantic Records).

the mellow sway of 'Ride On' was an ineffective drop in tempo.

The only other slow track on the album was another Scott special; with a title like 'Big Balls', even the subtleties of 'The Jack' went out of the window. 'Some balls are held for charity/And some for fancy dress/But when they're held for pleasure/They're the balls I like the best...' sniggered Bon, and the legend of the lecher lived on.

For the fanatical fan, 'Dirty Deeds...' was just what the devil ordered – 0% progression, 100% AC/DC. But a step sideways hardly placated some critics, who observed that the band could well be hurtling towards a 'too much too soon' scenario.

"It was a bit too rushed," Evans admits, "and I think it suffered a bit from that. All of the albums I did with the band were done quickly, but 'Dirty Deeds...' was taking it a bit too far. It ended up being a bit of a stop-gap album."

Fortunately, perhaps, all three of AC/DC's albums to date had been issued in Australia only, and this allowed them to gear themselves up for a stab at international recognition in the safe shadow of their own doorstep. With support from their fiercely patriotic countrymen who believed that at last they had a rock'n'roll band to match those they'd been force fed from Britain and America, AC/DC could be allowed to tread water for a while, before taking the plunge into the deep-end.

The real plunge was taken in April 1976, when Browning took his boys to Blighty for a sustained crack at the UK market. Some Aussie fans felt the band was turning its back on them, betraying their roots by pandering to the poms, but AC/DC had effectively reached the

pinnacle of commercial success in Australia, and to slog around the same rusty circuit clocking up thousands of miles between each town to play to converts seemed as unchallenging as it did unappetising.

In any case, AC/DC's popularity in Oz at this time was such that when the band were booked to do a week of lunchtime gigs at the Miss Melbourne department of the Myer superstore in Melbourne during the Spring, just before leaving for London, over 10,000 fans turned up for the first performance, forcing them to abandon the show before they'd even started and run for their lives.

"We were supposed to do five shows," says Mark Evans, "but we didn't play a note! I remember there being a ridiculous amount of people crammed into the women's department of this store, and then suddenly all hell broke loose. The people went wild, smashing the place up and stealing anything they could lay their hands on. Bon got chased up some escalators and through some other stores, I ended up in just a pair of jeans and one shoe... I was absolutely scared shitless at the time, but it seems very funny now."

There was no such nonsense in Britain, however. When the band arrived in London on April 1, the day after Angus' 21st birthday (although for publicity reasons they decided to claim he was only 17), they were ushered straight into a dirty dive in Lonsdale Road in Barnes, just the other side of Hammersmith Bridge. The house was so filthy, sympathetic staff from Atlantic's

Pandemonium at the pub!
Onstage in Britain, early '76.

making the front page of every newspaper in the country, AC/DC were in prime position to exploit the notoriety of the moment.

Yet where the likes of The Sex Pistols, The Clash, The Damned, The Stranglers and The Jam were championed solely by the new model of juvenile delinquency, AC/DC's appeal tended to cross over to the more traditional palates of older rock fans. Here was a band sucking from the roots of the blues, vaulting off the volume of heavy rock and exploding with all the power of punk; a devil-child with an unmistakable resemblance to its parentage, dangerously shaped by the rebellious insolence of adolescence.

AC/DC declined to make their British début supporting Afro-funksters Osibisa in Brighton for £10 – their first offer – and instead played their first gig on UK soil at the Red Cow pub in Hammersmith during April, followed by some low-key gigs around the country at the Nashville in Earls Court, the Retford Porterhouse and Manchester's Electric Circus. Atlantic decided to pursue a two-pronged attack, flirting deliberately with a 'Punks From Down Under' tag to ensure column-inches in the trend-conscious press, while simultaneously targeting an older and more traditional audience by slapping them on (Back Street) Crawler's long-awaited UK tour. It was a definite result.

Back Street Crawler was the band assembled by guitarist Paul Kossoff who had been determined to get out on the road again with a classic British blues band since his departure from Free in 1973. Bouts of ill-health allied to chronic drug problems had dogged Kossoff's career since the halcyon days of Free, but while things temporarily looked up for him the previous autumn and details of the tour with AC/DC starting on April 25 were finalised, Kossoff died of heart failure on March 19 while asleep on a plane bound for New York.

Within a month, however, Back Street Crawler had replaced their tragic mentor (with former If guitarist Geoff Whitehorn) and announced themselves fit to oblige their touring commitment, under the shortened name of Crawler. For Atlantic this was something of a relief, as for them the pairing of the old and the new – the name band with a pedigree and the angry upstarts with a point to prove – was an ideal way of promoting both concerns. Crawler, without the attraction of Kossoff, would benefit from having an opening act capable of generating some ticket sales themselves; AC/DC would

London office even offered to scrub the place themselves. But then, a touch of squalor seemed appropriate for Atlantic's proposed marketing strategy, and a controversial fight at a pub in North Finchley (where Bon used to work when Fraternity visited the UK in 1973), which ended up with the unfortunate singer getting his cheekbone broken, didn't lose its publicity value either.

Britain, after all, was gripped by the early stages of punk. The bloated, lazy, middle-class notion of superstar rock bands with Bel Air mansions and Swiss bank accounts was about to be exploded by the violent, subversive and confrontational attitudes of a new generation. Technical expertise was out, rampant aggression was in. Rules were for fools, letting rip was hip. Suddenly, the satin-jacket-and-snakeskin- boots guise of mid-Seventies rock was hung, drawn and quartered by the ripped T-

shirts and tartan-bibbed mutant of youth. The rock scene wore its hair in a lime-green mohican, a safety-pin through its nose and pad-lock around its neck as it spat, vomited and cursed its way into the headlines.

Image-wise AC/DC were hardly sartorial visionaries of the punk era, but in terms of attitude and aggression they were definitely in the same street. "I remember the first night they got here," says Steve Payne, who handled London promotions for Atlantic at the time. "We went to a pub in Mayfair, just around the corner from the Hard Rock Café, and within minutes they wanted to start a fight with someone. They couldn't understand why I was so surprised, they said it was just the usual thing for Australians to do after a few beers!"

Shrewdly, Atlantic seized the chance to align their new protégés to the swiftly escalating movement. By the time The Sex Pistols had set punk's touch-paper ablaze by swearing at Bill Grundy on Thames TV's Today programme and have the perfect opportunity to steal the thunder from beneath the snouts of their elders.

As the tour rumbled into May it became increasingly obvious that AC/DC were stealing the thunder, and as the sleeping giant of the music press gradually woke up to witness the truth about AC/DC at first hand, the word on the typewriter was that this 'Chunda From Down Under' lot weren't simply a gaggle of antipodean deadheads on a beano from the outback. The earliest reviews reflected a general opinion of 'enormous potential', while interviews with the pugnacious yet pixie-sized perpetrators themselves uncovered a loud-mouthed loutishness which was interpreted as lovable rather than laughable.

In the midst of the madness, Atlantic hit the British public with a belated and restructured version of the 'High Voltage' album. 'It's A Long Way To The Top...' (coupled with 'Can I Sit Next To You Girl') had become AC/DC's first official release in the UK when it was marketed to coincide with the band's arrival in April. But 'High Voltage' – a corner-cutting hybrid of its Aussie namesake and the follow-up 'TNT' – was earmarked as the début album.

Released on May 14, 'High Voltage' UK-style turned out to be rather more 'TNT' than anything else: Side One was the opening side of 'TNT' to a tee... with the addition of the track 'TNT' itself; Side Two (I hope you're following this) included only 'Little Lover' and 'She's Got Balls' from 'High Voltage', as both 'Can I Sit Next To You Girl' and 'High Voltage' itself came from... 'TNT'! If the band's image hadn't confused the public enough...

Yet in spite of such inconsistent cross-pollination, the British 'High Voltage' proved a cocktail of enough potency to attract more positive reviews than negative. Some inevitably objected to the 'sexist' nature of Bon's lyrics, some cruelly claimed the band only knew three chords, but most agreed that it was ferocious, infectious and fun. Which was all it was really meant to be.

After introducing the band on the Crawler jaunt, Atlantic decided on a more novel strategy for AC/DC's follow-up tour, their first as headliners. Conspiring with Sounds, the weekly rock magazine launched in 1970, they planned a co-promoted tour package of videos and live music for a specially low entrance fee of 50p. This would not only help kids digest the onslaught of

some favourable press...

Twenty venues were chosen for the experiment, modest places like Birmingham Mayfair, Southport Floral Hall, Liverpool Stadium, Cardiff Top Rank and Bedworth Civic Hall. At each show the audience would be 'warmed up' with videos of rock's aristocracy (The Stones, The Who, Zeppelin, Free, etc), before the pugnacious proletarian pandemonium of AC/DC would be let loose in the shape of 'Live Wire' from 'TNT'. This would normally be followed by 'She's Got Balls', 'It's A Long Way To The Top...', 'Soul Stripper', 'High Voltage', 'TNT' and then 'Baby Please Don't Go', during which Angus performed his comic/macabre strip-tease ritual before being hoisted through the crowd atop Bon's brawny shoulders.

It was an odd spectacle for those unprepared for the sight of a pimply, short-haired midget in a white (although sometimes blue, sometimes green) blazer and shorts, throwing a tantrum in the middle of the stage like he'd just been given extra homework, but it seemed to work overall. Naturally Sounds proclaimed the idea an unqualified success, but in some towns the so-called 'Lock Up Your Daughters Tour' ran into low-attendance problems, suggesting that perhaps some parents had locked up their sons as well, just in case.

"It was a real hit-and-miss affair," admits Dave Dee. "Sometimes the places were empty, sometimes there were just a few kids, sometimes it was packed. Dave walked all around the country with a guy called Don Morris who worked for Sounds, and we really did graft at getting a buzz going – sometimes, even arriving at a town at 3am to put up posters for that night's gig! It was totally illegal, but we did it. Morris, Carson and I pushed all the way – just pilfering money from our promotions budget really – but in the end we started to see some results."

The climax to the tour was at London's Lyceum theatre on July 7, and the success of this particular show papered over any cracks which appeared the week before. Compered by Radio One DJ John Peel, whose reputation as one of the most influential rock voices in the country added some kudos to the event, the show also included the slapstick sideshow of a 'Best Dressed Schoolboy/Schoolgirl' competition – won incidentally, and this despite entries from some of Atlantic's own female staff on the insistence of Michael Browning's sister Coral, by a certain Jayne Haynes, who skipped off home to Harrow in Middlesex that night clutching an Epiphone Caballero folk guitar as her prize.

By now AC/DC were well entrenched in London. They usually hung out at the Bridge Hotel pub in Barnes or gatecrashed their way into the ostensibly members only Speakeasy club near Oxford Circus and generally enjoyed their first year away from home. Indeed, the rehabilitation was complete when the band were booked by the capital's legendary Marquee Club for a weekly Monday night residency starting on July 26.

"We still had a bit of a problem with the press at this time," says Dave Dee, "because all the comics were a bit too trendy to touch a bunch of unfashionable long-haired yobbos from Australia. But what we were beginning to discover was that the band had a real 'street' thing going, a word-of-mouth reputation that was hotting up all the time, and when they did the Marquee there were queues right around the corner. I mean you just can't ignore that can you?"

"There was big competition at that time between AC/DC and Eddie & The Hot Rods," says Michael Browning, "they'd break the house record one week and then we'd break it the next week. I mean, we'd get 1200-1300 people in that tiny little place, much more than it was supposed to take, and it was ridiculously hot. Remember, that was the long hot summer of '76, and there was sweat literally running down the walls like a waterfall."

Visitors to the cauldron-like Wardour Street club were treated to all manner of Angus theatrics, from running through the audience to jumping off the top of the PA stack, and the energy of the performances at a time when twenty minute drum solos were de rigueur in rock ensured that the grapevine buzzed favourably. In response, Atlantic released 'Jailbreak'/'Fling Thing' as a single, the UK's first official taste of the 'Dirty Deeds...' album, which was by now creeping into import shops at sadly exorbitant prices.

Back at the Marquee, eye-witnesses

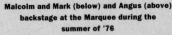

Malcolm and Mark (below) and Angus (above) backstage at the Marquee during the summer of '76

had been shocked by the presence of Ritchie Blackmore one night. Blackmore, the tetchy and darkly enigmatic guitar god who'd left Deep Purple the previous year to front his own band called Rainbow, was rarely seen in public, and given his renowned unsociable reserve could hardly have been expected to be an AC/DC fan.

In fact, Blackmore hated AC/DC, a grudge which went back to January 25th the previous year when AC/DC had played with Deep Purple at the Sunbury Music Festival in Australia. AC/DC were due to go on after Purple at around two o'clock in the morning, but Purple didn't want any band to follow them and kicked up a fuss as AC/DC's crew insisted on

loading their gear on to the stage. The whole episode ended in an onstage punch-up between AC/DC and Purple's road crew, an incident Michael Browning remembers well.

"Purple were headlining the event, of course, so they would go on in the mid-to-late evening slot, but there would also be bands going on after them, right into the early hours. The trouble started when Purple's manager decided he wanted to have all of Purple's gear taken off stage after their set, which would've meant us going on at something like 4.00am. So I said to our crew, 'Right, start putting out gear onstage NOW!' But as they were putting it on, Purple's guys were taking it straight off, and it ended up in a major shitfight. I remember standing on the side of the stage with George Young, Purple's manager and Purple's tour manager, Bruce Payne. At one point Payne made the mistake of saying to George, 'Don't mess with me, I'm from New York'. So George just looked at him and replied, 'So fucking what, I'm from Glasgow...' BANG! He punched him right in the face. The next thing we're all involved in this punch-up – me, George, Harry Vanda, the band... it was like, choose your partner and get stuck in!"

Blackmore had hardly forgotten this set-to when AC/DC were put forward as a possible support band for Rainbow's 19-date European tour in August, but seemed to have forgiven them. He had in fact turned up at the Marquee to check the band's suitability but, unbeknown to him, Malcolm had got wind of his intentions beforehand and decided that, with Atlantic having already paid the £10,000 'buy-on' fee for the tour, the band needn't pander to him. Thus, at the end of the show when Blackmore told one of AC/DC's roadies that he'd like to jam on the encore, Malcolm immediately agreed, keeping the band in the dressing room until Blackmore had climbed up onstage and was busy tuning his guitar in preparation, then leading the band in a dash for the street!

"No-one mentioned any of this during that whole tour," Browning laughs, "until one night in Hamburg when someone brought it up while we were in the bar of the hotel. We all had a laugh about it. I don't think Ritchie was too bothered... he was too busy trying to dodge his ex-wife or something!

"There were terrible problems on that whole tour though, especially with that rainbow which Ritchie used to have over the stage. Every night there'd be a

problem with it; it wouldn't fit into some halls, it wouldn't light up properly in other places, there'd be something wrong with other bits of equipment... every night someone would say, 'Oh Ritchie's not going on tonight because something's wrong'. It was a nightmare."

AC/DC still got through the tour though, returning to England three weeks later at the end of August with the seeds of a fan base sewn in Germany, France and Scandinavia. The next major move was a 15-date tour to take the band through to mid-September with another expedition muted for October/November.

Around this time the band made their first appearance on British TV, opening an odd three-act bill which also featured ex-convict Leapy Lee – who'd had a UK hit in the Sixties called 'Little Arrows' before his spell in jail – and main-attraction Marc Bolan. It was AC/DC's job to warm the crowd up, and they did so with the likes of 'Can I Sit Next To You Girl' and 'It's A Long Way To The Top...'. Filmed at the Wimbledon Theatre in London, the programme was aired on Friday, August 27, and the band watched it anxiously in the landlord's lounge upstairs at the Red Cow, unable to make it back to their house in time after their gig at the pub.

Two days later, on Sunday, August 29, AC/DC appeared on the bill at the Reading Festival, the traditional August Bank Holiday weekend bash. Once again the company was mixed: the Sutherland Brothers & Quiver, Brand X, Ted Nugent, Sassafras, The End, Black Oak Arkansas and Back Door. But Reading became an important showcase gig for the band, even if the man who'd championed their cause by plugging their Aussie-only records on his radio show for six months before they'd arrived in Britain didn't get to see their moment of glory.

"John Peel came up to see us at the Reading Festival," recalled Malcolm, "but unfortunately one of the security blokes chucked him off when we were playing. So he wrote in the newspaper, 'That's the last time I play one of these guys' records! Who do they think they are?'"

In the cold light of day, the band weren't too impressed by their own performance either. They hadn't played too well, the audience had more or less given them the cold shoulder, and the mood in the camp afterwards was black. Back at the band's latest house in Finborough Road, West Brompton – just off the Fulham Road and a stone's throw from Stamford Bridge – George read the

riot act to everyone, and it ended in an incredible three-way fight between the brothers.

Blissfully unaware of the dissent in the band, Atlantic clearly thought AC/DC were on the threshold of the Big Time by now, and announced a third headlining tour of the UK in five months during October. The venues selected this time were of university/civic hall stature, but while few doubted AC/DC's grass-roots-level popularity at this juncture, some observers considered a third tour so soon at best ambitious, at worst a case of overkill.

And so it proved to be. Moreover, if some half-full houses and a few hasty media reassessments didn't clip their wings ("One reviewer," Angus told the author, "even said, 'If I ever meet these guys I'd personally pay their fare back to Australia!'"), some adverse publicity clearly did leave its mark. Angus's by now essential buttock-baring routine had led to student union snobs at Oxford Poly banning AC/DC from a proposed gig there, for example. And to make matters worse, another single from the 'High Voltage' LP, the title track (coupled with 'Live Wire'), didn't even trouble chart compilers.

True to form, the band soldiered on regardless, once again blotting out any discrepancies in the provinces by pulling out all the stops for the harsh spotlight of the capital – this time at the prestigious Hammersmith Odeon on November 10, 1976, where the band were introduced by Dave Dee.

"Bon had been on at me about introducing the band," says Dee, who today runs a variety of entrepreneurial operations from his West London office, including the management of snooker stars like John Virgo. "I think he was just about old enough to remember a few of my hit singles with Dozy, Beaky, Mick and Tich. I think he was a bit of a fan in the early days, and he kept saying he wanted me to get up and say a few words. In the end he wound me up enough, so I just ran through a brief history of the band before they came on, and it was great.

"Actually," continues Dee, "that was the gig at which Phil Carson and I finally knew we'd cracked it with AC/DC. We only had about two-thirds of the stalls full – and that was only because we brought all the kids who'd bought tickets for the upstairs down to the stalls – but the reaction of the fans to the band was phenomenal. I saw five kids dressed up as Angus – cardboard guitars, the lot – and I said to Phil,

Angus in long trousers?
Shurely shome mishtake...

Mark Evans: decided he'd leave
before he could be sacked.

That's it, we've done it!', because I could see that at last people were beginning to associate themselves with the image of the band as well as with the sound. That was a truly great night."

The tour finally ended on November 13 at Newcastle University, the last remaining beads of British sweat having been wrung out of 1976. A month later, Atlantic finally released the 'Dirty Deeds...' album in the UK, albeit with a couple of alterations to the Aussie original. Strangely, the single 'Jailbreak' was omitted, along with 'R.I.P. (Rock In Peace)' (which had appeared on the B-side of the 'Dirty Deeds...' single Down Under). In their places came the frenetic 'Rocker' from 'TNT' and 'Love At First Feel', which despite being a new track was about as familiar as you could get, right down to the seedy chuckle of Bon's lyrics: 'I didn't know if you were legal tender/But I spent you just the same...'

Quite why the changes were made no-one seems to remember (or want to admit), but it hardly improved the package. Nor did a change in sleeve design; Hipgnosis, the company given the task of designing a cover, specialised in the kind of surreal images used by arty bands like Pink Floyd, and couldn't have been a more inappropriate choice for grungy urchins like AC/DC. The result was a puzzling picture of seven curious characters on the forecourt of a motel with their eyes mysteriously blacked out... hmm, quite. Atlantic's marketing seemed to have gone awry just when the band needed it most.

"The cover was something the record company tried to use to give the band a level of sophistication that they thought might broaden their audience," reckons Michael Browning. "Hipgnosis were the biggest noise around in record sleeve designs in those days and Atlantic gave them free run to do whatever they thought was right. I guess they felt they could use the same sort of ideas which had worked with other bands, but I must admit I think the whole concept was wrong. It just didn't work."

Meanwhile over in America, the UK-style 'High Voltage' album (now with yet another cover, this time a snap of Angus being zapped by a lightning flash) had been released during October, gaining some favourable reviews – most importantly from the influential Billboard, who assessed the band as a hybrid of Led Zeppelin and the Sensational Alex Harvey Band. It was just the boost the band needed at the end of an exhausting year, and Michael Browning

planned to take advantage of it by busily arranging some US dates for the New Year.

Having spent the best part of eight months on the road, the AC/DC entourage returned home to Australia for Christmas to recharge their batteries. 1976 had been an incredible year – three UK tours, a maiden European trek, festivals, residencies and two albums to promote – but 1977 wasn't going to be any easier.

Australia hadn't actually seen much of their loudest ambassadors since the previous winter, and it didn't look like they were going to for a large part of the coming year. But that hadn't retarded the growth of their notoriety at home.

"There was a women's magazine in Australia that really upset my mum," Angus told the author. "While we were home she called me into the room to show me this story that had a picture of a nice, clean-cut pop star on one page, and a picture of me on the other page. It said: 'This nasty little piece of work is Angus Young – and this is what the juvenile delinquents of today are turning to'."

The remark hurt, but the 'Seedies' (as they were affectionately known by their fans at the time) didn't take it seriously. After all, the backlash from conservative Australia was always busy whipping up all sorts of distortions to promote their attitudes.

"They accused us of causing violence in the suburbs, they accused us of inciting kids to get themselves tattooed," Angus said, "just because Bon had a few tattoos on his arms! Some Minister even stood up in the Australian Parliament once and blamed us for all the tattooing going on! Imagine paying your taxes just to have some jerk wasting everybody's time about us and tattoos!"

Bon, incidentally, got his tattoos from hanging out with a few unsavoury characters in his youth: "He'd go out cray fishing with these really rough redneck Aussies," Malcolm explained, "and they made him get all these tattoos. Basically, if he didn't he'd get the shit kicked out of him!"

"I could never see what the problem with tattoos was," Angus mused. "I mean, the world is full of evil people, and we were getting abused because Bon had a parrot or something painted on his arm..."

The best thing the band could do was send up the whole situation . On the back cover of the UK and US versions of 'High Voltage', a letter penned in a

childish scrawl from a fictitious conquest of Bon's called Helen read: '... My dad also says if he ever sees you face to face he will erase your tattoos... by pulling off your arms...'.

With all limbs still intact AC/DC started 1977 the way they began 1976 – ensconced in Sydney's Albert Studios with the Vanda/Young team. By the end of February they emerged clutching a mastertape of what many fans – and indeed Angus himself – consider to be the band's finest hour. The Who's Pete Townshend has even gone as far as saying it's his favourite hard rock album ever.

Indeed, the giant leap AC/DC made from 'Dirty Deeds...' to 'Let There Be Rock' still comes as quite a shock when listening to the albums back-to-back today, some 13/14 years on. If 'DDDDC' sounded slightly stale, then 'LTBR' was as fresh as a cold shower. If last year's model sounded dated within a year, the new one came without a sell-by date. Show me a rock enthusiast who doesn't own a copy of 'Let There Be Rock' and I'll show you a geologist. A deaf one. So what happened? How did they do it? What were they on? And... where can you buy it?! Angus tried to explain it all some years later.

"My brother George asked us what kind of album we wanted to make and we said, 'Well, it would be great if we could just make a lot of guitar riffs'. We were all fired up after returning from a lot of touring, and we just had a real 'gung-ho' attitude about the album.

"That album sort of put us on the road and I think it also set the style of the band. It had some great tracks – 'Whole Lotta Rosie' and 'Let There Be Rock' for a start – and I think that set the standard for us."

Such was the 'gung-ho' attitude, George didn't even want to stop one of his kid-brother's most ferocious solos despite the fact that an amp blew up half-way through. "...Towards the end (of the solo)," Angus remembers, "they're all looking and I'm wondering what's going on. The amp was on fire, smoke coming out of the back and everything! The sound was still coming out though, and George was telling me to keep going. I think he was hoping that the amp would actually blow up and he'd get an explosion on the end."

That didn't happen, but then it hardly needed to as the band's performance was explosive enough. For the first time AC/DC had a real metal edge to their boisterous bluesy boogie, an extra heaviness which packed a fearsome kick into tracks like 'Bad Boy Boogie' and 'Hell Ain't A Bad Place To Be'. The band refused to admit they had become a heavy metal outfit – and still do with some frustration – but 'Let There Be Rock' undoubtedly teetered on the edge of the much maligned genre, and its influence on a future generation of unashamedly metal bands remains unquestionable.

Much subsequent infamy has of course centred around two tracks in particular – the title track itself and 'Whole Lotta Rosie'. The former chugged along like a drag-racing juggernaut, sucking at the very roots of r'n'b and spewing forth a venomous, vulgarised version at vicious velocity. The latter, a wickedly contorted step-child of Led Zeppelin's 'Whole Lotta Love', crashed down like a ton of bricks on its way to blistering climax, as Bon shared another of his dubious sexual conquests with the world. This time the victim was a Tasmanian wench with reputed measurements of 42-39-56.

"Bon said she was HUGE, about the size of a football pitch!" Angus explained. "We were staying at a seedy little hotel in Melbourne – we'd just started out – and when Bon left the place this girl shouted 'BON SCOTT!' and grabbed him.

"She had a friend with her and they took him home with them, at which point she told him about all the people she'd slept with. 'I've been with 28 people this month' she said, before throwing Bon into the bedroom where they had a drink and a pretty wild night. Next morning, thinking Bon was asleep, she leaned across to her friend in the opposite bed and said, 'Twenty nine!'

"Actually," Angus added, "we saw her again in Hobart when we visited Tasmania, but she'd lost a lot of weight by then and Bon was very disappointed. She knew the song was about her though, and she took it as a compliment!"

Bon's other lyrical gem this time was 'Crabsody In Blue', which could well have been the sequel to 'Whole Lotta Rosie', dedicated as it was to a crab-treatment cream called 'Blues' ointment. He certainly seemed to know what he was talking about when he crooned with flesh-crawling credibility: '…And you start to scratch, when they start to hatch/Walking sideways…/Give me the Blues… And when you start to scream, that's when you'll buy the cream, Blues ointment/Yeah, and when they start to itch, you go out and you take the bitch, for an appointment…'

It was Bon's follow up to 'The Jack'

and 'Big Balls' in terms of risqué content, not so much near-the-knuckle as embedded-in-the-bone! Bon was rapidly becoming to poetry what Soho was to virginity.

But it all worked, ground into the grime of what was probably AC/DC's sleaziest album. 'Go Down', 'Dog Eat Dog' and 'Overdose' rounded the record off with pounding primeval beats, and the Vanda/Young production ensured that every wrenched riff, every gasp of adrenalin and every mistake remained full in your face, as raw as a grazed knee. This was as live as a studio album gets, like having the band set up in your bedroom, yet somehow achieving the acoustics of your bathroom. It steamed like a kettle.

Not everyone rallied behind the band though. Elements of the Australian media, keen to exploit the band for some cheap controversy, preyed on rumour, half-truths and sheer fiction in their attempts to rattle the band's cage. One TV station invited the band onto a chat show to promote their new album, harbouring the ulterior motive of exposing the band as foul-mouthed yobs – just as Bill Grundy had done with The Sex Pistols in Britain a few months earlier. Before the programme started the TV crew were the definition of hospitality, but as soon as the cameras rolled the band were introduced as 'notorious' and asked to say something sick. Malcolm immediately stomped off the set in disgust, only to be chased by the director who pleaded with him to get back on the set and storm off again, because he hadn't caught it on camera the first time!

There really couldn't have been many grounds for complaint, though, as AC/DC seemed determined to push their rebel rocker image and toilet-wall humour to the bounds of decency. It was all a big send-up of course, the sort of giggle that goes on in all back-alley bars after a few beers, but they couldn't have expected everyone to get the joke and grin at the sins.

The promo video for 'Let There Be Rock', for example, may have just been a light-hearted skit on a Biblical phrase ('Let there be light, let there be sound… let there be rock!'), but it was ripe for a rollicking from religious robots. Filmed later in 1977 after the departure of Mark Evans, it featured the band thrashing it out in a church, kitted out in full clergymen regalia (Angus complete with a cardboard halo!), until Bon rips off his robes to leap from the pulpit for the finale. Wickedly unsanctimonious.

In the Britain of 1977 though, a bit of notoriety wasn't a bad thing. Punk was still raging, the press were still championing the yobbish likes of Eddie & The Hot Rods, The Stranglers, The Clash and The Sex Pistols, and AC/DC's return in February was keenly awaited. A 26-date tour had been booked to take them from Edinburgh University on February 18 through to Hemel Hempstead Pavilion on March 1, taking in such unlikely haunts as Maidenhead Skindles, Plymouth Fiesta and Cleethorpes Winter Gardens, and the publicity machine purred excitedly. A riot in Edinburgh which halted the second number of AC/DC's new set, 'Dog Eat Dog', seemed to happen right on cue for those who believed the hype.

Back in London the band filmed a special slot for the Fifth Anniversary show of Countdown, the Aussie equivalent of Top Of The Pops. Introduced by Leo Sayer they mimed their way through 'Dog Eat Dog', Angus for once in a T-shirt and Bon fluffing his words with a devil-may-care grin. It was a relaxed and high-spirited skit which showed what fun the marauding Aussies were having on the other side of the globe to those who watched it back home. But trouble was around the corner.

The band's next assignment was as European tour support to metal's heaviest perpetrators of the age, Black Sabbath. Sabbath had virtually drawn up the blueprint for HM seven years before, but by 1977 the lumbering monster had suffered some internal ruptures and the problems between singer Ozzy Osbourne and guitarist Tony Iommi were exacerbated by the relatively poor sales of their latest album, 'Technical Ecstasy'. Even so they were still a big draw on the live circuit, and as such were the perfect vehicle for AC/DC to hijack.

It didn't quite go as planned. In fact they were thrown off the tour, the result of an incident in which Malcolm hit Sabbath's bassist Geezer Butler, after Butler had pulled a knife on him. Few in AC/DC's entourage could actually believe it when Malcolm actually apologised to Sabbath the next day, such was his remorseless pride, but the damage had been done and AC/DC flew back to London after the show in Helsinki.

"Geezer was just being an asshole," says Ozzy Osbourne, "he'd bought this flicknife and started waving it about in the bar. Mind you, he was completely pissed at the time – we all were – so of course things just got out of hand. I told Geezer to stop it, but he carried on and had a go at Malcolm, and Malcolm took it really personally. I don't blame him. I would've taken it personally if someone had threatened me with a knife!

"It was a real shame what happened, because I got on really well with the guys in the band – especially Bon and Angus. Angus used to crack me up; he'd sit in the dressing room and smoke 500 cigarettes and drink 50 cups of tea before he went onstage. I couldn't believe it! And then Bon… he'd usually have a half-pint tumbler full of Jack Daniel's!

"We got on great. I used to wear those brothel-creeper shoes onstage in those days and Bon loved them. The next time I saw him he had a pair on as well, and we had a laugh about it. What happened on that tour with AC/DC had nothing to do with us, it was just a thing between Geezer and Malcolm, the sort of stupid thing that happens when you're out of your mind."

The Sabbath tour was also to be Mark Evans' last contribution to AC/DC. When the dust had settled and the band had regrouped in London, a personality clash between Evans and Angus rose to the surface. Without Mark's knowledge the band had a meeting at Angus and Malcolm's London flat in Portobello Road, and all the grievances were aired. Later Phil told Mark of the meeting, and Mark decided he'd take the hint and leave before the situation mushroomed into a full-scale war.

Evans flew back to Australia during the summer of 1977 and, joining up with vocalist Owen Orford and drummer Peter McFarlane who'd been playing with the band Finch, he swiftly put together an outfit called Contraband and recorded an album entitled 'Nothing To Hide' for the Portrait label, which was released during 1978. Evans recorded three albums with Contraband, but by his own admission they were "too middle-of-the-road and nowhere near ballsy enough", and ultimately the band failed to take off.

Mark also had spells in Swanee (formed by John Swan, the brother of Aussie superstar Jimmy Barnes) and Heaven, for whom he played rhythm guitar – "doing my Malcolm Young impressions!" Heaven were actually managed by Michael Browning at the time, and looked set to make significant progress with their 'Where Angels Fear To Tread' album in '82. But once again, nothing came of it.

Since Heaven, Mark has been back in Australia tackling a variety of jobs. For a while he enjoyed a spell in publishing

with Rondor Music, still keeping his hand in by playing the occasional session. These days he works in an equipment store in his hometown of Sydney called The Bass Centre and gigs around "with a few mates, just for fun" in the evenings.

At the time of going to print however, a new project seems likely to bring Mark back into the public eye. He's set to go to LA to record an album for Capricorn Records with a new band called The Zoo, which features Mick Fleetwood from Fleetwood Mac on drums and Aussie legend Billy Thorpe on guitar. There's also talk of a tour for 1992.

Back in 1977, AC/DC replaced Mark Evans the way they have replaced every departing member since him, with the minimum amount of fuss.

"The day after Mark left," says Michael Browning, "I called this guy who used to keep his ear to the ground for me and said, 'I need a bass player pretty quickly. If you can find me one there's a ten quid 'spotter's fee' in it for you'. So this guy says, 'Yeah, I know someone called Cliff Williams who'd be ideal for you'. Cliff probably doesn't know it to this day, but it cost me just ten quid to find him!

"So I got in touch with him and as soon as I saw him I thought he'd be great, because apart from anything else he looked great and I knew he'd fit in visually.

"The problem was… Malcolm and Angus were keen on getting in this guy from Manfred Mann's Earth Band (Colin Pattenden) who I didn't like because I thought he was too old and didn't look right for AC/DC, so when Cliff came to audition I tipped him off about certain things… 'use a pick because the guys want someone who plays with a pick… learn these songs this way because that's how they like to play them…' So Cliff walks in and does everything the guys want from a bass player and gets the job! I had to laugh because obviously Cliff never told the band he'd been tipped off and obviously I didn't want the band to know that I'd tipped him off. So nobody knows the truth about how he got the gig."

Cliff Williams, already experienced in a string of lower-league bands, was born on December 14, 1949, in the Essex town of Romford, just outside London, and moved to Liverpool as a nine-year-old where he spent his teens. His first job was as an engineer at a factory just behind Lime Street Station in Upper Mill Street. By the end of the Sixties he'd had enough, and quit to try his arm at becoming a professional musician.

Linking up with singer Mick Stubbs, guitarist Laurie Wisefield (later to join Wishbone Ash), keyboard player Clive John (who went on to play with Man) and drummer Mick Cook (who, in turn, teamed up with The Groundhogs), Williams found himself playing bass for a band called Home. By 1970 the group's progressive brand of both hard and soft rock had earned them a deal with Epic Records, a subsidiary of CBS, and a début LP was released the following year under the title 'Pause For A Hoarse Horse'. In November of 1971 Home supported Led Zeppelin at the Wembley Empire Pool on the second of Zep's 'Electric Magic' concerts which featured circus acts as well as rock bands!

During 1972 Jim Anderson replaced John on keyboards and Home released a self-titled follow-up album, going on to have their one and only hit with 'Dreamer' in November 1972, which peaked at 41 in the UK album charts. 'The Alchemist' followed in 1973 but by then the band seemed to have run their course, and when controversial folk troubadour Al Stewart suggested they back him on his first American tour in March 1974, Stubbs went his own way and the others became The Al Stewart Band, burying the name Home for good.

With Stewart retiring to the studio to record his 'Past Present And Future' concept album immediately after the tour, Williams returned to Britain to put together a new group, Bandit. Featuring guitarists James Litherland and Danny McIntosh, drummer Graham Broad (who later played with Britain's somewhat feeble answer to Abba, Buck's Fizz) and singer Jim Diamond (who had limited success with PhD in the early '80s, and even sang the theme tune to the TV series Boon), Bandit were signed up by Arista and eventually released an eponymous début album of hard-edged blues-based rock during 1977.

That summer Williams found the lure of AC/DC too much to resist and slung his hook. Inspired by McIntosh, Bandit stumbled onward with a different line-up to record 'Partners In Crime' for the Ariola label in 1978, but the flame had died. Williams, meanwhile, the most unassuming bass player of them all, was about to embark on a rollercoaster ride to fame and fortune, something he later confessed was a feat beyond his wildest dreams.

Slipping into Mark Evans' shoes may have been one small step for man, but it was one giant leap for Cliff Williams.

Chapter V

If You Want Bucks
(...Enter The Power Age)

After rehearsals in Sydney had broken-in Cliff Williams, AC/DC steadied themselves for their most ambitious step since leaving their homeland two years earlier. The lure of the dollar was simply too strong to resist – still is for any band with an ounce of ambition – and Michael Browning planned an extensive bout of touring in the US for his boys to take them right through the rest of the summer and into the autumn.

Starting in the southern States they warmed up with ten club dates which took them from Texas to Florida, where they played their first major gig in front of 13,000 people at the outdoor Hollywood Spartatorium. The event had been organised as a fund–raiser for a muscular dystrophy charity, and as a show of appreciation the Mayor of nearby Miami presented the band with the keys to the city.

"We were particularly big in Jacksonville and this proved to the people at Atlantic in America that AC/DC could be a headline act," says Browning. "If it hadn't have been for that I think Atlantic may well have dropped the band. In fact, they were going to drop AC/DC when the first option was up after 'High Voltage', but we managed to persuade them to keep us on by suggesting that they cut our advance. Phil Carson called me in Australia one day and told me the Americans weren't going to pick up the option, so I asked what we could do to change their minds. In the end we told Atlantic in America that we would accept a $5,000 cut in our advance and they went for it. It sounds ridiculous when you consider the amount of money that changes hands today, but in those days $5,000 was the difference between AC/DC having a record deal and not having a deal."

Meanwhile, over on the West Coast, AC/DC played four nights at the Old Waldorf club in San Francisco, attracting capacity 750 strong crowds, but they found the going tougher in Los Angeles where less than a hundred turned up at the famous Whiskey A Go Go club on Sunset Boulevard for their Hollywood début.

"It was a typically cynical LA crowd," remembers journalist Sylvie Simmons, who worked for Sounds at the time, "more interested in looking cool than looking at the band. But it was a great show, completely different from anything I'd seen in a long while. The power was almost overwhelming."

Later Sylvie interviewed the band by the pool on the roof of the Hyatt House Hotel, further up Sunset Strip. "I was shocked to find that Angus only drank tea," she says, "but relieved that Bon lived up to his stage image. He was the classic rock'n'roll singer – a Page Three-type blonde on one arm, a bottle of booze in his other hand. That's how I'll always remember Bon..."

The band were certainly having fun, but the treadmill ground on. Nightclubs, bars, support slots, festival openers... AC/DC chewed up the miles and spat them out, cramming in everything they could in one huge, gruelling promotional push. They went from the Jacksonville Coliseum, where they played in front of 7,500 fans in supporting REO Speedwagon, to the much cosier climate of the New York Palladium, where they opened for The Dictators... sprinting down Manhattan Island later the same evening to fit in a headline set there at the infamous CBGB's club. "This was done purely as a publicity stunt – two gigs in one night – because we wanted to make a splash in New York," says Browning.

But perhaps more significant than the back-breaking feat of endurance the band performed that night was Angus's discovery of a guitar innovation at the Palladium. Previously, Angus had had to conduct his primordial choreography with the handicap of a flailing guitar lead, which hardly slowed him down but still made stunts like the crowd-pleasing 'walkabout' all the more difficult. In New York he was introduced to the Kenny Schaeffer wireless guitar which needed no cord as it worked on the principle of a transistor, with a small box fixed to the guitar strap sending radio-wave signals to the amplifier. Angus tested it out in the dressing room of the Palladium and his mind raced with thoughts of its potential.

"It was amazing to see," said Bon, recalling how he'd walked into the dressing room to see Angus playing at one end of the room with his amps at the other end. "Angus had this Cheshire cat grin all over his face, and evil thoughts seemed to be going through his brain as to what havoc he could wreak with this evil little invention."

To some Americans though, Angus himself was the 'evil little invention'. Not everyone fell in love with the brat and his weird new guitar with a mind of its own, vulgarising the blues at ear-splitting volume. When 'Let There Be Rock' was released in the States during June, some reviewers spoke of the disgust they felt at its raucous onslaught, particularly as it appeared on the label (Atlantic) which was once the home of 'God' (aka Eric Clapton). AC/DC may have been championed by the kids, but they were not for purists.

The reaction was similar in Britain when the record finally saw the light of day in October, held back as it was to coincide with another UK tour. Some lauded it as the rebirth of heavy rock, others felt all the band were doing was turning Black Sabbath upside down and the wrong way round. The band just shrugged and got on with it, promoting 'Let There Be Rock' (the album and the single) with 18 shows on the Continent (including France, Holland, Belgium and Germany) and then a 14-date fling from October 12th-30th around their adopted homeland, which included their first sold-out show at London's prestigious Hammersmith Odeon. This was an achievement made sweeter by its locality – a guitar lead's length from the Red Cow.

The album, meanwhile, had climbed to a respectable 75 in the UK charts,

not bad for a band still effectively in its infancy. Yet although the hard work was beginning to pay off there was no time for celebration, as a second bout of American concerts supporting big name acts like Rush and Kiss stretched through November and into December. And if the band thought Hammersmith Odeon was a big step up, opening for Kiss at Madison Square Garden in New York elevated them to a new level entirely.

"It was funny because Kiss had so many security guards around them they wouldn't let us in," Angus laughed. "I'd go to the backstage door and say, 'We're the support act' and they'd go, 'Nah! Where's your limousines for a start?' They couldn't believe that these scruffy little kids could be in a rock'n'roll band."

Also in New York the band performed a special set for radio-broadcast at the Atlantic Studios on Broadway, on December 7. Kicking off with 'Live Wire', they showcased with 'Problem Child', 'High Voltage', 'Hell Ain't A Bad Place To Be', 'Dog Eat Dog', 'The Jack', 'Whole Lotta Rosie' and 'Rocker', and the set was sent out to radio DJs as a 'For Promotional Use Only' LP, in the hope that snippets would be aired by way of a prelude to the next AC/DC studio album.

These days very few copies of that limited edition record exist, but those

lucky enough to possess a copy will find it an interesting if slightly odd recording, suffering from a virtually silent audience and an occasionally erratic mix which boosts the bass too high during '... Rosie', and wobbles all over the place during 'Rocker'. For sheer intimacy with the band though, few live recordings will ever beat it.

British fans did get a treat in the New Year though, with the BBC airing the band's show at Essex University in Colchester on Sight And Sound In Concert, a simultaneous radio and TV broadcast. It was an important breakthrough and a great performance, the live transmission beginning with 'Problem Child' (probably the second

The new line-up after a close encounter with a zealous barber.

song of the set, after 'Live Wire'), then continuing with 'Sin City', 'Bad Boy Boogie', 'Whole Lotta Rosie' (dedicated to "the biggest, fattest woman who ever fornicated"), 'Rocker' and 'Let There Be Rock'. As with the 'Live From The Atlantic Studios' record though, recordings (either video or taped from the radio) of the programme remain hard to come by.

In what was becoming a tradition for AC/DC, the New Year was spent back home in Sydney, where a short break was followed by the inevitable return to Albert Studios with brother George and Harry Vanda. Recording took place

between February and March, and to complete the re-run of a tried-and-trusted formula, the Young brothers wrote the music and left Bon to write the words.

The album was called 'Powerage', but it might just have been titled 'Ditto'. AC/DC had clearly decided that to change their style now would alienate the fans who loved them for the three chord wonders they were. The new album simply perpetuated the AC/DC thud, and if it wasn't as powerful as 'Let There Be Rock', then it would certainly do for now.

The only noticeable hint of evolution this time around was a faint commercial sheen which could be detected in the almost danceable throb of the bass on 'Gimme A Bullet', and the very-nearly-melodic hook in 'Cold Hearted Man'. To complement this, the production wasn't as raw as it had been the previous year, and while the record certainly didn't pull any punches it didn't hit below the belt either.

There was nothing as potent as 'Whole Lotta Rosie' this time, but 'Kicked In The Teeth' was pretty close. 'Sin City' boomed with malicious intent, a perfect vehicle for the red-light howl of Bon, and 'Up To My Neck In You' jerked along a well-worn path as if it were charting new territory. Best of the lot, though, was 'Riff Raff', destined to open many an AC/DC show in future, which slid along a running Angus riff like a battered old banger with a Rolls Royce engine. To this day, it remains one of the band's finest five minutes.

Indeed, 'Powerage' was pretty well received almost everywhere, although some critics pointed out that a change of studio and producer wouldn't be amiss if AC/DC wanted to avoid stagnation or becoming a parody of themselves. However, Sounds described the record as '...Testimony to the rawest and most uncompromising sclerosis, no room for rebuttal'.

AC/DC, the experts agreed, still had teeth. Angus, budding dental surgeons would have noticed, actually had new teeth! Glowing like a Ready Brek kid on the cover, electric cables running up both sleeves, he sported a new set of gnashers which gleamed like white ivory where in days past his few manky molars drooped like ancient headstones. Clearly, the kid wasn't only interested in school caps...

Indeed, there was plenty of teeth-grinding to do in the coming months, as a huge world tour sprawled before them. To promote the release of 'Powerage' on April 28, AC/DC were scheduled to return to Britain for a 28-date tour opening on April 26 at Wolverhampton Civic Hall but Angus picked up a foot infection on the trip over to England, and the first three dates had to be cancelled. Another date at the West Runton Pavilion was also pulled at short notice, leaving support band British Lions playing somewhat awkwardly to a surly crowd.

The tour finished on May 29 at Dundee Caird Hall, and AC/DC took flight for America once more for support slots with Rainbow, Savoy Brown, Alice Cooper, Journey and Aerosmith, not to mention an appearance at San

"Now Angus, remember your table manners..."

happening in Tasmania!"

Clearly the traditional Yankee diet of glitz and hype wasn't washing with the altogether more down-to-earth Aussies. "The worst thing about these American record companies," said Malcolm, "is they want to make you feel like a star. It's embarrassing."

"We went into the office in Chicago," continued Angus, "and everybody stood up and clapped us. What can you do?"

"They take it so seriously," commented Bon.

"What with the star trip and the coke," Angus snorted, "the Yanks don't know where they are."

One story that is often repeated in AC/DC folklore concerns the time Bon had sharp words with an American record company employee while standing in a toilet. The American inquired, somewhat facetiously, "Are you AC or DC, lovey?" to which Bon replied, "Neither... I'm the lightning flash in the middle!" and landed a smart upper cut on the hapless halfwit's chin.

Another amusing incident involving the band and their beloved American record company occurred backstage at the Tower Theater in Philadelphia where they were appearing with British band UFO. Because it was AC/DC's first show in the area, various senior staff from Atlantic made the journey from New York

Francisco's major summer festival, The Day On The Green, during August. The band's reputation was growing considerably in the States, but the feeling certainly wasn't mutual; at one of the Rainbow gigs Angus got involved in a spitting match with one particularly pugnacious punter, while in Detroit Malcolm butted a promoter after he pulled the plug on the band for

exceeding the 98-decibel noise limit. Threats of arrest were countered by suggestions that the band would sue for $15,000 worth of damage to their equipment, and both parties retreated swiftly. "Detroit... rock'n'roll city?" snapped Malcolm. "There's more

to Philly to impress their new clients. "After UFO had finished their set," recalls Ian Jeffery, "Pete (Way, their bassist) and Phil (Mogg, their singer) came into our dressing room for a chat, then suddenly we were joined by all the guys from Atlantic. One of the main men walked straight up to Phil Mogg, shook his hand and said, 'Bon! What a great show!'... and we hadn't even been on yet! Well you can imagine, Malcolm and the others looked at each other in amazement."

The UFO tour, a co-headlining affair with each band topping the bill in the areas in which they were most popular, threw up some interesting contrasts,

" ... Oh well, obviously not"

especially between Pete Way and Angus, who formed a close friendship.

"Angus was amazing," says Pete, "I loved him. He doesn't drink, doesn't do drugs... and yet he'd stay up all night on his own energy. Often he'd come to my room for a chat or whatever, and he'd be drinking cups of tea while I was doing my white powder. He'd say to me, 'Why don't you give that stuff up and have a good breakfast instead?' He was great, totally unique.

"He was a fiery little character as well sometimes. I remember once in Columbus, Ohio, seeing him and Malcolm rolling round on the floor on the side of the stage, fighting over what they were going to do for an encore. And I remember Malcolm hitting the promoter at another gig...

"They were great fun to be with on those tours, but very different from most bands. They didn't feel in competition with any other bands around at the time, and didn't even bother to listen to

anyone else's albums. We'd go, 'What do you think of so-and-so's new single?' and they'd be like, 'Well it doesn't pay our rent...' They didn't care. They were just into the old bands like The Who and the Stones, and if you mentioned someone like Foreigner to them it'd be, 'Nahhh, bloody cabaret act!' They didn't like any fuss and they hated anything that was a bit flashy; being from Australia they had this sort of macho attitude to everything. Paul Raymond (UFO's keyboard player/rhythm guitarist) used to wear some bright clothes and have his hair pushed up, and the AC/DC lads used to go, 'Nahhh, he looks like bloody Shirley Bassey!' Paul's never been able to live that nickname down to this day.

"It was a great tour because both bands were breaking at that time and the buzz was a big one. I think it must've been one of the first times that two bands of that nature were paired, because in America before we'd play on the same bill as Marc Bolan and Blue Öyster Cult... a real mixture. But AC/DC and UFO was a much closer match, and we drew a much more hardcore audience, the kind of kids who weren't into hit single bands."

AC/DC could have been forgiven for not knowing where they were half the time. Zig-zagging across the States almost without a breather, they trudged through no less than 76 shows during the summer. It was hard graft, but the band were philosophical. "It's sometimes a drag, being in a different hotel every night," said Bon, "but it's not as bad as being stuck in front of a lathe every day of your life for fifty years. I am here and I am free and I'm seeing new faces every night and touching new bodies or whatever. It's great, there's nothing like it."

Also, the returns were finally making

things worthwhile. The tours may have been, as Angus put it "real low-budget tours; five of us in a tiny station wagon, packed in like sardines", but by the time they returned to Europe for yet another whirlwind tour throughout October and November, 'Powerage' had sold close on a quarter of a million copies in America.

Atlantic were warming to the task, too. The album had breached the Top 50 in the UK, and a single which wasn't even on the LP called 'Rock And Roll Damnation' – a slab of prime-time AC/DC simplicity – reached No. 24 in the charts during the summer. There followed the unlikely spectacle of Angus & Co. headbanging deliriously through the ludicrous lip-synching charade that is Top Of The Pops.

"There was this stupid rule that said nobody could mime to the actual recording of the song on Top Of The Pops," recalls Browning. "So you had to re-record the song before you went on the programme. We went to Island's studios in Basing Street to do our song, only we didn't actually do anything. We just pretended to re-record it. We ended up giving the guy at Top Of The Pops the same tape back. Of course, they didn't know the difference.

"The only other thing I remember about Top Of The Pops was that the producer was gay and obviously fancied Angus. All he did was show shots of Angus in his shorts running around, and I remember having this argument with him saying... 'Show the singer as well mate, show the singer!' But all he wanted to do was look at Angus."

Flushed with the success of 'Rock And Roll Damnation', the powers-that-be prepared a live album from tapes collected during the earlier months of 1978, and by October – a mere six

Vanda (right) and Young mixing 'If You Want Blood...' at Albert Studios in Sydney.

months after the release of 'Powerage'–
'If You Want Blood... You've Got It' hit
the streets to exploit the rising demand
for anything AC/DC.

In retrospect, it's difficult to make a
case for any AC/DC album being a
better-timed and more crucial release
than 'If You Want Blood...'. Releases
both before and after the band's only
official live album to date were both
important and significant in their own
way, but in the greater scheme of things
'If You Want Blood...' was a sucker
punch which galvanised all previous
support into fanaticism, hauling the
band from a cult level mid-table position
to the brink of the big league.

For an essentially live band it was a
natural step forward, too. Suddenly, all
those who'd merely made a vinyl
acquaintance with AC/DC in the past
were transported into the cacophonic
cauldron of a sweaty concert hall hell,
like walking into some incredible New
Year's Eve party in the middle of August.
The band's entire past was condensed
into one glorious hour, forming a popular
launch pad from which they would soar
to even greater heights in future.

'If You Want Blood...' was the fans'
album, and the fans responded by
planting it as high as No.13 in the UK
charts, and breaching the Top 50 in
America for the first time too. The sight
of Angus impaled on his guitar amid a
pool of blood became one of rock's
most striking images of the year. The
album's cover was plastered over the
walls of record shops nationwide and
AC/DC's powerful, Gothic logo adorned
the backs of denim jackets everywhere,
making a welcome return to the fold
after the weaker, shattered-glass style
incarnation on 'Powerage'.

Unlike the majority of live albums
which, especially in the Seventies, tended
to be double-record extravaganzas with
tedious solo sections and 30-minute
versions of five-minute LP tracks, 'If You
Want Blood...' smacked you straight
between the eyes and disappeared
before you could blink. A single disc in a
single sleeve, it was singularly direct and
dangerous, impossibly raw and ragged
at a time when it was the norm to
overdub live records until they sparkled
with the polish of a producer's touch.

'Riff Raff' set the standard; hit the
volume knob and you were in the front
row peering up Angus' shorts. Then
there was 'Hell Ain't A Bad Place To Be',
'Bad Boy Boogie', 'The Jack' with new
words from Bon, who still recounted the
tale with an evil glint in his eye, and
finally the zombie stomp of 'Problem

Child', almost drowned out by the hysteria
of the audience at the beginning.

Side Two was pure tennis-racquet
Nirvana. The by-now anthemic 'Whole
Lotta Rosie' (the new maxi-single no
less), the recent hit single 'Rock And Roll
Damnation' previously not available on
record, 'High Voltage', 'Let There Be
Rock' and, sprinting for the line, a
speeded up version of 'Rocker', for
which the band must surely have been
on double-steroids. If producers Vanda
and Young could have chosen their
swansong, they couldn't have made a
better choice.

Within a fortnight of the album's

release AC/DC had returned from a
short bout of European shows to begin
their eighth UK tour in two and a half
years, an extraordinary feat which was
executed fittingly by squeezing 16 gigs
into just 18 days. Such was the ground-
swell of popularity for the band now,
they added extra nights at venues like
Newcastle's Mayfair (the first band ever
to do so) and London's Hammersmith
Odeon, where fans were treated to
AC/DC's first real attempt at a proper
'stage-set', a towering walkway behind
Phil Rudd's drum-kit across which Angus
could scuttle to his heart's content,
occasionally with a smoke canister going
off inside his satchel.

The tour didn't pass without amusing
incidents either. On the third night of the
tour at Glasgow's Apollo, after he'd
dumped Angus back onstage following
the 'walkabout' stunt, Bon ran around
the side of the auditorium to get back

on stage as well and took a wrong turning
in the maze of corridors. Confused, he
pushed through a door which slammed
behind him... and found himself standing
in the street outside. There followed a
heated exchange with the bouncers on the
front door as Bon tried to persuade them
that he was actually the lead singer of the
band which was currently on stage. He
finally convinced them by asking why else
would he be wandering around the streets
of Glasgow in winter without a shirt!

Tackled about the Apollo incident in
Newcastle by one intrepid scribe, Bon
claimed, "I can't remember that – it was
two days ago."

Another extraordinary incident
happened on the final night of the tour,
November 16 at Hammersmith Odeon,
when AC/DC provided the author with
one of his most lasting memories of the
band. Disappearing offstage for his
usual 'walkabout' whilst Malcolm, Cliff
and Phil thrashed out the rhythm to
'Rocker', Angus suddenly reappeared
from nowhere right under the author's
nose... in Row S of the circle! It seemed
an impossibly long way from the stage,
especially as he would've had to run
through the Odeon's foyer, up the stairs
and through the public bar – still playing
his solo – to get to the circle, but there
he was, draped over Bon's shoulders
and surrounded by a few tracksuited
security goons, coating the entire rear
circle with sweat for a full five minutes.

In 1978 if you wanted blood and sweat
from AC/DC... you certainly got it. Tears?
They were just around the corner...

Chapter VI

Shot Down In Flames
(...On The Highway To Hell)

T he live album effectively closed the first stage of AC/DC's career and their immediate future needed careful planning. By the end of 1978 Atlantic could argue that their boys-from-the-outback were up there with the best of them in metal's own little universe, but they still needed a record which would guarantee airplay and open up an even broader market.

With this in mind, Atlantic suggested a change of producer. For four years Harry Vanda and George Young had moulded and shaped the AC/DC sound, turning them from boys into men along the way. But with '... Blood...' proving something of a watershed, it was agreed by all that fresh blood was needed in the studio if progress was to be made.

Eddie Kramer, who engineered much of Jimi Hendrix's work during the late Sixties and worked with Led Zeppelin on three of their albums, was the first choice to produce AC/DC's next LP but Kramer and the band failed to gell. "They were in Florida with Eddie and things weren't going well," says Michael Browning. "One day I got a call at my apartment in New York from Malcolm who said... 'You've got to get rid of this guy and find us someone else. He's no good at all.'

"Now at the time I was sharing an apartment with Mutt Lange's manager and when he called I was actually sitting next to Mutt. So as Malcolm's ranting down the phone, I turned to Mutt and said, 'Look, would you please do this record for us?' And he more or less agreed right there. So we came back to London and I got the boys together with Mutt, but they'd had such a bad experience with Eddie Kramer they weren't too sure about anything."

Robert John 'Mutt' Lange, a Rhodesian veteran of some repute in hard rock circles, had worked with the likes of City Boy, Boomtown Rats, The Outlaws and Graham Parker. As well as changing producers, AC/DC also changed studios, electing to record outside Australia for the first time. They were booked into London's Roundhouse studios which abutted the former engine shed turned rock venue in Chalk Farm Road.

Even more out of character for AC/DC was the length of time spent working on the new record. For a band who would have considered six weeks a bit over-indulgent before, the six months that AC/DC spent working with Lange was virtually a lifetime.

But then 'Highway To Hell' was as different a record as AC/DC had made since the quantum leap from 'Dirty Deeds...' to 'Let There Be Rock'. Anyone with a passing acquaintance with hard rock would have recognised it as AC/DC immediately, but there was a new grasp of melody in Bon's singing, a new dimension in 'hooky' choruses and an overall radio-friendly gloss which took it from the clubs to the stadia.

"It was the record they needed to make," says Tony Platt, who mixed the album at Basing Street Studios near Ladbroke Grove in West London. "At this time there were still factions who took them to be a punk band, but they of course were very much heading for a straight rock sound, while trying to open up the American market at the same time. I remember being very impressed by the way they worked at getting the balance just right.

"It was a very exciting album to work on too; we mixed it in something like eight days, and it was all very intense. I'd worked with bands like Free in the past and had kind of got used to the way those musicians worked, so to come across a band like AC/DC who just rolled up their sleeves and bashed it out was very refreshing.

"I was very impressed with Bon; his sense of humour, his attitude, his general demeanour... One of my most vivid memories of him on that record was when he was doing 'Night Prowler'; he more or less just made the lyrics up on the spot! Apparently that's the way he wrote most of his lyrics, just sitting in the corner of the studio scribbling down a few ideas, until it was time for him to sing... then it'd just trip off his tongue. Apart from that, the record was great to work on because it was the first time I'd worked with Mutt..."

Lange's influence shone through the record like a beacon. With an apprenticeship based mainly in pop some may have thought him the wrong choice for a band who generally stood as the antithesis of mainstream Muzak. But the combination of polish and power, shot through a glut of top quality tunes, elevated 'Highway To Hell' into the realms of immortality for many fans.

The title track embodied AC/DC's new sound in three minutes and 26 seconds of air-punching, lung-wringing catchiness – sort of a runaway terrace-chant with melody. Lange had obviously worked hard on Bon's voice, honing it from a strangled-wallabee yelp into an altogether fuller sound which, combined with stronger backing vocals, made for huge tidal-wave choruses.

'Walk All Over You' was another, 'Shot Down In Flames' and 'If You Want Blood

(You've Got It) two more, but perhaps the finest example of all was 'Touch Too Much', which hit the nail right on the head. This was exactly what the record company bods wanted, especially the ones at Atlantic in America, where radio-play can determine an artist's career.

Angus had the bit between his teeth, too. 'Beating Around The Bush' was the result of a startling straight-from-the-hip riff which hit you in the pit of your stomach, while 'Girls Got Rhythm' found him in a more subtle mood, getting almost funky. And Cliff Williams even got in on the act, laying down his most ambitious bass-line to date on 'Love Hungry Man', which bobbed along in an almost pleasant fashion, most unlike AC/DC.

Bon was still on top form though, ever the dirty old man you simply couldn't dislike. Titles like 'Get It Hot', 'Girls Got Rhythm' and 'Love Hungry Man' spoke for themselves, while 'Night Prowler' which closed the album howled like a werewolf-on-heat. Once again Bon was the Prince Of Promiscuity, one of the lads just out for a bit of fun. But sadly 'Night Prowler' was to cause a storm of controversy in America a few years later... as indeed was the album's sleeve, which featured a picture of Angus with horns coming out of his cap. As the band's popularity in America soared, it seemed, so did the number of detractors out to vent their pseudo-religious paranoia on any rock'n'roll band within spitting distance.

For those who didn't take tongue-in-cheek imagery so seriously, 'Highway To Hell' (the nickname, incidentally, which Angus had given to one of AC/DC's gruelling US tours a few years earlier) was a modern day classic. Released on July 27, it quickly became the band's first UK Top Ten hit (peaking at No.8) and their first US Top Twenty (reaching No.17), comfortably outstripping the sales of all previous albums. AC/DC had arrived in the big time, and Bon was crowing from the rooftops: 'Hey Satan! Paid my dues – playing in a rockin' band/Hey Mama! Look at me – I'm on my way to the Promised Land/I'm on the highway to hell...'

But despite their upwardly mobile status there was unrest in the AC/DC camp at this time, and shortly after the new album hit the streets the trouble bubbled to the surface. "After the album was done I'd gone back to Australia to do some business," says Michael Browning. "We'd all agreed to rendezvous in America at a later date. At this point none of us had any money,

things were really difficult financially, so I decided to enter a partnership with a guy who could help us out with some money, someone who could give us a much-needed injection of cash. But during this period there were certain things going down... I guess there were problems between me and the band, there was a certain amount of upheaval going on, certain things got blown out of proportion... it was a very unhappy and unstable time for us.

"In the meantime certain people were talking to the band, maybe applying some pressure on them, and my position was being very much undermined. It all came to a head in America, and in a very emotionally-charged atmosphere I left. I haven't spoken to them since."

AC/DC had in fact been 'courted' by rival manager Peter Mensch for some time. Mensch worked for the powerful CCC (Contemporary Communications Corps) management company in New York, who handled Aerosmith and Ted Nugent. At a time when breaking the American market was crucial to the band, the Youngs obviously felt that having big time US management was important, and Browning was banished rather cruelly, especially considering the years of hard work he'd put in on behalf of AC/DC.

Browning would go back to Sydney and start his own record label (Delux Records, who at one time had INXS on their roster), going back into management with an LA-based metal act called Warrior in the early Eighties, as well as the aforementioned Heaven. Today he's still very much involved in the music business, running another label of his

Phil Rudd simply shrugs, "Why, do I need a ticket?" When asked what he thought of Angus, Malcolm's opinion is: "He's better than Mick Jagger... and Elton John... and Rod Stewart... and Paul McCartney..."

The whole thing is a bit of a sham, which is sad as it makes the band come across as numskulls. What with film of Phil racing across an airfield in a Porsche hotly pursued by Cliff in a bi-plane, much of it is also completely irrelevant. But Bon comes out of it with his lovable personality intact, although he unwittingly tempts fate with a few self-effacing tongue-in-cheek jibes. Asked why the rest of the band call him 'special', Bon laughs, "I'm a special drunkard – I drink too much." Pressed

"All he kept talking about was how fantastic this next record was going to be," recalls photographer Robert Ellis, who worked closely with the band at the time. "He carried this pad full of lyrics around with him, and he'd read them out to you whenever he could. He just kept on about the new album, how it was going to be the best thing AC/DC had ever done, and he was so fired up about it you couldn't help but believe him."

During the first weeks of February Bon hung around in London with friends, penning lyrics, working on ideas for the new record with Angus and Malcolm, and drinking at his favourite haunts. One of the happiest knees-ups was at Angus' wedding to his Dutch girlfriend Ellen;

On arriving home, however, Kinnear found he still couldn't wake Bon and decided the easiest thing to do was

...hrowing some blankets over him and ...ocking the car doors for safety, he ...eventually retired to bed.

Kinnear claimed he slept for some 15 ...hours, well into the early evening of the ...following Wednesday. Remembering ...where he'd left Bon, he nipped outside ...nto the dark, cold February night and to ...his horror found Bon was still ...unconscious in his Renault 5. He still ...couldn't wake him, but this time he ...knew Bon wasn't merely drunk. Fearing ...he worst, he rushed his friend to King's ...College Hospital where the nightmare ...became sickeningly real. The doctors ...pronounced him dead on arrival. ...Sometime during the night Bon, who'd ...been lying in an awkward position with ...his neck twisted, had vomited and ...choked to death.

The circumstances surrounding Bon's ...death didn't seem suspicious at the ...time but subsequent investigation ...suggests there might be more to the ...tragedy than was originally believed. ...There is strong evidence to suggest that ...Alisdair Kinnear was, in fact, a false ...name given to the police and press to ...conceal the true identity of the man who ...accompanied Bon on the last night of ...his life. Another name that crops up ...regularly during investigation is Joe King ...– itself apparently a nickname, as in ...joking' – who was a known drug ...(especially heroin) dealer in London ...around this time and who was a close ...friend of Bon's. There's even a ...suggestion that heroin had something to ...do with Bon's death, especially as the ...two most familiar after-effects of heroin ...use are drowsiness and vomiting. What ...is certain is that very few people know ...the full truth about what happened to ...Bon that fateful night, and those people ...are determined to make sure it stays ...that way.

The man known as Joe King was last ...seen at the Sunset Marquis Hotel in Los ...Angeles shortly after Bon's death and is ...alleged to have confided in friends that ...it was time he returned home to ...Australia to "lay low for a while". Only ...one conclusion can be drawn from that.

Whatever happened though, shock and ...confusion buzzed around the phone ...lines that night. Kinnear's (or perhaps ...King's) girlfriend phoned Angus, Angus ...phoned Malcolm, they phoned Ian ...Jeffery, Peter Mensch and the hospital. ...Angus thought and hoped Kinnear's (or ...King's) girlfriend had got it wrong and ...that the man in the car wasn't Bon; the ...hospital wouldn't give Angus any ...information as he wasn't next of kin. ...Mensch rushed to the hospital himself

...and identified the body.

Slowly the facts emerged to the inner circle of the AC/DC camp; even slower would they sink in. Malcolm phoned Bon's parents in Perth and broke the heartbreaking news. No one could believe it. Bon was not ill, for a regular drinker he hadn't drunk that much that night, and after all it seemed such a feeble way to go. Everyone was numb.

"The first I heard of it," says Pete Way, "was when Paul Chapman (UFO's guitarist) rang me the next day. He said he'd just had a call from Joe King's girlfriend, and that Bon was dead. He asked me if I knew any of the band's phone numbers, and I think I gave him Angus's number. I called Angus myself later to say how sorry I was about it all and Angus was terribly upset. He said he still had a lot of Bon's stuff at his flat and he couldn't look at it…"

Out on the streets of London news of the tragedy spread like wildfire. The author found out during the rush-hour in Piccadilly Circus when a newspaper stand selling London's evening paper The Evening Standard was daubed with the headline: 'ROCK STAR FOUND DEAD IN CAR!'

'Rock player Bon Scott of the Australian-based band AC/DC has been found dead in a friend's car…' ran the story,'… The 34 year-old singer was left in the car after a heavy drinking session. He was dead on arrival at King's College Hospital, South London. Scott, who had built a reputation for hard-drinking and hell-raising, was in London with the band to make a record'. On the Tube that night the author remembers seeing one youngster burst into tears while reading the story.

The following day all the British dailies ran their hashed obits. Like the Standard's story, most were riddled with inaccuracies: Bon was 33 not 34, he didn't die of alcohol poisoning, he wasn't a drug addict (although, like most people in rock, he occasionally took pills such as barbiturates and on a couple of occasions ended up in hospital after overdosing), he wasn't the 'wild man of pop' hellraiser bent on self-destruction… but the papers wanted him to be, so that's how they portrayed him. To some, Bon was just another sorry statistic of that ghastly, seedy rock'n'roll culture: Jimi Hendrix, Janis Joplin, Jim Morrison, Keith Moon… Bon Scott. Seven months later Led Zeppelin drummer John Bonham would go the same way, choking on his own vomit after a heaving drinking session. Wasn't it just typical? Inevitable? Fitting?

Actually, no. Far from being the result of a kamikaze boozing bout, Bon's death seems to have been nothing more than a tragic accident. At the inquest the coroner reported that Bon's liver, kidneys and general health were in excellent condition, and while his stomach did contain 'the equivalent of half a bottle of whiskey', this was not the kind of amount which would normally have troubled the singer.

The friend publicly known as Kinnear told the inquest Bon had downed at least seven double whiskeys at the Music Machine that night, but Mensch and the rest of the band commented that this was not unusual. Bon had always liked a drink and had a pretty high capacity; the band had played 250 shows during 1979 and Bon hadn't missed one. In fact, the band told the inquest they could remember one only occasion when Bon had been too drunk to do a show, and that was when he'd had a few drinks on a flight and accidentally got off at the wrong airport.

"All that stuff about drinking was a myth," says Ian Jeffery. "Bon liked a drink, sure, but only socially. OK, so he'd go on binges, but he'd also go two or three months without a drink – he wasn't a habitual drinker at all, and he wouldn't drink before going onstage. The only time he was ever drunk was at the Southampton Gaumont. We'd had a big party the night before and Bon was still going – but that was the ONLY time he ever drank before a show."

That Southampton show, of course, was Bon's last-ever gig. The irony was painful, the title of AC/DC's latest single – 'Touch Too Much', which included a live version of 'Shot Down In Flames' on the B-side – tragically prophetic. But then, as the coroner concluded in recording a verdict of 'death by misadventure', Bon had been 'the captain of his own destiny'.

He'd also had a great life. He'd lived life to the full in his 33 years, travelled the world, made a lot of people happy, made a bit of money, achieved what most people can only ever dream of achieving… and did it all with an irrepressible smile across his face. He was the kind of guy to whom fans could definitely relate because he was real and not some untouchable superstar in a Hollywood mansion. He was like your best mate up there on stage, giving it his best shot but having a laugh at the same time. His across-the-board popularity was his most fitting testament.

Tributes from around the world came

thick and fast. French band Trust dedicated their 'Repression' album to Bon (Bon was great mates with the band, and had planned to translate the lyrics of their album into English), American AOR outfit Nantucket called their album 'Long Way To The Top' LP out of respect to him, and Canadian trio Santers did the same with their next record, 'Shot Down In Flames'. In Nice, Cheap Trick and Angel City got together for a version of 'Highway To Hell'. In Scotland, Girlschool paid their tribute by adding a cover of 'Live Wire' to their set. Down in London, the Bandwagon pub in Kingsbury held a Bon Scott benefit night.

Perhaps the most controversial tribute though came from Ozzy Osbourne, who was writing songs for his first solo album after leaving Black Sabbath when Bon died. With guitarist Randy Rhoads, who himself would meet a tragic fate two years later, Ozzy wrote 'Suicide Solution' about the perils of alcohol, with Bon in the forefront of his mind. Six years later in December '86, Ozzy faced an ultimately unsuccessful prosecution in the Californian Superior court after the suicide of a teenager allegedly under the influence of 'subliminal messages' in the song hit the headlines.

"I've taken so much stick over that song," says Ozzy, "with people reading all sorts of things into it. But really it just came about because we were all so bummed out about Bon's death. Bob Daisley, who was my bass player at the time, actually came from Australia, and he knew Bon back in the really early days. He was sick when he heard the news, we all were, so I sort of dedicated the lyrics of that song to Bon. I mean, I've had my problems with alcohol too, a lot of us in this business have, but it's still a real shock when someone you know dies like that.

"Bon was one of the nicest guys I've ever met, I really mean that. I mean, if he was an asshole I'd tell you, I'm not just saying it because the poor guy's dead. He really was a lovely guy... it was a great loss."

The music media in Britain were busy recording their obituaries. In Sounds, the country's most sympathetic rock magazine of the time, journalist Dave Lewis added his thoughts about Bon The Boozer. "...I never saw him surly or aggressive no matter how much booze he had inside him. If after-gig exuberance led to a food throwing fight or whatever, you could be sure Bon would be at the centre of the action, but he never sat back on his star status and was always happy to shake hands or

sign autographs for fans – particularly if they were female.

"Basically, the phenomenal success of AC/DC opened the doors for him to indulge in all the fun and games that his denim-clad followers can only dream about. But, as rock's grisly roll-call of terminal casualties proves only too well, it's a dangerous game to play and sadly Bon went over the top just once too often."

Mark Evans tends to agree with the notion that Bon wasn't the hopeless drinker with a deathwish that he was made out to be.

"Sure Bon liked a drink," he says. "Who doesn't? But he only drank the same as any guy who works down the road and has a few beers in the pub at the end of the day. Occasionally he'd have too much and you'd find him crashed out on a hotel room floor, but then we've all done that from time to time! Bon certainly wasn't an alcoholic."

Pete Way, who became a great friend of Bon in the last couple of years of his life, spoke for a lot of people in the industry when he described his feelings to the author recently. "It was real sickener because Bon was such a great bloke," he says. "I know that sounds like a cliché and it's the sort of thing that everyone says about someone who's just died, but it was true about Bon, it really was... he was a genuinely great bloke, really friendly, really good fun, and very inspirational.

"The other thing was... Bon wasn't an alcoholic no matter what some people tried to say afterwards. I mean, what's an alcoholic? To me, an alcoholic is someone who lets drink interfere with their work; like, someone who gets to work late because he's too drunk to be punctual. Bon never let alcohol interfere with his work – which was basically doing the business onstage – and in fact if he did have a few beers before he went on then it was probably to enhance his work.

"When it happened though we all got a big jolt, y'know, because I think a few of us felt... God, that could've been me! I mean, we all drank a lot and took drugs and whatever, and half the time we were so out of it we didn't know what was going on. But I suppose we all felt that it wouldn't happen to us, that we were OK. When Bon died though it made you think... y'know, you have a few drinks, crash out in the back of your car and... that's it. Such a terrible way to go... I still miss Bon."

"He was the real spirit of AC/DC," says Tony Platt, "the glue that held the

"Anything Rolf Harris can do…"

band together. It was such a tragedy because he had everything to live for... but the strange thing was, someone told me he had visited a clairvoyant shortly before all this happened and she told him he would die in his 30s. I can't remember where I heard that, but...

"Anyhow, I think the best thing I ever heard about Bon came from Malcolm. He said to me while we were recording 'Back In Black': 'Sometimes Bon would disappear after a show and we wouldn't see him until just before we were due onstage the next night. But although he wouldn't turn up until the last minute, you knew he'd be there, you knew you could always depend on him. The hardest thing will be getting used to him not being there...'"

"I was very upset when I heard the news about Bon as you can imagine," says Michael Browning. "He certainly flirted with death before, living life very much in the fast lane. And he even told me he thought he wouldn't live to be 40, which was slightly strange... But it was still a shock. He was a likeable guy, there's no doubt about that."

Angus, meanwhile, remembered Bon as the happy-go-lucky rascal who just couldn't refuse a good time. "Often Bon would trail off with fans who came backstage after a show and go off with them to a party," he chuckled. "He judged people as they were and if they invited him somewhere and he was in the right mood to go, he went. It didn't matter to him if they had a name or were a 'star', he just went with them. We used to call him 'Bon The Likeable'.

"We could be somewhere where you would never expect anyone to know him, and someone would walk up and say, 'Bon Scott!', and always have a bottle of beer for him. It was uncanny. One time we were broken down in a bus outside this little town in Australia and some guy came walking along with his surfboard and a whole crate of beer. And it was really hot and we were dying for a drink. Anyway, he walked by the bus and looked in, saw Bon and suddenly yelled, 'BON SCOTT!', and came running in and handed out all his beers, and everyone was there for hours having a party while the bus was being fixed.

"He made a lot of friends everywhere and was always in contact with them, too. Weeks before Christmas he would have piles of cards and things, and he always wrote to everyone he knew, keeping them informed. Even his enemies, I think.

"He certainly was a character..."

Chapter VII

Back In Black
(...And Over The Moon, Brian)

he last week of February 1980 seemed to last a year. Somewhere among twisted feelings of sadness, anger, confusion and despair lay an aching dilemma: whether to continue without Bon and honour recording and touring commitments which stretched before them, or split up and to hell with it all?

"Everyone was walking around in silence," said Angus. "Nobody knew what to do, we were so depressed. We were so close! It was like losing an arm..."

"We sat around Peter (Mensch)'s flat for days wondering what to do," Ian Jeffery told the author some years later. "We weren't even sure if we should go back to Australia for the funeral, and there were actually a few days when the band wasn't sure if it would carry on.

"In the end, we decided to go back for the funeral - just for the sake of Bon's family - and the thing that really sticks in my mind is when we went to Bon's mother's house, she pulled out five chairs for the band... and then suddenly realised Bon wasn't there anymore. She broke down. She was saying things like, 'It can't be true – look, he's having a swimming pool built for us in the garden...' It was a very traumatic experience."

The band were also faced with the task of cleansing Bon's name from the mindless mud-throwing favoured by the ever antagonistic Aussie media. Angus, who was particularly affected by the death of his 'sixth brother', was determined that Bon's parents weren't distressed by the exaggerated 'wild man of rock' sensationalism. Instead, they spoke of a hard-working professional who never let them down, whose only crime was to enjoy a good time.

All of this seemed lost now, a sickeningly rude awakening. Yet it wasn't long before Malcolm decided he'd had enough moping around, and got on the phone to Angus. The two decided Bon would have wanted AC/DC to continue, and that was enough to fire them up into getting back to work. "So we got a little rehearsal studio and the songwriting became our therapy," Angus explained. "Then our manager kept pestering us about what we all dreaded: 'Don't you guys want a new singer?' We kept putting it off..."

The band were scheduled to spend Spring writing the next album, but Mensch suggested they use the time to find a replacement for Bon, and work the mourning out of their system that way. Reluctantly, the band agreed.

By mid-March the rumours were flying. Melody Maker suggested former

Easybeats vocalist Stevie Wright was being considered for the role (although he'd left the business with a drugs problem some time before and was now working for the Salvation Army in Sydney as a drugs counsellor). NME counterclaimed that a relatively unknown Aussie called Alan Friar from a band called Fat Lip from Elizabeth, near Adelaide, was in fact the man for the job (Friar actually ended up in Heaven with Mark Evans). In fact, countless applications for the job of singer with AC/DC were received and systematically sifted.

"Mutt used to pick me up in the mornings and we'd go through tapes on the car cassette whilst driving up to the studio in Willesden," says Tony Platt. "We'd have a new tape each day, and there'd be four or five singers on each

tape. This went on for at least a week. Some of the people who sent in tapes... well, it was hilarious. I mean, some were so far away from what AC/DC were about it was embarrassing, and some thought they could bring a certain kind of personality into the band just like that... it showed how naïve people could be."

One of the more promising applicants was Gary Holton, a chirpy Cockney who'd sung with The Heavy Metal Kids before going on to star in the acclaimed TV comedy series Auf Wiedersehen Pet. Holton was a renowned boozer, though, and he failed to show up for the audition three days on the trot as he couldn't get

Animals appeared on the scene in Newcastle, and Jonna suddenly discovered he wanted to be like Eric Burdon.

"I used to go and see The Animals in Newcastle when I was still at school," he said. "We'd sneak into the Club A-Go-Go and watch them playing... although eventually someone caught us and we were thrown out for being under age."

He had the bug though, as well as a stack of Animals albums. Taking up singing on a more ambitious level ("I swear I've never been able to play an instrument in my life – my fingers are too big!"), he saw out the Sixties without making much of an impression and seemed destined for obscurity during the glam era of the early Seventies. In February 1972 he joined a local outfit called USA – who changed their name to the far more appropriate Geordie a few months later – and by the end of the year the band slipped into the mould created by bands like The Sweet, Slade, and T. Rex, winning a recording contract with EMI and hitting the Top 40 with their début single 'Don't Do That' (which reached No.32). "The speed with which everything happened was amazing," he said. "It seemed as if we only just got together when the record was in the charts!"

Another hit, 'All Because Of You', came in March 1973 (it reached No.6), and later 'Can You Do It' peaked at No.13, while support slots with the likes of Slade (at the London Palladium) and The Sweet (at the Rainbow Theatre in London) cemented the band's following and status. As the glam era thrived so did Geordie, although after 'Electric Lady' slid out of the charts, only reaching No.32 in August of 1973, the band began to go out of fashion along with flared Levis and stack-heeled clodhoppers.

Geordie – which included guitarist Vic Malcolm, bassist Tom Hill and drummer Brian Gibson – continued to play the club circuit and released three albums during the Seventies – 'Hope You Like It' (1973), 'Don't Be Fooled By The Name' (1974) and 'Save The World' (1976) – as well as one compilation album, 'Master Of Rock' (1974). The ride was over though; things were pretty good on the Continent, but in the far more fickle UK another pop craze had taken over and the fleetfooted industry had once again left stragglers like Geordie behind.

To add to the misery the band had management problems – "Basically, we were getting ripped off," said Brian later

himself together. Clearly the band didn't need that so soon after Bon's demise, and their judgement proved sound when Holton himself died from over-indulgence in 1985.

"They kept sending guys down," said Angus, "and it was making us even more depressed... we didn't like anybody!"

Eventually a shortlist of two was drawn up: Terry Schlesher and Brian Johnson. Bon's comments about Johnson, recalled by a fan in Chicago who'd bought an import copy of the Geordie album 'Hope You Like It' to check the singer out, and then forwarded a tape to the CCC management offices in New York, swung it for the band. Johnson was a wanted man. Mensch put the word out.

At the time 'Jonna', as he's known, was busy trying to get Geordie back

together. They'd been his only serious band (although he did admit to spending two and a half years with an outfit called the Gobi Desert Canoe Club!) and after several years out of the music business due to disillusionment over management problems, he felt it was time for another go.

Geordie was, after all, what Brian Johnson was all about. Born in the Newcastle district of Dunston on October 5, 1947, he grew up with all the grit and wit that's synonymous with the North East of England, a product of the post-war baby boom in one of the most working class areas of Britain. As a kid he performed Gang Shows with the Scouts, appeared in a TV play and even joined the local church choir. But rock'n'roll seemed a far more tempting proposition right from the time The

Geordie circa '74 -
at the height of sartorial elegance.

Pimlico rehearsal studio 45 minutes late, they ran through a couple of numbers – 'Nutbush City Limits' and 'Whole Lotta Rosie' – and... "It just felt so comfortable". At home the following Saturday Brian received a call from Malcolm, who told him he'd just had a nice little win on the Grand National and then muttered something about coming back to London as soon as possible to get started on an album... "... It was the greatest day of my life," Brian beamed later, "I joined on Grand National day and I now always pick a horse with an 'A', a 'D' or a 'C' in the name!"

A few days after his appointment he went out on the town to celebrate and ran into his younger brother, an avid AC/DC fan, who simply refused to believe what Brian told him, not least because it was April 1!

But it was true. Brian Johnson, the Geordie, had become an honorary Aussie. Geordie, the band, was dead... at least until the end of the year when Red Bus put out a cash-in compilation album under the title 'Geordie Featuring Brian Johnson'. Incidentally, the single the band were cutting when Jonna was poached, 'Treat Her Like A Lady'/ 'Rockin' With The Boys' was shelved.

Geordie stumbled on for another couple of years, ironically with Terry Schlesher on vocals, but to no avail. Going their separate ways, one member became a chip shop manager, one a mechanic and another continued to look

for a break in the music business. Jonna, on the other hand, was given a £5,000 signing on fee and a car after joining AC/DC, then whisked off to the Bahamas to begin work on their next album.

"Frankly, it scares the shit out of me," he told Sounds, "'cos some of AC/DC's most fanatical supporters come from Newcastle and if any member of this band has so much as a bad tooth, that lot would sense it. But I suppose I'm a lucky lad in a way 'cos I've never ever seen AC/DC play live or even on the TV, I've always been too busy gigging myself. I've heard all about them and their fantastic show of course, and I've got all their albums in the house 'cos it's my kind of music and I love 'em. I mean, I'm an out-and-out basic man and to me they are one of the best rock'n' roll bands in the world."

After a few rehearsals at E'Zee Hire Studios just off the Caledonian Road in North London, the heat of the Bahamas beckoned. The band had considered a number of alternative locations, including Abba's Polar Studios in Stockholm, which Led Zeppelin had just used for 'In Through The Out Door', but lack of availability and the temptation of tax evasion won the day for Compass Point Studios in Nassau.

"Jonna really couldn't believe he was in Nassau," laughs Tony Platt, who

– and disillusionment set in. "We were doing Top Of The Pops so everybody thought we were millionaires," he explained, "but we were actually on £40 a week."

Before long they called it a day. Jonna turned his back on the business in disgust and carved a niche for himself in the motor trade, settling into a cosy North Shields world of nights in front of the telly, a few beers with his mates and golf every Wednesday and Sunday. It suited him down to the ground until itchy feet during the first few months of 1980 got him thinking about giving music another go.

The re-formed Geordie dusted itself down and creaked back around the northern club circuit, picking up a deal with the Red Bus label, initially for one single. When the AC/DC camp finally tracked him down to Newcastle, he treated the offer of an audition very casually. "I got this call from the band saying come down and look us over," he explained. "I said, 'Listen, I can't spare much time, can we make it quick?'"

They could. Brian waltzed into the

Portrait of a man as
a fashion victim.

**Déjà-vu? Jonna in Geordie...
and (right) rehashing an old trick in AC/DC.**

steer and edit the whole process."

Despite recent events Platt found the band remarkably resilient during the recording of 'Back In Black', full of determination to prove they could bounce back and also keen to 'do it for Bon'. Jonna had fitted in quicker than anyone could've hoped and was surprising everyone with the effort he put into his performance. Slowly the pain was erased by rising spirits.

"The band do have a great sense of humour," explains Platt, "and Jonna was such a character that he was keeping everyone laughing. Meanwhile we had stacks of comedy videos and tapes to listen to; Malcolm discovered the comedian Jimmy Jones and would listen to his stuff all the time. There were a few funny incidents... like the time we all went on a fishing expedition for the day. We caught all this tuna and the cook at the studio filleted it all and put it in the fridge ready for cooking the next day. Anyway, during the night it all shifted and knocked open the fridge door, spilling out all over the place. By the time we got up in the morning the sun had come up and... well, you can imagine the smell!"

The band's idiosyncratic sense of humour even came across in their tributes to Bon. Some observers felt titles like 'Have A Drink On Me' and the sound effect of an eerie tolling bell on 'Hell's Bells' were in dubious taste considering the tragedy of a few months before, but they were just missing the point.

"There is a tongue-in-cheek element to everything AC/DC do," agrees Platt.

"Everything was done out of the highest possible respect for the memory of Bon, but at the same time I think Bon would've appreciated that sort of humour.

"Recording the bell was a real laugh though. The band were having a foundry in Loughborough cast a huge bell for them to take out on the road, but by the time we got round to recording it for 'Hell's Bells' it wasn't ready. So we ended up finding another bell at this belfry somewhere, and I rigged up a mobile to record it chiming... not knowing that as the belfry was full of birds all we could hear was this deafening chirruping going on! Eventually I borrowed Ronnie Lane's mobile and we got it done in time, but it was a struggle."

'Back In Black' was finished by the end of May and in the shops on July 31. Its all-black cover was a sombre, silent tribute to Bon; its storming, steaming soundtrack a tribute to the way AC/DC

engineered the record under the production guidance of Mutt Lange. "He was walking around on cloud nine, full of beans. It was a real kick to see how excited he was."

Most of the new album, 'Back In Black', had been written by the time the band arrived at Compass Point in mid-April to start recording. As usual, the basic riffs had been bashed out by the Youngs in rehearsals, with Cliff and Phil brought in later to work the ideas up into

full arrangements, sometimes for up to seven hours a day. Bon's lyrical ideas – Ian Jeffery claims he still has the folder of lyrics for 15 songs written for 'Back In Black' by Bon – were abandoned, as some felt it wouldn't be right for Brian to be singing them.

"The lyrics on that album were a real joint effort," says Platt. "Everyone pitched in with ideas. Malcolm used to go on about the 'newspaper headlines syndrome' – y'know, titles that catch the eye and stick in the memory. Brian was still a bit reticent as he was new, but he joined in too, and of course Mutt would had hauled themselves back on the tracks. The Lange/Platt team deserved all the credit they got, too. The production was even more polished than 'Highway To Hell', yet none of the band's aggression had been sacrificed. Suddenly, the full force of AC/DC came screaming into focus with pin-point precision.

The quality of the songwriting particularly stood out; 'Shoot To Thrill' was a top-gear tearaway laced with lashings of melody, 'What Do You Do For Money Honey' and 'Given The Dog A Bone' (subtle as ever) stomped and honked with animalistic tenacity, while 'You Shook Me All Night Long' – a commercial rock classic – remains to this day one of the band's best songs.

But then, wherever you looked on 'Back In Black' AC/DC were attaining new heights; Angus' playing sounded more stylish than ever before, Brian's higher-pitched voice was evidently easier on American ears, and the overall demeanour of the record was definitely Eighties, not Seventies. It should have been a vehicle for Bon to reach his peak, instead it was a fitting testament to his memory.

On the day before the album's release the new-look AC/DC were in America, preparing for the acid test of their first tour with Brian. Some warm-up dates in Holland and Belgium at the beginning of July had confirmed that the band were as popular as ever, and at the end of Brian's début (at Arlon in Belgium on July 2) the crowd dispelled any doubts by chanting his name. But how would America react to AC/DC without Bon? How would Brian react to the close scrutiny of Bon's fans, who suddenly saw a stranger filling their hero's shoes?

"All I can really say is that Bon is still around and watching," said Brian. "I can't tell you any more because it's all so personal. But at night in my hotel room I had proof that he was there in some form. I know he approves of what the new line-up is trying to do. He didn't want the band to split up or go into a long period of mourning. He wanted us to build on the spirit he left behind.

"That poor boy was loved by thousands of people worldwide," he continued. "When we did a warm-up gig in Holland this kid came up to me with a tattoo of Bon on his arm and said, 'This bloke was my hero but now he's gone. I wish you all the luck in the world'. I just stood there shaking. I mean, what can you say when people are prepared to put their faith in you like that? Since then I feel like I've been singing for that kid and so

many others like him. I hope I've been accepted by AC/DC fans…"

The 'Back In Black' tour started for real on July 30 at the County Fieldhouse in Erie, Pennsylvania, with the deathly sound of a tolling bell. The band freighted the one and a half ton bronze monster embossed with the AC/DC logo over from Britain, and it was lowered by a giant crane above the lighting rig for Brian to strike with a hammer at the beginning of 'Hell's Bells'. It was the first time a stage prop, apart from the school uniform, had been used by a band strictly against any showbiz

ostentation, but AC/DC had long since proved they could play without the aid of gimmicks, and besides, it was better to include the real thing in the show than have the tackier task of running a tape of the bell. It was, dare I say, a sign of the chimes…

Needless to say, the fans loved it. The new improved AC/DC presentation simply served to underline the fact that the band had arrived in the big league, and the impact shuddered across the Continent. Radio stations at last welcomed them with open turntables, magazines scrambled for interviews and

attendance figures doubled at a rate of knots. At last money began to roll in, which was something of a relief for a band who, even during the recording of 'Back In Black', had to club their per diems together in order to go out and celebrate the birth of Malcolm's first child!

Just over a week into the tour, while playing at Norfolk, Virginia, news filtered over from Britain that 'Back In Black' had topped the UK charts (the feat was achieved during the week of August 9, and it stayed No.1 for two weeks). In September, 'You Shook Me All Night Long' reached No.38 in the singles charts, and a tour booked for October was selling out fast. Without doubt, while the mushrooming success in the States was obviously more lucrative, spiralling fortunes in Britain meant more to them.

Jonna, who with his battered jeans, faded T-shirts and cloth cap looked like he should still be dossing around the boozers of Gateshead, could scarcely believe how quickly it was all happening to him. "I'm used to being a legend in my own lunchtime," he laughed, "not my bleedin' life!"

After two solid months in the States and Canada, AC/DC finally began their UK tour on October 19, at the Colston Hall in Bristol. This time around they played two or three shows at more or less every venue – six in London, equally split between Hammersmith Odeon and Victoria Apollo – and every date was sold out. Unfortunately the bell was too big to be used at certain venues (including, much to Jonna's dismay, Newcastle's Mayfair or City Hall), but overall the reception the band got was triumphant.

There was icing on the cake too. Ignoring criticisms of nepotism, Malcolm and Angus took their nephew Stevie Young's band Starfighters on the road for the tour, helping to sow yet another family seed in the business.

Five days after the British tour finished on November 16, a new single was released in the UK from the 'Back In Black' album: the lumbering, brooding 'Rock And Roll Ain't Noise Pollution'. The band didn't hang around to see it become their most successful 45 to date – it reached No.15 – they were busy making their first visit to Japan, where their popularity had flourished despite their absence.

The set at this time had become pretty well established, a generous balance between old and new. 'Hell's Bells' boomed out at the beginning, a startling introduction which sent a shiver down the spine. Then two oldies, 'Shot Down In Flames' and 'Sin City', followed, before 'Back In Black', 'The Jack', 'What Do You Do For Money Honey' and 'Bad Boy Boogie' led into 'Highway To Hell' and 'High Voltage'.

'Whole Lotta Rosie' was next, complete with the "Ang-gus! Ang-gus!" chants even in Japan, and then 'Rocker' found Angus in walkabout mode, this time on the shoulders of a roadie, before climaxing the show with his guitar solo/freakout spot. Encores usually came in the shape of 'You Shook Me All Night Long', which tumbled straight into 'TNT', and then finally 'Let There Be Rock'.

Johnson sounded like he'd been there all his life. His voice was not too dissimilar to Bon's, but he was certainly no clone, establishing his own strong identity very quickly, and achieving an almost instant rapport with the audiences. Even in Australia, where Bon remained something of a national hero, Jonna survived unscathed when the band wrapped up 1980 with some long awaited 'homecoming' concerts in December.

Bon would surely have approved.

After the usual New Year break AC/DC returned to work in January to find they'd scaled even greater heights. During the third week of the New Year, 'Back In Black' officially became their biggest selling album to date, reaching No.4 in America and turning platinum to boot. The demand for the band on the richer side of the Atlantic would keep them away from Europe for virtually all of 1981 – the first time they had switched their priorities since 1976 – but who could blame them for striking while the iron was hot?

The first US stint during '81 lasted a

mammoth five months, from February to June. Capitalising on the demand for new AC/DC product, Atlantic finally released 'Dirty Deeds Done Dirt Cheap' (the UK version) in May, and even though it was nearly five years' old and featured a singer who was no longer with the band, it soared to No.3 in the charts (a position it held from May 23 to June 20) and, incredibly, even topped 'Back In Black'. Angus was quick to see the irony in this. "The Americans turned down 'Dirty Deeds...' (initially) because it didn't sound American," he laughed. "Yet years later they ask us for the album!"

Inevitably there were those who tried to cash in even more crudely on the band's rising profile and wealth. A couple from Libertyville, Illinois, took out a $250,000 lawsuit claiming AC/DC were responsible for a string of offensive phone calls after the title track of the album mentioned their phone number. The line in question, '...Call me anytime/ 36 24 36/I lead a life of crime...', was of course pure fiction from Bon Scott's mischievous mind, but the couple whose home number was 362-436 weren't amused, and their lawyers demanded that the record be withdrawn until the words were changed.

"The numbers don't refer to any particular telephone," Angus told the press. "They are simply my dream girl's vital statistics. I thought any red-blooded male would realise that." The judge turned out to be a red-blooded male, and the case was dismissed.

Nevertheless the whole episode highlighted the irritations of having a high profile, and these added to the strain of the band's bloated workload. To help cope with some of this they devised a form of escapism in the shape of their own backstage bar, christened the Bell End Club (sometimes also known as the Bell Inn, or Hell's Bar), complete with dartboard and all the trimmings. Membership tickets would have to be bought like any normal club, and bets would fly back and forth during darts tournaments.

"The great thing is," Jonna enthused, "when you go backstage first of all and you're playing darts, those 15,000 or 20,000 kids waiting for you don't seem such a threat anymore – because you're worrying about getting through to the next round of the darts final. At $10 a head... why, that's £200! It's good because it makes you feel a little bit like home."

Home was something the band wouldn't see for some while yet though, although in Britain during June their status amongst rock fans was underlined when the very first issue of the Sounds spin-off magazine Kerrang! ran the results of a Sounds readers' poll which found 'Whole Lotta Rosie' heading the Heavy Metal Top 100 Tracks chart. Appropriately, Angus adorned the inaugural cover of the mag, which has since gone on to become metal's very own Bible/comic, making another small slice of history into the bargain.

Before reaching Britain though there were more dates in Japan and Australia, as well as a new album to record. In fact, their one and only appearance on British soil during 1981 turned out to be the Monsters Of Rock festival at the Castle Donington motorcycle racing track in the East Midlands.

The recording of 'For Those About To Rock (We Salute You)' straddled the Donington début. Once again Mutt Lange was at the controls, but the location this time was Paris, where the band spent three weeks in late July/early August rehearsing Angus and Malcolm's riffs in an old abandoned factory. Trouble arose, however, when Lange couldn't get the 'live' sound the band wanted in the studio, and another studio had to be tested out just as the band had to leave for England, leaving the job frustratingly incomplete.

The break seemed to work, though, allowing the band a chance to clear their heads. At Castle Donington on August 22, the second year of a festival which thrives to this day as Britain's premier rock beano, AC/DC lined up next to Whitesnake, Blue Öyster Cult, Blackfoot, Slade and More, finishing off a day otherwise spoilt by an iffy-sounding rain-soaked PA in traditional headliners-on-heat style.

"That was the first time we'd played together for months," said Jonna. "We were shitting ourselves. And all these other bands are in the middle of touring and they're red hot! But we had the biggest ball of our lives."

Not everyone thought AC/DC ran away with the day's honours – some observers thought Slade and particularly Whitesnake (who even played a longer set than AC/DC) were top dogs – but wherever preferences lay, few in the officially estimated 65,000 crowd could have argued that the band hadn't given it their all, as usual. It was a particularly proud moment for those who'd worked so hard on the band.

"That was such an emotional day," Ian Jeffery told the author, "because I'd gone from pulling kids off the street in London and dragging them into a pub to see the band play, right through to their biggest tour in America. Now, suddenly, they were headlining Britain's number one rock festival. When Brian hit the bell at the beginning of 'Hell's Bells', me and Maurice Jones, who'd been their promoter since day one (and also promoter of Donington), just fell into each other's arms, crying. I honestly mean that. To see all those years of hard work and effort finally paying off was fantastic.

"Actually, Maurice was on crutches that day, because two weeks before we'd all gone round to his house after seeing Whitesnake play at Bingley Hall in Stafford and we were all pretty drunk. After a while, we started mucking around in the garden, and Malcolm pushed Maurice into the pond. Unfortunately, his foot got stuck between some rocks and he broke his ankle! But that didn't

stop him feeling incredibly proud of his boys at Donington."

Another unfortunate mishap almost stopped the band from making the gig that day too; the band very nearly didn't get onstage... "The lights had gone down and the crowd were cheering like mad," Brian laughed later, "but as we were going up the steps to the stage some security guy says to Malcolm, 'Come on get off - you haven't got a pass!' So I said, 'Oi, he's in the band!', and the guy says, 'And you can shut up – you ain't coming up here either!'"

The band had similar problems in America, where even hotel porters would refuse them admission to their own five star accommodation, and their entourage now included a team of security guards to pave their way as well as protect them. But despite the aggro, the band took pleasure in the knowledge that their highly deliberate 'just everyday blokes' routine was still genuine enough to fool people.

Back in Paris after Donington, the task of making another multi-million selling album wasn't proving easy. Lange was still having problems getting the right 'feel' and the project was slipping behind schedule. In the end, they decided to switch the operation back to the factory where they'd rehearsed, using a mobile recording unit brought over from England, and in the nick of time everything fell into place.

The result, officially accredited as having been recorded at H.I.S and Family Studios, was released in December during yet another mammoth tour of the States. In years to come the band would

come to regard 'For Those About To Rock...' as one of their least favourite albums, and Malcolm would be particularly scathing about the amount of time that was spent mucking around with the sound, but as the follow-up to 'Back In Black' it didn't disappoint many fans.

Most importantly, it bore another classic cut to sit alongside 'Whole Lotta Rosie', 'Let There Be Rock', 'Hell's Bells' and the rest. The title song, complete with authentic sound effects of exploding cannon fire, easily proved the album's standout track as it lurched with surging momentum towards a personal Armageddon. In a single stroke it not only ensured the new record's appeal, but heightened the curiosity of those on the periphery of the band's following.

Those who were checking AC/DC out for the first time wouldn't have found much of the grimy elbow-grease which characterised earlier recordings. Lange, who'd styled them for the American market from 'Highway To Hell' onwards, had achieved perhaps his most radio-friendly product to date. But while this seemed to please their American management and record company, within the band itself it sowed seeds of discontent which would soon lead to far reaching consequences.

On balance, 'For Those About To Rock...' was a good album, but not quite in the 'Back In Black' league. While Side One prospered with 'Put The Finger On You', 'Let's Get It Up', 'Inject The Venom' and 'Snowballed' – all pretty safe-but-sound AC/DC fare – Side Two lost the thread, and slower tracks like 'Breaking The Rules' forced the record to go off the boil.

In Kerrang! Angus and Brian offered their own listener's guide to the record.

'For Those About To Rock...' (Angus): "We had this chorus riff, and we thought, 'Well, this sounds rather deadly'. We were trying to find a good title... and there's this book from years ago about Roman gladiators called 'For Those About To Die We Salute You'. So we thought, 'for those about to rock'... I mean, it sounds better than 'for those about to die'.

"Actually, that song's got a lot of meaning to it. It's a very inspiring song. It makes you feel a bit powerful, and I think that's what rock'n'roll is all about."

'Put The Finger On You' (Angus): "That's basically a gangster line, like they do in the movies. The heavy bit. We're not putting the finger on anyone in particular... it's always the other way round!"

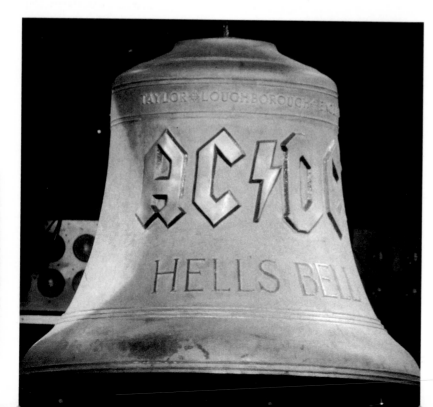

'Let's Get It Up' (Brian): "Filth, pure filth. We're a filthy band!"

"It was just a line that sprang to mind, and it sounded better than 'Let's Get It Down'." (Angus)

'Inject The Venom' (Angus): "That's a power thing, like 'For Those About To Rock...'. It means, 'have it hot'."

"There's one line that says, 'If you inject the venom it will be your last attack' – which is like a snake, once it bites you it's got nothing left." (Brian)

"Do it once, do it hard and do it good, or you're finished. It's a real rock'n'roll line." (Angus)

'Snowballed' (Angus): "Meaning you've been conned, fooled again. And we figured we'd been tricked enough in our time, so we came up with that. It could be the woman you're paying alimony to, anything."

'Evil Walks' (Angus): "As the name says, evil walks - it's everywhere! When we were playing it at the beginning I said, 'Those chords sound dead evil' - and that's how we do it, just sitting around and nattering and jamming away... and someone says something like 'evil walks', and that's it!"

'C.O.D.' (Angus): "Most people think of C.O.D. as cash on delivery, or cash on demand. I was sitting around trying to come up with a better one, and I came up with 'care of the devil'. We're not black magic Satanists, or whatever you call it. I don't drink blood. I may wear black underwear now and then, but that's about it!"

'Breaking The Rules' (Angus): "It's like when someone says, 'you can't do that'... they were always saying that to me at school. You do it anyhow."

'Night Of The Long Knives' (Angus): "It sounded nice."

'Spellbound' (Angus): "That's a tricky one. It's a slower one for us, but we liked it anyhow. It's one of those moody ones."

"You know when you get one of those days when it's like a trance. It's hard to describe really, but that's 'Spellbound'. We set it to a man driving a car, blinded by a bright beam. But it could be any situation." (Brian)

That was it, simple. Nothing deep, nothing ambitious. But it didn't have to be. AC/DC's popularity was rocketing, particularly in the States where attendance figures on the ensuing 'For Those...' tour trebled and in some cases quadrupled from the last outing. The band even found themselves reluctantly (or so they claimed) becoming strangely attractive to women. Could it be Jonna's flat cap, beer gut and Whitley Bay

Working Men's Club charm had at last turned him into a sex symbol?

"Who me? You're joking!" he cracked. "The boys were sitting around in the dressing room last week and saying, 'Do you know this is the first time we've actually had girls screaming at us (outside Australia)?' Because in England it's nearly all lads. Most of the audience is fellas in America as well, but since this tour there's been a lot of girls. I don't know why, I think it's because we're on the radio so much. I don't think it can be for me good looks!"

Whatever the reason, the band's pulling power was peaking. And as a salutation to those who came to rock, 21 cannons were added to the ever-expanding show, operated during the appropriate track by tour manager Ian Jeffery, who produced the deafening sound of the explosions on a Prophet synthesizer, while the guns puked smoke.

This increasing compromise of the band's 'no nonsense' policy weighed heavily on the conscience of the Youngs in particular. Caught between their belief in minimalist principles and the need to increase the spectacle of their show in proportion to their new-found status as an arena act, they trusted the advice of those who vouched for getting in on the gimmick act. But it was clearly working, proving effective on two levels: giving the fans something to remember, and stirring up yet more notoriety – as in the incident at Hartford, Connecticut, where the band almost ended up in jail after fire marshalls had complained to the local police that the harmless props were unlawfully dangerous.

AC/DC's show – bells, cannons, huge lighting rigs and all – was now costing a fortune to haul around the world, but record sales revenue was keeping

production costs manageable. During the first few months of 1982 'For Those...' turned platinum in America, hitting the Billboard No.1 spot for the first time in the band's history, while 'Back In Black' continued to sell at an extraordinary rate.

In Britain fans got to see some of the US show when a new BBC2 series called Late Night In Concert introduced by Annie Nightingale presented highlights of a show at the Capitol Center in Washington DC, including 'Put The Finger On You', 'Back In Black', 'Highway To Hell', 'Let's Get It Up', 'Let There Be Rock' and 'For Those About To Rock'. Typically, the programme faded out before the cannon climax of the final song, but it was a sign of their massive popularity that the boring old Beeb even broadcast the band in the first place.

Statistically, AC/DC couldn't be denied. 'For Those...' peaked at No.3 in the UK albums chart, with 'Let's Get It Up' becoming the band's biggest hit single to date, making No.13 in February. Later in July, the title track itself made No.15 in the charts, consolidating further the success of the new album.

Indeed, when the 'Cannon And Bell' tour finally reached the UK in October 1982, AC/DC could afford the luxury of two nights at London's Wembley Arena – a prestigious step-up from Hammersmith Odeon – as well as another landmark notch on the guitar strap, Birmingham's huge National Exhibition Centre. The giddy heights they'd reached seemed unfeasible for a band who still looked like a bunch of ruffians from the local Youth Club, but up there with the élite they most certainly were.

The only question remaining was, where did they go from here?

Chapter VIII

Bedlam In Belgium (...And Brazil, And Boston, And Birmingham...)

A fter the exertions of the previous year, the first half of 1983 was more or less erased from AC/DC's diary. The last tour had been their most resoundingly successful so far, their vinyl output platinum at a touch, but cracks had appeared in the armour: drummer Phil Rudd's behaviour was becoming increasingly bizarre, a situation not entirely unconnected with his indulgence in certain 'cerebral entertainment chemicals' – those closest to the camp noticed that he smoked so much pot he began to hallucinate regularly and he even ended up in hospital on two occasions – and disagreements with management merely compounded a number of other problems.

The band needed a decent break, something even Bon's death hadn't allowed them. Thus, Malcolm and Phil returned home to Australia, Angus spent some time in Holland, Cliff retired to his new house in Hawaii with his wife Georgann (an ex-air hostess) and Brian, after reluctantly deciding to quit Newcastle ("I said I'd never leave England for tax reasons until I saw the figures in front of me!"), settled into residence in Florida with his wife Carol.

It was several months before AC/DC reconvened, this time at Compass Point Studios in Nassau again, to begin work on their next album. But changes were afoot: Peter Mensch and CCC Management had been dropped, with Ian Jeffery effectively taking over the organisational role; and Mutt Lange's services were no longer required by a band who were determined to do things their way this time.

"The band effected a quite incredible clear out of personnel at this time," says photographer Robert Ellis, who'd worked closely with them since 1979 but who'd found himself part of the 'purge'. "Their management went, roadies, other members of their entourage... a lot of people who'd been with them for a long time. Their oft-quoted ethic was: We carry no excess baggage. But I think it went further than this. They were in a state of paranoia, feeling that all eyes were upon them. They guarded their privacy jealously and didn't like people to know them too well. When certain people got too close, they backed off. The band are terribly worried by informality but I can't see why because they have nothing to hide. I personally was accused by Angus of doing all sorts of things. They were concerned I was being intrusive but basically they are ultra-sensitive about all relationships. When they made this clear out, it was totally

unwarranted and unexpected behaviour and I was totally shattered by it. They are their own masters and I have the greatest of respect for them but what happened at this point in their career is something I could never understand."

Tony Platt, whose commitments with the Swiss band Krokus had prevented him from working on 'For Those...', did find himself back on the team, engineering and mixing an album which the Young brothers had decided to produce themselves.

"Malcolm was basically running the entire show by this time," he explains, "and he was determined to get the band away from the kind of smooth production which 'Mutt' had made his trademark. He came in one day with a copy of Muddy Waters' 'Hard Again' LP, which was produced by Johnny Winter, and played me the track 'Mannish Boy'. In the background you can hear all this shouting and screaming going on, a real rowdy atmosphere as if there was a party going on when it was recorded... and the principle idea was to recreate that feeling on the new AC/DC record.

"The problem was, some of the band's inspiration had gone by this time. They'd done a lot of touring and were showing signs of fatigue. Plus there were a lot of little niggly things which were going on, problems which on their own probably wouldn't sound anything worth worrying about, but added together made for a certain amount of discomfort in the camp. The band weren't in the best of moods, there was definitely tension in the air, and things came to a head..."

Midway through the recording sessions, Phil Rudd found himself out on his ear. Initially the reasons for this were kept close to the band's collective chest, with the old 'musical differences' excuse inevitably trotted out. But years later, with Rudd's drug problems no longer a secret, the truth emerged...

"On the tour before we went to the Bahamas," Ian Jeffery explained, "... it got to the point where he began imagining there were people in his room and things like that. During the break we had before recording began he seemed to pull himself together, but when we went to Nassau he finished his drum parts pretty quickly... and you can imagine what it's like being on an island in that part of the world with time on your hands!"

To make matters worse, Phil had become 'involved' with a female relation of Malcolm's... and just prior to this he'd ditched a French girl who he'd managed to get pregnant. The situation had

become complex and embarrassing, causing a lot of friction between the people involved, and the outcome was as abrupt as it was dramatic.

"In the end," Jeffery revealed, "there was a bitter confrontation between Phil and another member of the band – physical blows were exchanged – and I put Phil on a plane home two hours later. He was out. Gone."

Rudd had clearly burnt himself out. Angus said later he'd never really got over Bon's death, that he felt the tightness of the 'family' unit of the early days had died with Bon, and that he'd become hell bent on living the high life whatever the consequences. "If he hadn't stopped," Angus said, "... he'd have gone overboard and done something drastic either to himself or to someone else."

Ultimately thankful that he didn't go the way of Bon and relieved to have escaped with his sanity intact (just), Rudd retired to Rotorua in New Zealand, where he invested in a helicopter business. The band, meanwhile, finished the record as best they could, leaving it scorchingly raw in the final mix.

"Because 'For Those About To Rock...' had been such a long album for them," says Tony Platt, "they wanted to get the next one done as quickly as possible. Unfortunately though, the climate in which the record was done sort of showed in the finished product... the band were unsure of which direction to take because there were so many bands around at that time who were jumping on their bandwagon, and there just wasn't the same kind of determination there as there was when we did 'Back In Black'."

Nevertheless, 'Flick Of The Switch' had the kind of chewed-at-the-edges charm that some of the earlier albums had, and certainly jabbed a middle finger in the direction of those who'd criticised the band for becoming 'too polished'. If anything, some complained, the band had over-compensated for Lange's commercial leanings in the recent past...

But if the new album didn't have any concert-closing classics like its cannon-firing predecessor, it did have a clutch of bristling 'filler' material, beefier than a butcher's shop window. The title track and 'Bedlam In Belgium' (about a riot at one of the band's gigs) are two of the tracks which usually spring to mind, but 'Rising Power', 'Guns For Hire' and 'This House Is On Fire' were all unmistakably cast from the same unique AC/DC mould, while 'Landslide' wreaked all sorts of havoc with the senses as it

brazenly broke the speed limit.

"I mean, stuff yer concept albums and that," Jonna spat. "Rock'n'roll is supposed to be a laugh… and we've done a hell of a lot of it!"

'Flick Of The Switch' may not have been destined for legendary status – indeed, some fans consider it one of the weakest AC/DC albums – but for its sheer attitude, power and energy it ranks as one of the author's favourites. Released in August after the longest yet gap between AC/DC albums, 21 months, it eventually reached No.4 in the UK charts.

Returning to London the band desperately sought a replacement for Phil Rudd. Several candidates were flown out to Nassau during the recording of 'Flick Of The Switch', and several were auditioned while the album was being mixed in New York, but finding someone whose personality would suit the close knit AC/DC unit was no easy task.

Eventually an anonymous ad was placed in the music press, and applicants were invited to audition at Nomis Studios, just behind the Olympia complex in Kensington. Some guessed it was the AC/DC job they were going for, others didn't have a clue.

"We hired two rooms at Nomis," Ian Jeffery explained, "with a drum kit, a tape machine and our roadie in one, and the band in the other. Then, instead of auditioning 200 candidates and getting into embarrassing situations where the band would have to kick people out after one number, the drummers would go into the first room with the roadie and play along to a tape; only then, if the guy was really good, would he be asked to go through the door leading to the room where the band

were waiting for a proper 'play'."

After a number of trial runs, 20-year-old Simon Wright from Manchester was given the nod. A sober, unassuming, easy going lad with a profile lower than a snake's belly, he was ideal for AC/DC; the sort who'd turn up, bash it out with the minimum of fuss, and disappear quietly. Also, he was a huge fan who'd been annoying his flatmates in Kilburn, North West London, by constantly playing along to AC/DC records and videos.

Wright had learnt his trade the hard way: slogging around the northern circuit in small-time local bands. At 18 he made the step up from an unknown Manchester based band called Tora Tora (who released just one self-financed single, 'Red Sun Setting' on the Mancunian Metal label) to AIIZ, who had a record deal with Polydor and had released an album called 'The Witch Of Berkeley' in 1980. With AIIZ he cut one single, 'I'm The One Who Loves You' (b/w 'Ringside Seat'), but despite the promotional push of a major label and the pro-metal atmosphere of the early Eighties, the band never managed a breakthrough.

By the end of 1982 Wright had moved to London and joined the more promising Tytan, a powerful British band of fluctuating personnel who sounded like a cross between Black Sabbath and Whitesnake. The outfit had released one excellent 12-inch single, 'Blind Men And Fools', and were recording a début album called 'Rough Justice' when Wright took over from ex-Judas Priest drummer Les Binks (Wright did three tracks for the record), but problems with a record company heading for liquidation threatened the band's existence from its infancy.

"We had a year of doing nothing, except one gig in Belgium," says Simon. "It was just an endless bout of 'umming

AC/DC marched steadily through the winter on yet another American and Canadian tour, usually doing two and a half months on the road, then having two weeks off. As before, the addition of a new member went more or less unnoticed, such was the emphasis on Angus.

The band had become quite adept at keeping a low profile off stage by now, too. The 'purge' which had been executed earlier in the year (dropping CCC Management, Mutt Lange and Phil Rudd) had washed over into other areas of the band's entourage as well, and the 'family' unit had become even more select in the process. Those in contact with the band sensed a strange atmosphere around the camp, a situation agitated by a deliberate lack of contact with the press in Britain. Some suggested they were cracking under pressure, but in a rare interview Jonna, who'd just opened a studio in Newcastle "...for young bands who want to have a go at it – it's nice to be in a position now where we can put something back"), shrugged it all off with typical earthy honesty. "If it all fell through, then we'd probably turn around and start back on the pubs again."

The pubs were a long way off though. Simon Wright's British début came on August 19, when AC/DC became the first band to return as headliners at the fourth Monsters Of Rock festival at Castle Donington. Canadian trio Rush had initially been asked to top the bill, but had dithered too long over their reply, so AC/DC were put forward as an alternative and quickly confirmed their availability, making the 1984 line-up the most impressive bill to date: Mötley Crüe, Accept, Y&T, Gary Moore, Ozzy Osbourne, Van Halen and AC/DC. The question British rock fans who hadn't

seen AC/DC for two and a half years asked themselves was: could Angus & Co. justify their lofty positon in such a competitive running order?

In the build-up to the event there was much press talk about the rivalry between the WEA stablemates Van Halen and AC/DC, a situation inevitably fuelled by Van Halen's outspoken frontman, David Lee Roth. The enormously popular and gloriously ostentatious LA band hadn't played in Britain since 1980, but had just scored a Top Ten hit in the UK with the US chart-topping single 'Jump', so while much of the rivalry could be put down to hype, it was going to be interesting to see which of these two vastly different bands came out on top.

In a photo finish, most observers claimed AC/DC clinched it. Benefiting from all the usual headliner perks – a full light show, a full set, gimmicks (bells and cannons a-go-go!), fireworks at the end, the lot – AC/DC emerged with their reputation enhanced by their brush with America's finest. Of course they didn't do anything out of the ordinary to press their claims, they just plugged in and played like they'd always done. But by now that's all anyone expected from them, so nobody could be disappointed.

"It was a great gig," Simon enthuses proudly. "We started with 'Guns For Hire' from the new album, which I always thought was a great opening track, then we did stuff like 'This House Is On Fire', 'Nervous Shakedown' (which Atlantic had released as a multi-track cassette single to coincide with the festival, backed by live recordings of 'Rock And Roll Ain't Noise Pollution', 'Sin City' and 'This House Is On Fire' from the last US

tour) and, of course, all the classics like '...Rosie' and 'Let There Be Rock'. Some complained that we always played all those old songs, but that was the material that made that band's reputation, they're brilliant songs, and if we hadn't have played them there would have been an uproar!

"Anyway, I remember that everyone was there for that gig; friends, relatives, neighbours, the guy from the fish'n'chip shop... everyone! And all I was worried about was getting there early to catch all the other bands on the bill! It was some day..."

After Donington the band undertook a series of dates on the Continent, which included more 'Monsters Of Rock' shows. However, the biggest festival of all came in January, when AC/DC joined a glut of rock heavyweights including Queen, Ozzy Osbourne, Yes, Iron Maiden, Whitesnake and Scorpions, as well as more mainstream acts like George Benson, Al Jarreau, James Taylor and Rod Stewart, in the very first Rock In Rio extravaganza in Brazil.

The event pronounced itself The Greatest Show On Earth (this was six months before Live Aid, remember), and on the surface at least this seemed a fair assumption. The acts on show were all Big Names and crowd estimates ran into hundreds of thousands. But the reality was that Rock In Rio was a financial disaster (the $11.5 million purpose built site was pulled down shortly after), and the corrupt and incestuous nature of Brazilian politics, on which the whole promotion hung like a thread, ensured that the original notion of an annual Rock In Rio withered in the palm of a hand whose fingers were severely burnt.

Rio seemed an odd choice of venue for such an ambitious and lucrative operation, anyway. The ethics of those who stood to make a mint from rock in one of the world's poorest countries were continually questioned, but such was the blind euphoria and hype surrounding the event that few of the acts booked were aware of the more mercenary attitudes of the promoters.

"It was a weird experience," Simon Wright reflects, "being in the Third World with all that poverty right before you. It was real sad, seeing all these shanty towns and beggars and kids with nothing on their feet, just yards from the big flash hotels and tourists loaded with money. The difference really hits you in the face.

"The gig itself was great though, really unusual. I remember seeing Ronnie Biggs

Rock's answer to the Chippendales flex their goosebumps in Rio.

on the side of the stage at one point, and I also remember I kept getting over-whelming wafts of hamburger smells halfway through the set, as there was this huge McDonalds stall set up in the middle of the crowd! It was all very bizarre…"

AC/DC did two nights at the festival, appearing on the same bill as the Scorpions. Once again their low profile caused some critical comments from gossip-hungry hacks, and only served to heighten a certain sense of mystery around the band at this time.

After Rio they took time out from touring, a break that all welcomed after the excesses of previous years. Mindful of the dangers of allowing repetition to translate into complacency, the Youngs made a conscious decision to back off from the road. "We felt it might be becoming a bit predictable," explained Malcolm, "going around the same places every year, people might get the attitude of 'Ah, we won't bother seeing them this year, they'll be back again next year!' It's a bit like a circus coming to town, you know. And there was ten years of doing that, so I think it's quite understandable to take a break – from the road anyway."

The band eventually regrouped during the Spring at Mountain Studios, an old disused casino which the band promptly converted into 'home', near Montreux in Switzerland. "If I remember rightly the first thing we did was set up Hell's Bar," laughs Simon, "nothing like getting your priorities right! Actually, the studio was a strange place, a huge circular room about the size of a football pitch, with padded walls, gantries and all that stuff. All the speaker cabinets were covered in fur as well… it looked like some sort of jungle scene, although it was freezing!"

Despite the relative commercial slip of 'Flick Of The Switch', Angus and Malcolm decided again to produce by themselves. Reluctant as they were to admit it, the last album had missed the golden touch of a top producer like Mutt Lange and 'only' reached No.15 in America as a result. But the brothers were happy with the raw sound they'd achieved before, and wanted a similar approach with the new album, a decision that perhaps reflected the need for someone with sufficient influence to persuade them that they needed outside help. The group was now managerless, a situation which had been allowed to continue since their decision to cut down on touring commitments.

So the recording of 'Fly On The Wall' was the usual turn-it-up-and-slap-it-down

"Oops sorry! It must've been the curry…"

exercise at which AC/DC excelled. Even Simon Wright, working on his first proper album, found himself thinking it was a piece of cake. "Everything came so easy," he says. "The band worked so quickly and so simply. It wasn't like I was in some massive band doing an album, it was like we were just putting down a demo or something. I remember thinking, 'Jesus, this is great!'"

The finished record wasn't one of AC/DC's best, however, and even their staunchest fans had to admit it. As would be the pattern on future releases, Side One proved to be far stronger than the flip, but in essence 'Fly On The Wall' lacked the style of 'Back In Black', the songs of 'For Those About To Rock…'

The band receive their 'Fly On The Wall' gold discs along with various members of Atlantic Records and Part Rock management backstage at Wembley Arena.

and the edge of 'Flick Of The Switch'.

Its highlights were, without question, the title track, 'Shake Your Foundations' and, perhaps best of all, 'Sink The Pink', on which Angus used the finger/thumb picking technique he'd mastered so effectively on 'Shoot To Thrill', 'Put The Finger On You' and the intro to 'For Those About To Rock…'.

When the band got the balance of groove, melody and energy just right, they were still capable of mixing it with the best, but most of the rest of the album sounded lacklustre. 'Danger', the first single (released in June, as was the album), plodded rather laboriously through its paces, 'Stand Up' was instantly forgettable and 'Send For The Man' was a throwaway B-side. In fact, half of the songs on 'Fly On The Wall' wouldn't have made it onto any post-'Let There Be Rock' AC/DC album.

Malcolm defended the new record to the hilt though, explaining in June how

Jonna enjoys the odd gallon of Champagne.

he band had stuck to their simple-is-
best philosophy despite having more
ime on their hands to make the record.

"We spent a year on this album –
about a year on writing songs and pre-
production. We thought we'd sit back a
it this time. There was no pressure on
s for another album or anything, so we
hought we'd take a bit more time, and
think it's come out better as a result.

"We've got a set style, and when
ou've done so many albums and you've
ot to come up with something without
epeating yourself, get songs that are
ood and don't require too much
verdubbing – in some ways it's much
arder to be simple than be all long and
nvolved."

The album did chart respectably high,
eaching No.7 in the UK despite the flop
f the lead single, which only made
No.48. There was also the added bonus
f a 'Fly On The Wall' promotional video
ackage, which featured six songs from
he album strung together on a slapstick
toryline. Written and directed by Brian
Ward, the concept was based around
he band playing a gig in a tiny New York
leazepit full of shady characters, a
cene surreptitiously surveyed by the
artoon fly which appeared on the album
leeve. The set, a disaster at first as
he modest crowd hardly acknowledges
he band, progresses with 'Fly On The
Wall', 'Danger', 'Sink The Pink' and
Stand Up', and each track is linked
ather tenuously by the goings on
around the band.

Finally, as they play 'Shake Your
Foundations' and the locals begin to
how their appreciation, the building
egins to shudder and crumble, torn
apart as if an earthquake had just hit
own, leaving the band concluding their

set before a backdrop of the Manhattan
skyline, much to the astonishment of
the club's owner. Corny it may have
been, another careful concession to the
MTV age, but as promos go this was 27
minutes of harmless, quirky fun, and the
band escaped their most stage-managed
brush with self-promotion with their
tongue-in-cheek reputation intact.

Ironically, elsewhere in America,
AC/DC's reputation was about to be
dragged through the mud yet again. Ever
since 'Highway To Hell', with its picture
of Angus and a pair of plastic devil horns
on the cover, the so-called Moral
Majority had picked on the band (in fact,
they picked on most rock bands) in futile
efforts to ban both their records and
concerts. But during September, as they
were taking the 'Fly On The Wall' tour
across the States, the gruesome case
of a murderer responsible for a spate of
killings around the Los Angeles area
threw AC/DC in the dock once more.

Nicknamed the Night Stalker (some
claimed a connection with the track
'Night Prowler' from 'Highway To Hell'),
the murderer haunted the American
public for some time before the police
finally caught up with him. When they
did, they claimed he was wearing an
AC/DC T-shirt, had left an AC/DC hat at
the scene of one of his crimes, and had
quoted from the band's lyrics. Friends of
Richard Ramirez, the Night Stalker, told
the press he was a big fan of the
'Highway To Hell' album.

Horror and consternation flew around
the country. Parents, many of whom
believed the AC/DC's sexually
suggestive lyrics were a bad influence
on their children, doubled their
opposition to the band. Church leaders,
outraged by what they called 'Satanic
glorification', called for widespread bans
to be enforced. In Springfield, Illinois,
the City Council not only tried to prevent

a scheduled show from going ahead, but
barred the band from even staying in the
area.

"They accused us of turning butter
rancid in their fridges," said Brian. "They
said we were making their kids' teeth go
bad... they had lists of things we were
supposed to have done, it was
hysterical."

"They're the ones who're breaking the
law," Angus told the Los Angeles Times
when tackled about the Springfield
incident. "We're protected by the First
Amendment, which supports freedom of
speech. After the Council banned the
show we had to spend a week with all
the legal hassles of getting the show
back on. These people are so high and
mighty. You know what's ridiculous?
Right behind the concert hall are
brothels and massage parlours. And
they say we're contaminating their town!

"When is all this going to stop? We're
not doing anything illegal. We don't have
any evil intentions. Yet people are
attacking our freedom to say what we
want to say. It's ridiculous for people to
be so narrow-minded. These people live
in the dark. If they think their kids are
going to be harmed by what they see at
our shows then they should just keep
the kids at home. But don't try to stop
the whole show. This is the 20th century,
not the Spanish Inquisition.

"'Highway To Hell' has nothing to do
with devil worship," he stressed. "It's
about a band that was on the road a lot.
We toured for four years at a stretch
with no break. A guy asked me how you
would best describe our tours. We said,
'A highway to hell!' The title stuck with
us and we used it for a song. It was a
frivolous thing.

"What happened to people's sense of
humour? There's nothing evil about what
we do, it's a joke, we're kidding. We're
more of a tease than anything... more
like naughty little boys than out-and-out
villains."

The Springfield show eventually went
ahead, with around 5,000 kids turning
up instead of the anticipated 8,000
("There were only three days to let the
kids know it was still on," Angus
complained), but the band couldn't find
any accommodation in Springfield, and
had to stay 100 miles away in St. Louis.

The following month, on Tuesday
November 19, the author caught up with
the band in Washington DC and found
them still smarting from the way the
Night Stalker episode had affected the
tour, some places having given them the
kind of welcome usually reserved for
plague carriers.

"We've had a lot of shit thrown at us," Malcolm cursed. "This kid (Ramirez) had an AC/DC T-shirt on, and of course the religious fanatics put 'Night Stalker' and 'Night Prowler' together. What they can't see is that 'Night Prowler' is just about creeping around at night on a couple of old girlfriends and doing 'the business' – having a bit of fun, y'know? It's not about raping and pillaging...

"A lot of our songs have double meanings – because you can't just say, I'm gonna stick my **** right up your ****', you've gotta cover up the filth somehow – and we look for nicer ways of expressing things. But you get these people who pick up the title of a song and put their own stories into it, and before you know it everything has been twisted around.

"So... some of his friends said he was AC/DC mad. So what? So some loopy loves your band and wears your T-shirt while he's bumping people off. We're not telling the guy to do it! I even saw one article on the Night Stalker where they'd got a picture of his face and placed a picture of Angus (from the Highway To Hell' cover) next to it! I know it's only silly sensationalism and that those kind of papers just do it to try and sell more copies, but that's taking it too far. I mean, we're only a rock'n'roll band for fuck's sake!"

Not all the press in America hounded AC/DC; indeed, some chronicled passionate cases for the defence. But the censorship issue in the States during the mid Eighties was becoming big news, with the PMRC (Parents Music Resource Center) taking the case for the so-called Moral Majority to the courts and publicly pushing strongly for the right to enforce a rating system on records.

Bolton who?
Angus fails the audition for club mascot

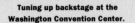

Tuning up backstage at the Washington Convention Center.

The PMRC was a self-appointed organisation which, without the jurisdiction of a legally-elected body, took it upon themselves to act as 'the conscience of society' and define the terms 'art' and 'morally acceptable'. Supported by the powerful lobby group PTA (America's Parent Teacher Association) and comprising influential and politically connected Washington wives (Susan Baker, the other half of US Government Treasury Secretary James, and Tipper Gore, spiteful spouse of Senator Albert), the crackpot do-gooders argued the case for having stickers on records warning of 'explicit lyrical content'. Thus, X = profanity and sex, D/A = glorification of drugs and/or alcohol, O = occult and V = violence.

"I think to use that in this day and age is ridiculous," said Malcolm. "But then I suppose it's just like what they're doing with cigarettes now – you've gotta put a health warning on the packet – and all of a sudden it's music's turn.

"I really don't care what they do, it won't change us from singing about what we want to sing about. I think they're talking about making bands put their lyrics on the cover of the record so parents can see what their kids are buying. But that'll only sell more records because if kids know they're not allowed something they'll go out and get it to try it out, y'know? It's the same thing with cigarettes and drugs, isn't it?

"If this censorship thing does come

off, I don't think it'll hurt anyone. Look at all the old songs, like Eric Clapton's 'Cocaine', The Rolling Stones' 'Sympathy For The Devil', Cliff Richard's 'Devil Woman'... will they put X-ratings on those records? It might damage Cliff Richard's career and those of people like him, but it's not gonna hurt us."

The crusade won sympathy from the middle-aged-mind of conservative America, but hardly cut any ice with AC/DC, one of the artists at the top of their hate list along with Prince, Madonna and WASP. Among the PMRC's most virulent critics was Frank Zappa who spoke out passionately on radio and television against what he saw as an infringement of free speech.

AC/DC's show that night at the huge Washington Convention Center certainly wasn't that of a wounded beast. Opening with 'Fly On The Wall', 'Back In Black' and 'Shake Your Foundations', the band immediately fell into a routine which, had any amnesia-sufferer wandered into the auditorium, would have been instantly recognised. The most surprising aspect of AC/DC was that they could still put so much effort into such a familiar drill.

"I used to watch Angus every night, and I'd never fail to be amazed by him," says Simon Wright. "He might not be feeling too well during the day or whatever, but he'd get out there, shake his head like mad and give it 200%... it must've been all that English tea he drinks! I honestly don't think I ever saw him play a bad gig, he really is something special..."

The others played their parts with almost robotic accuracy, too. Malcolm and Cliff still stood rooted to the stage either side of the drum kit, timing their arrival at the microphone stands at the front of the stage during the choruses to synchronised perfection. And Jonna, floppy flat cap and sleeveless denim jacket welded to his stocky frame, still stomped around with knees bent, fists clenched and veins bulging like hosepipes on the side of his neck. It was like watching your favourite Monty Python sketch for the hundredth time: you knew exactly what was coming next, but you still sat on the edge of your seat and lapped it up.

The set list didn't disappoint any of the hysterical American fans either: 'Dirty Deeds...' was followed by 'You Shook Me All Night Long', 'Sin City', 'Jailbreak' (with obligatory striptease), 'The Jack', 'Shoot To Thrill', 'Highway To Hell', 'Sink The Pink', 'Whole Lotta Rosie' and then 'Let There Be Rock' before the encores

of 'Hell's Bells', 'TNT' and 'For Those About To Rock...' (this time with two cannons firing from twin hydraulic platforms) wrapped it up in style. By the end the floor of the hall was literally shaking.

Backstage moments later the author found himself assuming the 'fly on the wall' role, watching the band tuck into a dinner of liver and bacon cooked by Angus's wife Ellen who, far from being the aloof Wife Of Superstar, always liked to muck in. First impressions were of how relaxed and laid back everyone was... except Brian, who'd nicked one of the roadies' walkie-talkies and was busy winding up the rest of the road crew. Constantly playing practical jokes on unsuspecting members of the entourage

Jester with his job on the line, Jonna proved as lively offstage as Angus was on it.

An hour or so later at the plush Four Seasons Hotel, after the band had been refused entry to the hotel bar and the nightclub next door for not being properly attired, everyone congregated in Cliff's room for a nightcap. As Jonna continued to pull tricks and wheeze through a procession of pranks, the others confessed that when the going got tough on the road it was the jovial Geordie who made life bearable.

"Do you know he came all the way over to me onstage tonight just to drop a fart?" Cliff winced. "I could tell by the look on his face that that's what he was gonna do the minute he started coming towards me. Smelly bastard!"

"He used to do that to me," Malcolm replied, "until one night when I let one

It was a silent one, but really savoury and it just slipped out. A classic!"

Oblivious to the mock scorn of his colleagues, Jonna continued his one man show with a word-for-word re-enactment of a whole episode of 'The Young Ones', mimicking all the characters with incredible accuracy.

"OH NOOO! THERE'S SOMETHING, LIKE, HEAVVVYYY GOING DOWN..."

"SHUDDUP NEIL, YOU BORING OLD HIPPY FART!"

"It's unbelievable at times," Malcolm shook his head, "he does so many characters that once I walked past the bathroom and I heard about four or five different voices coming from inside. I thought, 'How many people has he got in there?', but there was only him – he was practising his accents!"

...And these were child-poisoning, sexually corrupt, murder-inspiring devil-

Chapter IX

Who Made You?
(...The Return Of
The Video Nasties)

Angus gets help with his homework from a few hundred fans...

After the traumas of America in 1985, the prospect of a return to Europe at the start of 1986 seemed a particularly good idea to the AC/DC the author met in Washington. And with all of Australia's most famous band now being British-born, the first UK tour for more than three years was anticipated with extra relish.

The British tour would also prove significant for another reason. It was the first full tour presided over by the band's new guardians, the London based Part Rock management team. Fronted by Stewart Young and Steve Barnett, Part Rock also handled the affairs of Gary Moore (and still do), and came with the kind of reputation with which the Youngs felt comfortable. After running the show on their own for nearly three years, and perhaps more importantly seeing their record sales slip during that period, Malcolm and Angus clearly felt it was time to lift the load off their shoulders and share responsibilities with an outside force, a force which could revitalise the set-up and focus the still-highly marketable values of AC/DC towards maximum commercial potential.

It proved a sound move. The band suddenly seemed accessible again, their relationship with the press was prised open and AC/DC loomed back into view bigger and better than before.

Not surprisingly the British tour was a sell-out, although it was the least amount of dates the band had undertaken on a UK tour for some time. After Manchester Apollo on January 13, there was one night at Whitley Bay Ice Rink, two at Wembley Arena, two at Birmingham NEC and two at Edinburgh Playhouse - a conscious attempt to stick to the larger arenas in order to ensure that fans could see the full stage show.

"The last time we were over there we had a lot of difficulty getting all the cannons in, fitting in the walkway at the back of the stage and that kind of thing," explained Brian, "and it's not fair if the kids have to miss out on certain things. We want to make sure they get value for money."

The shows were pretty much the same as the American version, in fact pretty much the same as any show in the Jonna era. Angus still 'mooned' at the cheering crowd during his strip-tease, Brian still went berserk with a sledgehammer at the beginning of 'Hell's Bells', and the cannons still deafened the first ten rows at the climax of 'For Those...' (although at the Wembley shows there was the added bonus of seeing the pink-lipsticked and mink-coated guests in the VIP enclosure get covered in pyro-ash from the fall-out!). The band had long since given up the idea of dropping their most famous party pieces.

"We have thought to ourselves, 'Oh, they must have got sick of that bell by now'," Malcolm confided to the author, "but when it comes down at the beginning of 'Hell's Bells' and the cheers go up, we think 'How can we get rid of that now?' Tracks like 'For Those About To Rock...' are such favourites that they'll probably always be with the band - if we dropped them the kids would wanna know why!"

After the UK tour and the subsequent 18-date romp around Belgium, Holland, Germany, Switzerland and Scandinavia, which took them up to February 16, the band returned to London to start work on a video for their next single. During January 'Shake Your Foundations' had become their most successful single since 'For Those About To Rock...' three-and-a-half years earlier, when it reached No.24. But the next 45 campaign would prove to be the most determined push for a hit yet.

During the American tour the previous year AC/DC were approached by renowned horror-writer Stephen King, who'd asked whether he could use some old material for the soundtrack of his forthcoming movie, Maximum Overdrive. King, a huge AC/DC fan, also suggested the band record some new tracks exclusively for the film and, after poring over the script, the band had agreed.

"We've always kept away from doing films and stuff before," Malcolm told the author, "but this one looks like it could be good. It's a pretty weird story, kind of real science fiction stuff, y'know? But we thought we'd have a go."

Recording took place at Compass Point Studios in Nassau when the US tour had been completed, with Harry Vanda and George Young flying over to produce the band's new material for the first time since 'Powerage'. In just two weeks they laid down three new pieces: 'Who Made Who', 'D.T.' and 'Chase The Ace'.

"We did it so quickly it seemed like it was all over in a flash," says Simon Wright, "but it was good fun because it was the first time I'd met George, and Stephen King even came down for a while too. 'Who Made Who' turned out to be one of our best songs for ages, but doing the other two (both instrumentals) was a bit different. We had these TV screens which showed us the relevant parts of the movie, and we had to fit the music to the action. I must say, playing along to the crash scenes in 'Chase The Ace' was very odd."

The film, written and directed (for the first time) by King, was based on the tale Trucks, from his collection of short stories called Night Shifts. The concept was that of machinery with homicidal tendencies, the dramatic after effect of a close call when a comet passes dangerously close to earth. And those brave enough to agree to star in a film with such an iffy storyline included Emilio Estevez, Pat Hingle, Laura Huntington and Christopher Murney.

Both 'D.T.' and 'Chase The Ace' were Angus/Malcolm compositions, rocked-up incidental music of a like rarely heard in the cinema, and also quite a rarity for a band who never usually strayed from the confines of their own well beaten path. But 'Who Made Who', the title track from the compilation album which constituted the movie's soundtrack, was the kind

Above: A heatseeking missile, or
one of those new chemical toilets?
Below right: Angus (centre) and
The Clone Rangers.

of mass appeal monster that wouldn't have been out of place on 'Back In Black' - straight from the Young/Young/ Johnson School Of Three Minute Wonders, naturally ear-marked as the new single.

The video, directed by David Mallet (who'd worked on Queen's 'Radio Ga Ga', Def Leppard's 'Photograph' and the impromptu Bowie/Jagger version of 'Dancing In The Streets' for Live Aid), was filmed at the Brixton Academy in South London at the end of February. Not noted for their love of new fangled notions such as promo videos, particularly ones which involve the

dreaded act of miming, the band weren't over keen on the idea. But, they were told, this was going to be different...

As it turned out it was a real case of 'send in the clones'. Hundreds of fans had been recruited from all over Britain - some through the fan club, some via announcements on Radio One, some simply through word of mouth - to act as extras on the set. Waiting for them were piles of specially made Angus uniforms - grey shorts, blue blazers, blue and white ties and curly black wigs - which they were asked to change into, thus producing the unlikely spectacle of an army of dodgy doppel-gangers.

Cardboard guitars at the ready, they were drilled with military precision into a number of synchronised manoeuvres

while Angus jumped off balconies and generally put his parenthood prospects at risk in a tight fitting harness. Then for the onstage sequences, hordes of the laughable likenesses were positioned on various walkways around the stage, headbanging in unison to hours of tape re-runs.

In between shots the band mingled with the fans, autographing their cardboard guitars and chatting casually. Some had slept outside the building all night to be sure of making the video (a strict first come first served policy had been enforced), but most survived the gruelling day's filming which lasted well into the early hours.

The band meanwhile spent the long periods between scenes playing darts, drinking tea and watching Yes Minister and The Comic Strip Presents videos. Friends and relatives called in through-out the day, and as usual Jonna kept everyone entertained... eventually (at around 1.00am, after close encounters with a bottle of Scotch) even managing to persuade the author to don the schoolboy garb and muck in with the mimicking.

"Why-ay, canny crack, mun!" the delighted prankster beamed, lying through his teeth. "Ah divven't knaa what Angus'll see like, but ah reckon yuz looks reet champ'yn. If urnly yuz worraboot two foot smaller!"

By May it had all proved worth it though. Boosted by the video the single reached No.16 in the UK charts, becoming a favourite on pub video jukeboxes the length of the country. The following month the album, for which King also chose 'You Shook Me All Night Long', 'Sink The Pink', 'Ride On', 'Hell's Bells', 'Shake Your Foundations' and 'For Those About To Rock...', hit No.11 in Britain.

'Maximum Overdrive', which opened in America on July 18, didn't have the same kind of impact. Many critics dismissed it bluntly, and even Angus admitted to the author later that he wasn't too enthralled by it.

"We only really saw the film on paper when we worked on those songs, and it did look great at that stage. But when they came to film the thing I think they just lost it somewhere. We only really did it for Stephen because he's such a fan of the band. We haven't been offered any more contracts like that and I don't think we'd do another soundtrack just for the sake of it, because it's so restricting having to write for a movie. We write for the fans - the kids who come along to our shows to have a good time and let off a bit of steam, y'know? - not for a bunch of actors to fool around to."

The band were getting used to fooling around on film themselves though. In June another David Mallet directed video was shot in London, this time at Jacob Street Studios just south of the River Thames near Tower Bridge. The track in question was 'You Shook Me All Night Long', due to be re-released as a single in August, but the real intrigue centred around what kind of extras would be used after the success of the Anguses.

They turned out to be models, scores of leggy lovelies wearing not very much at all. On the set the band and the male members of their entourage walked around rolling their eyes at each other and shaking their heads in mock disgust, as by mid-afternoon the old warehouse assumed the scenario of a cash'n'carry brothel. At one point, as a number of knee-trembling nubiles in rubber mini-skirts rode specially positioned bicycles high above the stage, Malcolm turned to the author and complained: "I'm not sure about all this... I mean, we're supposed to be a *lads'* band!"

Later, as top Page Three model Corinne Russell rode a bucking bronco simulator, Cliff had to look away, unable to take it anymore. Sadly, his comments cannot be recorded in a book of this nature.

The finished version proved to be even better than 'Who Made Who'.

Angus, Malcolm and Brian acted out different character roles for the first time - Brian as a hapless father who hasn't got the bottle to buy a packet of condoms in a chemist's, the brothers as his sniggering kids who watch him through the window - and the whole thing ends up with Brian being seduced by the busty Ms. Russell, until the bedroom wall splits in half revealing the whole band performing onstage in the distance.

Surprisingly the record wasn't a big hit, only just scraping into the Top 50 at No.46. But the memories (not to mention mammaries) of the day seemed to make it worthwhile anyway. "It made a few old men very happy," Angus laughed, "and it didn't exactly upset many of the younger ones either!"

By the end of July AC/DC were back on the road in America, kicking off at the Lakefront Arena in New Orleans, soaked in the searing bayou heat. For this tour the band took the 'Who Made Who' concept a step further, with a stage set designed to reflect the futuristic aspirations of the video and a sequence during the song itself which gave lucky fans (recruited again through radio ads, etc) the chance to take to the stage in full Angus attire and emulate their idol.

This scam usually opened the show: the first notes of 'Who Made Who' would sound as the figure of Angus, head bowed to conceal the fact that it isn't the real one, appears high above the stage on a walkway. As the crowd roars, another Angus appears, then another, then another... until there's a whole mob of them, leaving those far enough from the stage to actually be thrown by the stunt, wondering which one's genuine.

By now the band had more or less abandoned their previously fierce stance against too many gimmicks, aware that to keep apace of increasing competition they had to expand their production. The strategy was paying off: readers of Circus magazine in the States had already voted AC/DC as winners of the Biggest Comeback category in the annual Music Makers Awards Poll for 1985 ("Comeback Of The Year?" quizzed a puzzled Angus. "Where did

we come back from?"), and interest in the 1986 'Who Made Who' tour was greater than ever.

The 'Who Made Who' album didn't capture the fans' imagination though, and it struggled to make No.33 on the US chart. As simply a collection of Stephen King's personal favourites, which hardly constituted a 'Greatest Hits' package, its disjointed selection wasn't widely popular. And the cover left much to be desired too: an out of focus snap of Angus from the 'Who Made Who' video shoot superimposed on a horrible blue background. But having relinquished control over the record to King, the band didn't view it as an official AC/DC album, and weren't greatly worried over its poor results.

"Nobody can point the finger at us," said Jonna, effectively washing his hands of the whole project. As for the movie, he hired it from a local video store... and promptly took it back.

Originally planned to finish in September, the demand for extra dates prolonged the 'Who Made Who' tour until November. At the end of it the five retired to their own little corners of the globe for a two-month break, until thoughts turned to a

new studio album in February.

As ever, the new songs were conceived from knockabout jams between the brothers, and a whole batch of guitar riffs were put down on tape to play around with later. Brian then joined them in Australia to go over the ideas and consider his contributions, before melodies and choruses were juggled into place. And not surprisingly with the project getting kick-started in Sydney, extra input came from George Young.

After an extensive search for the right location, the studio chosen for recording was Miraval in the South of France. Although Angus joked that this was purely because there happened to be a decent golf course nearby, Miraval, an ancient building of immense character, had the right atmosphere for the band.

"It was a rustic old brick place," says Simon Wright, "right out of the twelfth century, or something. You'd see the odd scorpion scurrying across the floor from time to time.

"Out the back there was this huge medieval-looking black tower, with living quarters in it. Some of the guys actually slept up there, and I remember we'd finish work and leave the studio in the middle of the night saying to them,

'Brrrrr, rather you than me!'"

"We were working most of the summer," said Brian, "and there was no air-conditioning in the place. Hell, there wasn't even a fan that worked! On top of that Cliff and I had to stay in this little shack that was actually part of a church. It was an old stone building, and there were bats and spiders all over the place - very spooky. All we had in our rooms was a bare light bulb sticking out of the wall and a mattress on the floor. I felt like I'd been thrown in a dungeon.

"The second night we slept there the proprietor came up to us and said, 'Did the White Lady bother you last night?' I didn't know what he meant until he explained that the White Lady was the ghost of the house. It didn't take us long to get out of there after that."

Recording officially began in August, and it wasn't long before news leaked out that the Vanda/Young team were back in the production frame. It was an obvious move after the success of the 'Who Made Who' single, and one which Angus and Malcolm had wanted to make for some time. Although the Mutt Lange albums proved to be by far the band's most successful, it seems that Angus and Malcolm's attitude towards them was less than charitable, as if they begrudged Lange his success after their brother and Harry Vanda had done all

the groundwork on the early records. To increase the irritation their attempt at producing themselves hadn't been much of a success, so it was with great relief that Angus told the author the wheel had finally turned full circle.

"When we first worked with George and Harry they were mainly into doing commercial stuff, so they looked upon working with us as their pet hobby; with us it wasn't all arty-farty, it was just a chance to let their hair down and get stuck into some dirty rock'n'roll. So they've always had that fun attitude with us, and we feel loose and relaxed in their company. Plus, he's our brother, so there's no ego problems.

"They also like to work fast, as we do. We like to get in there, get a sound and get out. If we stay in the studio too long we get a bit stale. It has to be bang! bang! bang! for us because that's the kind of band we are. Also, George and Harry are honest enough to tell us if something is crap, and we don't mind them doing so if they're right. So in many ways working with them is better for us.

"Mutt is great, you can't take anything away from the guy because he's so successful. And 'Back In Black' was a good album... but that's because I think the songs were great. The difference between working with George and Harry

and working with Mutt is that George and Harry are always looking for something different, whereas Mutt is more interested in creating the perfect sound in the studio. Mutt would worry about the sound of a pin dropping half-a-mile away, but George and Harry would rather look for something different musically, and that suits us because we always try to come up with something different for each album."

Whether they were 'different' or not is very much open to question, but before long they had come up with no less than 19 songs for the new record. Angus admitted that if it was up to him all 19 would be on the album (although the idea of a début double-LP didn't appeal), but when the tapes were shipped across to New York to be mixed during the autumn, only the strongest ten survived.

"There's definitely NO BALLADS though," Angus stressed. "I have a great aversion to ballads... apart from anything else the world is saturated with the damn things - I don't think anyone needs another one."

The first single from the album, unquestionably no ballad, was a storming statement of intent. Released on January 4 and entitled 'Heatseeker' ("Well," Brian reasoned, "we couldn't call it 'The One Eyed Trouser Snake' or 'The Heatseeking Moisture Missile', could we?"), the track was an uptempo rocket-fuelled fighter, the most menacing AC/DC single for ages.

The by now essential David Mallet directed accompanying video had been filmed earlier in December at Elstree Studios, Hertfordshire - big budget stuff again featuring a massive Cruise missile model which crashes through a giant TV screen at the back of the stage at one point, the warhead flipping open to reveal (who else?) Angus in full freakout mode. And once again a few hundred fans were brought in as extras, making up the kind of wildly enthusiastic crowd usually reserved for American game shows.

There was a danger that the band's music might be regarded as secondary by those who'd been spoilt by an endless string of great promos, that the MTV monster would blur priorities and interfere with the basic qualities of good songs. This had certainly happened in the pop market - as long ago as 1979 The Buggles had claimed in their UK No.1 hit single that 'Video Killed The Radio Star' (which, ironically, became the first video to be shown on MTV when it opened on August 1, 1981), and throughout the Eighties increasingly expensive and extravagant videos seemed to eradicate the old fashioned art of songwriting.

In rock too there appeared to be a shift of emphasis, especially with the new generation of American bands who tended to be sold on their looks rather than their licks. The commercial potential of heavy rotation on MTV - and therefore the importance of the video over the song and the musician's ability to play it - had resulted in some record companies spending six figure sums on the small screen samplers, more than most metal bands would spend on recording entire albums.

But no-one could aim the same accusation at AC/DC. If ever a band succumbed to the pull of the promo yet emerged unscathed by its pompous pretensions, it was them. 'Heatseeker' was the best thing the band had done in ages, and it crashed into the British charts at No.17, eventually making No.12.

The album followed at the end of January, and as the gratuitous destruction of a TV set in the 'Heatseeker' video might have suggested, it was entitled 'Blow Up Your Video'. The phrase was actually coined from a line from one of the new tracks, 'That's The Way I Wanna Rock'N'Roll', and its irony at a time when AC/DC were making

something of a name for themselves in the video game didn't go unnoticed. But as Angus explained to the author back in December, the title was merely a call for a return to prominence of live music.

"These days there's all these cable TV shows and video channels, and people are getting used to sitting at home watching music on the box. But that's not rock'n'roll. We made our living out of getting up there and doing it onstage, and I don't think TV, radio or even maybe records can quite capture the excitement of a live gig.

"So with 'Blow Up Your Video' we're saying, 'Get off your backside and go and see a rock'n'roll show live!'"

Reaching No.2 in the UK charts (No.12 in America), the album proved how much the extra exposure afforded to the band by their videos had helped. Only 'Back In Black' had fared better in the British charts. But this time it wasn't just statistics on some product manager's wall-chart which proved AC/DC were buzzing again. With their influence on the rock scene more conspicuous than ever during 1987, a year in which they hardly poked their snouts above the ground, suddenly AC/DC were hip again. The Cult were ripping them off unashamedly (their hit single 'Wild Flower' was a ringer for 'Rock'n'Roll Singer'), New York rap sensations/ five minute wonders The Beastie Boys were sampling riffs left, right, and centre, rap-metal mentor Rick Rubin was proclaiming AC/DC as his favourite band, and Britain's latest joke superstar Zodiac Mindwarp based his few months of fame entirely upon rehashed AC/DC riffs.

Elsewhere, LA's latest exports Guns n' Roses included 'Whole Lotta Rosie' in their set during their UK visit in November 1987, promising Brit rockers Wolfsbane took to playing 'If You Want Blood...' in their set, and almost every pub band you came across seemed to be following suit. Only Led Zeppelin proved more popular with the plagiarists.

'Blow Up Your Video' simply continued the legacy. It wasn't quite a return to the worldbeating form of 1979/1980, but it was a definite improvement on 'Fly On The Wall', and that was more than enough for now.

Apart from 'Heatseeker' and the belching boogie of 'That's The Way I Wanna Rock 'N' Roll', standout cuts were 'Some Sin For Nuthin'' - full of lazy sleaze and brooding menace - 'Ruff Stuff', the blistering speed-of- light

'This Means War' and, best of all, 'Nick Of Time', which proved that Jonna could squeeze a wicked melody into his usual grit-gargling vocal-lines when he wanted to.

Even the sleeve design reflected the upturn in quality. Before Angus had been electrified with high voltage cables, stabbed by a bloodthirsty SG and depicted as the devil. This time he stood, fist raised in triumph, amid the shattering screen of an exploding TV set. The image was perfect, embedding itself in the mind faster than a chunk of flying glass.

As the album hit the shops the band were Down Under, preparing for their first Australian tour since 1981. Then, the hysteria of the homecoming had led to a show at the Myer Music Bowl in Melbourne being disrupted by a riot, with police reportedly baton-charging the crowd and making 60 arrests. And this time expectations were at fever pitch too, with many Aussie fans about to see the band for the first time. When tickets for the first Perth shows went on sale there were 56 arrests for a range of offences including assault, drug possession, and drunk and disorderly. One idiot was even caught wielding a machete.

The tabloids crackled with life, running stories about how the Americans had certified the band 'Satanic', of how the band had now shifted 38/41/50 million albums (figures varied wildly, of course) and of how scores of kids had camped outside a record store in Sydney awaiting the official launch of 'Blow Up Your Video'. At the beginning of the country's Bicentennial year, the timing of their triumphant return was spot on.

After three days of rehearsals at the Entertainment Centre in Perth the tour finally kicked off on February 1. It was the first show AC/DC had done anywhere in over a year, and to make the occasion even more special, Isa and Chick Scott, Bon's parents, were there as VIP guests.

"We gave them a special mention and it was wonderful to hear the crowd roar their welcome for them," said Brian. "It was the first time they'd seen the band in nine or ten years and it was a great feeling, like a welcome home. The crowd went crazy."

After two nights in Perth, four at the National Tennis Centre in Melbourne, three at the Entertainment Centre in Sydney, one at the Globe Derby in Adelaide and two at the Entertainment Centre in Brisbane, AC/DC had played to over 130,000 fans in three weeks.

The Aussies also got to be first to see the band's new stage set as well - a variation on the 'Who Made Who' design, with Angus rising out of transparent plastic tube at the start - and were treated to snippets from the new album, with 'Heatseeker' slipped in at first, 'That's The Way I Wanna Rock 'N' Roll' thrown in after a few shows, and more added later.

By the time they reached Britain in early March, the 'Blow Up Your Video' show was in full swing, and Angus on Fast Forward. Demand for the band in Britain was stronger than ever, especially after the hit singles of 'Who Made Who' and 'Heatseeker', but despite this the band's management had decided that they'd stick to playing just two cities in the British Isles - Birmingham and London - to enable all those who managed to get to the show to see it in its full glory, not just a neutered version which had been scaled

down to fit into smaller venues. Which is fine if you live near Birmingham or London, but tough luck if you live in Aberdeen or Plymouth.

It's an ancient dilemma and one faced by all successful bands when touring Britain. Unlike America, where there's a huge multi-complex sports arena around every corner, venues in Britain are so old and small that they simply can't cater for the overblown excesses of an extravagant modern rock show. So do the bands shed all the trimmings of their success and trudge out into the far reaches of the country to present the bare bones of their show to tiny crowds, or do they settle themselves into a couple of accommodating arenas and ask the fans to come to them?

Inevitably the bands choose the second option though fans who'll have to either miss the show or pay a fortune to travel several hundred miles in order to catch it hate the idea. Many would probably prefer to see their favourites in a more intimate environment anyway, rather than a cavernous surrogate aircraft hangar in which the stage is a hundred yards or more away. But a band like AC/DC can argue that they slogged around all the nooks and crannies - the pubs, clubs, bus shelters and phone

boxes - for years, and that this is their just reward for having graduated through the system. Besides, being a global success story means that their touring schedule elsewhere in the world is chock-a-block with commitments, and it simply wouldn't be possible to spend months in a relatively tiny territory like the UK.

It's a difficult one. But if the only way the band can compensate for that is to make sure that the shows they do put on are a bit special, then AC/DC could never be accused of letting their fans down. Over three nights at the NEC in Birmingham and three at Wembley Arena in the capital, despite Brian's touch of laryngitis ("The doctor gave me a shot up the bum, and although it helped clear my throat I could hardly walk afterwards!"), the band were as reliably entertaining as ever. In fact, it seemed as if they'd hardly been away.

After the second night in London, on a bright Sunday morning clogged up with busy shoppers at the weekly market in the car park of the Wembley complex, the band set to work on another video, this time for the second single off the new album, 'That's The Way I Wanna Rock 'N' Roll'. Facing an audience of empty red plastic seats, Angus hopped across the stage with all the enthusiasm

he'd mustered up the previous night. Quite how, the author has never been able to establish, but the grins and the constant joking around proved it wasn't a reluctant, through-gritted-teeth act.

In the illness-induced absence of David Mallet, the latest video was being directed by Brian Grant, Jiff Morrison and Peter Sinclaire. The concept was based around a number of fans who, for various reasons, couldn't make it into an AC/DC show, so Angus takes the show to them, crashing through a wall into a nearby pub, and miraculously materialising in both a local hospital and a schoolgirl's bedroom. Once again it was a gimmick-spiced collage of offstage stunts and the usual onstage stomping around, extremely well done.

"We just get out there and do it with the minimum of fuss," said Angus during a short break. "We don't wanna stand around posing with our mouths wide open like goldfish, the way some bands do. This is a rock'n'roll band, not a fashion parade."

"When we were in Japan," Malcolm added, "these journalists kept asking me what I thought about bands like Whitesnake and Bon Jovi. And I mean, to me it's disgusting to see men prancing around with make-up on and hairspray wafting around them.

It's sickening, isn't it? I told them I thought it'd taken David Coverdale 20 years to realise he's a pop singer. It's true!"

"The only thing they do to us before filming," explained Angus, "is squirt water on us to make it look like we're half-way through a show and we're sweating, y'know? Apart from that, what you see is what you get..."

In the dressing room, the band rested between 'takes' by catching up on the live football match on TV, while Jonna took the opportunity to deny a story which the Daily Mirror ran the previous September claiming he'd bought his beloved Newcastle United for £5 million. "I tell you," he spluttered through a beer, "I couldn't believe that when I read it... I mean, how the fuck can they make something like that up? Those people are plebs man, the scum of the earth."

With that he snatched up a copy of the Sunday People, pointing to a page long 'gay sex scandal' story followed by a tiny paragraph reporting that 90 people had been killed at a soccer match in Nepal. For once the ever grinning face of the jovial Geordie dropped like a sack of spuds.

The humour returned later when a hundred or so fans were let into the arena to pose again with cardboard guitars for the crowd shots. Some fans got to talk to the band, firing questions which ranged from where Angus got his uniforms (... "From a guy called David Chambers, a tailor here in London... and I've got hundreds of 'em!"), to the choice of songs in the new show. Earlier, in response to a similar inquiry, Cliff told the author why there were no tracks from either 'Fly On The Wall' or 'Flick Of The Switch' in the current set.

"I just think there's better songs for us to play," he shrugged. "After the 'big production' Mutt Lange albums that rawer production sound was just something we *had* to do, y'know? I wouldn't say those records were below par, just different that's all. Let's just say I prefer the new album!"

"The trouble is," Angus pointed out, "we can't play everything or we'll be onstage all night... and we don't wanna end up like Pink Floyd, growing old onstage!"

The idea of doing a medley of old songs, in order to pack more into the set, hardly appealed to the no-nonsense mentality of the band either. "We're not a cabaret band, we haven't hit Las Vegas yet," Angus shuddered. "You can't do a song justice if you only play half of it, so we'd rather play more of a song by jamming around in it, than cut it short. I think the fans prefer that too."

After Wembley the band took off for the rest of Europe, hitting Arnhem in Holland on March 15 and then working their way through 20 major venues in 10 countries before finishing in Stuttgart on April 11. Then, due to their extraordinary rise in popularity in Britain, they returned to London for a fourth night at Wembley Arena, a record-breaking achievement for a hard rock band. Indeed, such was the demand for tickets a fifth night could have been added if there'd been time.

Those who saw the extra Wembley show on April 13 saw all the familiar sights of an AC/DC show, probably the most forgivably repetitive show in rock. But how many spotted Malcolm Young leaning disconsolately against an amp at one point in the evening, and looking positively bored during Angus' strip-tease routine? Those who did wouldn't have been too surprised to hear that as AC/DC started the American leg of their world tour less than three weeks later, Malcolm was nowhere to be seen.

The makers of 'Blow Up Your Video' prove that they've been framed.

Chapter X

The Monsters Of Rock
(...Moneytalks, And Talks...)

of many bands, losing the very backbone of the team midway through a major tour would've been reason to cancel all remaining dates and scuttle off into hiding. Typically, AC/DC simply called up another member of the Young family, nephew Stevie Young, and continued as if nothing had happened.

What had happened was that Malcolm felt in desperate need of a rest from touring, principally to kick a drinking habit which escalated during long tours. No-one outside of the band had really noticed Malcolm's problem, and his albeit largely inconspicuous performances on stage hadn't seemed to suffer, but Malcolm wanted to nip the situation in the bud before it got out of hand. The 'official' reason (almost always a transparent fabrication) at the time of his departure was 'exhaustion', but Angus admitted the truth to the author later.

"He wanted to get rid of his booze problem and clean himself up. I think if you can do that of your own free will, then that's great; and having been through that situation with Bon, I don't think I could have gone through it again.

"Mal had been desperately trying to knock the booze on the head for some time, but he felt that he couldn't do it on the road. I mean, he's been drinking since he was 17 – nonstop! There's a few breweries who've gone out of business because of him, I can tell you! So Mal wanted to go home and beat the problem on his own, but we didn't mind... especially as I could bring in my nephew to replace him."

That the wound could be disguised so effectively was no fluke, although there was a touch of hereditary good fortune about it. Not only did Stevie Young know all of his uncles' songs off by heart – during his childhood in Scotland the Young family would send the early AC/DC albums over from Australia, and he'd religiously learn every note – but he was Malcolm's double physically as well.

"He had his own band up in Birmingham," Brian explained, referring to The Starfighters, who'd put out a couple of albums on the Jive label ('Starfighters' in 1981, 'In Flight Movie' in 1983) without ever breaking big, "and suddenly – bingo! – he was playing with us... to 20,000 people. We told him not to be shy, and he came out with a smile on his face. He knows exactly what to play, he's like a carbon copy of Malcolm...

"The Young family, I dunno... even their 55-year-old uncles look like they're 20 –

band looks like a kid, even Malcolm still gets checked for his ID card, and gets charged half fare. It's a problem I wouldn't mind having!"

Stevie's first show with the band was at the Cumberland Civic Center in Portland, Maine, on May 3. Later Uncle Angus admitted, "I think he was probably better than me... I was a bag of nerves, he was cool and calm."

"Stevie really did work out well," says Simon Wright, "so much so that sometimes I'd look across the stage and think it was actually Mal standing there. He was such a natural fit that it'd be like... hey, wait a minute, isn't that...? Oh no, Mal's back in Australia! You really had to think about it sometimes."

Complete with yet another new gimmick – a model of a heatseeking rocket which opened up at the start of the show to reveal the tiny figure of Angus – the '... Video' tour trekked on through the summer, spilling over into the autumn with promoters adding more dates by the dozen. One promoter, flushed with having sold out two nights with the greatest of ease, even came up with the ingenious idea of selling tickets for the band's rehearsal on their day off! (The band's reply remains unprintable.)

Within a matter of weeks 'Blow Up Your Video' had become AC/DC's biggest selling album in America since 'For Those About To Rock...', and even in Los Angeles – not the easiest of cities to conquer – there was a certain sense of DC-mania in the air.

"We were stunned," said Brian. "In the past we were never considered your hip band over there – they were still into Crosby, Stills & Nash. This time we couldn't believe it when we played Long Beach Arena, the reaction was fantastic. The kids over there don't buy a ticket for a show, they buy a season ticket for ANY concert – they cost about $5,000 and their mums and dads buy them – so of course they just sit there and go, 'Oh...wow'. But this time it was great, the kids went crazy."

Meanwhile back in Sydney, Malcolm's convalescence was progressing smoothly. Having plenty of time to spend with his wife Linda and two daughters was important, but he'd also bought himself a race horse and was indulging himself in the sport, in between dabbling around on the guitar and putting a few ideas down on tape for the next album.

By the end of the year AC/DC had bled America dry. During a particularly poor period for ticket sales – many of the rock'n'roll tour in the States during

Malcolm Young leaves, '...desperately trying to knock the booze on the head...'

'88 played to half-full houses, while the much heralded Monsters Of Rock tour (featuring Van Halen, Scorpions, Metallica, Dokken and Kingdom Come) died an embarrassing death – AC/DC sold out more or less everywhere they played. And far from being the perennial bad guys, the story that US troops had used deafening blasts of AC/DC to flush the ex-Panamanian dictator General Noriega out of his embassy lair and thus bring him to justice, almost made heroes of the band.

After the exertions of the tour the band took a well earned breather – Cliff moving from Hawaii to Fort Myers on the West Coast of Florida, just three miles up the road from Brian, Simon moving from Manchester to Fresno in California with his wife Desiré, Angus going home to Holland and Stevie returning to Britain, where he put together a new band called Little Big Horn (also managed by Part Rock) with ex-Starfighters bassist, Steve Redvers.

The first few months of 1989 were dormant, the only activity being a few demos laid down by the brothers in

"To baldly go..."
New drummer Chris Slade in action.

either London (where Malcolm, who'd declared himself fit to rejoin the band, still had a house) or Holland (at Angus' house). Purely for the purpose of establishing melody ideas Malcolm added rough vocal guidelines to the tracks, but when news of this leaked out rumours that Brian had left the band set the grapevine purring.

Brian hadn't in fact left (as his mother informed him during a panic-stricken phone call!), he was simply tied up in America finalising his divorce from Carol and straightening out various legal problems, complications which would prevent him from contributing any lyrics to the new album for the first time since he joined.

But there was a line-up change on the horizon: Simon Wright, who according to Angus had got "itchy feet", had taken up an offer from Ronnie James Dio to play on Dio's new album, 'Lock Up The Wolves'. And while initially it was claimed Wright was merely guesting on the record as a session drummer, a few months later it was announced that he'd been inducted as a full member of Dio's band.

Inevitably, varying rumours abounded. Some claimed he'd stolen some equipment from the band's poorly paid, some said the band were furious that he'd taken the Dio session, some suggested 'spouse interference' over his financial status with AC/DC had caused the split. Whatever the truth, Angus threw a wet cloth over the affair.

"He (Simon) couldn't expect to be paid the same as the members who'd been there for years. But hey, we all drank from the same teacup. I don't think he felt he was a member though. All the time I was around Simon I only heard two words: they were 'hello' at the beginning of a tour, and 'goodbye' at the end! I couldn't get a word out of him because he was so quiet. He always felt he was an outsider because we'd been doing it a lot longer than he had, so maybe that was our fault.

"But he always had this thing about Dio. When he first joined the band he was always talking about Dio. He had a very close thing with Ronnie and I don't know why; he always spoke very highly of the guy. At the end of the day I think he got bored sitting around waiting for me and Mal to get ready to go into the studio. He just got in touch one day and said, 'I'm off to do this Dio thing'. So we thought we'd better get someone else in, and that was it. It was a bit stupid on his part, but he'd moved to America and was under some outside pressure. I think he felt he wasn't being

Today, still living in Fresno and, at the time of going to press, putting a band together under the monicker of Mr. Rude, Simon reflects on his departure from AC/DC with just a tinge of remorse. "The band was taking some time off and I just wanted to work," he says. "Plus, I kind of got tired of the straightforward drumming that AC/DC requires – I wanted to do something different, I wanted to elaborate on my style and do something more with my playing. Not that I wanted to leave AC/DC – I spent seven years with that band and they were the best years of my life – but I wanted to expand into different areas, and obviously I couldn't have done both.

"Dio wanted a drummer quick, so quick that in fact I only had ten days to learn the songs before we went into the studio. But it was a challenge for me, a totally different style of drumming and the whole atmosphere was different as well. I just felt I could put more into Dio than I could AC/DC, I felt a lot happier about things. It only lasted for about a year (Ronnie Dio in fact disbanded his own group to rejoin Black Sabbath), but there you go... at least I had a go."

In November, 1989, AC/DC were in the middle of rehearsing the new material in an old converted farmhouse just outside Brighton. In need of someone to bash around on the skins for a while, the who'd helped Gary Moore – another of their acts – out in a crisis before. He wasn't offered a permanent position at the outset, but as work on the album progressed he was asked to join. "He jumped at it," says Malcolm.

Slade, with his distinctive bald head, was an odd choice for AC/DC: not only was he of normal human height, he was a journeyman drummer who'd made his name working with a string of top artists, unlike the relative unknowns the Youngs had chosen as replacements in the past. His career can be traced back to 1963 when he left school in South Wales during to move to London with Tommy Scott & The Senators, whose singer would change his name and identity to become the pelvis-twirling underwear magnet Tom Jones. Two years later, after Jones had signed to Decca Records and topped the charts with 'It's Not Unusual', he changed the name of his backing band to The Squires, consolidating his success with an appearance at the New Musical Express poll winners' concert at the Wembley Empire Pool (now known as Wembley Arena), appearing alongside The Beatles, The Rolling Stones and The Animals amongst others.

Jones took to using session men on the records that followed 'It's Not Unusual' but Slade was on hand to watch his extraordinary success from close quarters and it wasn't until early 1969 that he quit Jones's road band to join a fabricated group called Toomorrow whose focal attraction was a toothsome Australian blonde called Olivia Newton-John. Masterminded by US producer Don Kirshner, who also recruited Ben Thomas, Karl Chambers and Vic Cooper for the project, and formed principally to star in a lightweight science fiction musical comedy of the same name, Toomorrow flopped virtually overnight. British audiences weren't about to fall for the kind of instant concoctions that had previously fooled pop fans in the US, and both the movie and soundtrack album became tax-losses for Toomorrow's backers.

Returning to session work, Slade recorded albums with Tony Hazzard ('Loudwater House'), and Tom Paxton ('How Come The Sun'), both in 1971, before joining Manfred Mann's Earth Band in March 1972. He was to spend six years with Mann, recording no fewer than nine albums and achieving three UK Top Ten singles in the process: 'Joybringer' (No.9, October 1973), 'Blinded By The Light' (No.6, September 1976) and 'Davy's On The Road Again'

(No.6, June 1978).

After leaving the Earth Band he recorded two albums in 1979 – 'Falling In Love' with Frankie Miller and 'Crazy Love' with Kai Olsson – before joining Uriah Heep in time to play on their 'Conquest' album in 1980. But things didn't quite work out with Heep so he went back to session work, most noticably with Gary Numan (appearing on the 1982 'I, Assassin' LP) then with the ultimately abortive Mick Ralphs Band (1983) and Pink Floyd guitarist Dave Gilmour's touring band (1984), before joining The Firm, the band formed by Led Zeppelin guru Jimmy Page and ex-Free/Bad Company singer Paul Rodgers at the end of 1984.

The Firm never lived up to the reputations of its individual members, although they did produce two reasonable albums for Atlantic, 'The Firm' in 1985 and 'Mean Business' in 1986. When the group folded, Slade's meandering career eventually took him into Gary Moore's touring band, where he stepped into Cozy Powell's shoes just four days before the start of the 1989 'After The War' tour. It was at one of Moore's gigs that Malcolm saw Slade play, and although he was in LA putting together a band with ex-Aerosmith guitarist Rick Dufay at the time, Chris Slade didn't think too hard before flying back to England when offered the AC/DC drum stool.

"He's just what we needed," said Malcolm, "solid, hard and lots of energy. He fits in great."

After rehearsals in Brighton, AC/DC adjourned to Windmill Road Studios in Ireland with enginner Ian Taylor, to start work on the album proper. Vanda and Young were originally mooted as producers once again, then Young was to join Taylor in Ireland, but in the event the band elected to work with Canadian Bruce Fairbairn who was on a hot streak with Aerosmith and Bon Jovi at the time.

"Mal flew out to Canada to meet him," Angus explained to the author, "and thought he was great – y'know, no superstar bullshit or anything like that. From the start he said to us, 'Look, I don't want to change you – in fact, I'd prefer you to sound more like the old AC/DC than the new one, because the old records were much more raw and simple'. That suited us."

The album – the band's first for the Atco label, after their contract with Atlantic had expired – was completed within six weeks at Little Mountain Studios in Vancouver, the band banging down the tracks more or less live as

usual. Fairbairn worked hard in getting the production balance just right – not too polished, but with noticeable improvements in areas such as backing vocals – and the finished item sounded like their best in years.

Entitled 'The Razor's Edge', it was released on East West Records in the UK in September, and the marketing strategy was the same as 'Blow Up Your Video': precede the album with a blitzkrieg single (this time 'Thunderstruck', like 'Heatseeker' the first track on the new record) and sell the whole thing off the back of another David Mallet directed video featuring hundreds of specially recruited fans headbanging to order. Never change a winning formula they say, and as 'Thunderstruck' hit No.13 in the UK charts few could argue with that reasoning.

The single was a crafty crowd pleaser written specifically as a concert opener. Angus achieved a great 'over-lay' effect with his guitar on the intro – it certainly wasn't done with a synthesized tape loop – and as a chorus of guttural chants built up into a frenzy, it was easy to imagine the outstretched arms of the faithful clapping in time. Although fans of the new British band Thunder might've been particularly amused by it all...

After 'Thunderstruck' came 'Fire Your Guns', a sort of double quick distant relation of 'Whole Lotta Rosie' which pumped you full of lead and then disappeared down some dark alley before you could even reach for your holster. Then 'Moneytalks' shaped up as the most commercial song the band had attempted since 'You Shook Me All Night Long', all melodic guitar chimes and tuneful singalong sensibilities, daubed with as much FM sheen Fairbairn could get away with.

Next there was the epic melodrama of the title track, a real left turn for AC/DC terms and another example of the extent of Fairbairn's input. It was serious stuff, most unlike AC/DC... although 'Mistress For Christmas', with its ludicrous behind-the-bike-sheds innuendo, seemed to confirm that even though Angus and Malcolm had written the lyrics this time, the band hadn't lost any of their renowned smut.

On the whole 'The Razor's Edge' was on par with probably every album since 'For Those...' – some high points, a couple of duff tracks, but overall worth adding to the collection. With 12 tracks, it was the band's longest record to date, and perhaps a bit of loose flesh could have been lost if the usual 10 track format had been repeated. But few fans complained; once more AC/DC had stuck to their guns, not to mention their chords, and produced an album which greeted you like an old friend.

After the album's launch at the School Dinners restaurant just off Baker Street in London's West End (a dubious eaterie where waitresses dress as sexy schoolgirls in stockings and suspenders and discipline 'naughty' customers with whips...), the exhaustive round of press interviews was held at Part Rock's offices in Chelsea. There, clutching the ever present mug of tea, Angus explained the concept behind 'The Razor's Edge'.

"It's thinking about the moment just before a big storm when you look in the sky and see huge black clouds coming over," he squinted mysteriously at the author. "People used to say, 'Here comes the razor's edge', and we thought that fitted in quite well with what's happening in the world at the moment...

"... Not so much in the Middle East with Iraq – that situation just seems like one big soap opera to me... I'm still waiting for Joan Collins to show up in it somewhere! No, we're thinking about the ongoing thing between the Russians and the Yanks. I mean, they've always been at loggerheads, but recently it has died down a bit and everything seems peaceful. But the world's never really been like that, so I guess it's just our way of warning about Armageddon. "Armageddon outta here!"

And so he did, to America, where another mammoth tour lay ahead, and where the band couldn't have received a better welcome. In October the RIAA (Recording Industry Association of America) announced that sales of 'Back In Black' had officially reached the ten million mark – making it the joint highest-selling metal album ever, with Def Leppard's 'Hysteria' – while the November 10 edition of Billboard pronounced ten of the band's albums platinum (1,000,000 sales), with 'Who Made Who' double platinum (2,000,000), and 'Highway To Hell' and 'Dirty Deeds...' triple platinum (3,000,000). 'The Razor's Edge', meanwhile, took AC/DC's total global LP sales past the 60 million mark.

With a whole new stage-show, including huge inflatable models and titanic telescopic cannons, the AC/DC monster was more grotesque than ever. The sheer size of the production proved that money didn't just talk, it bellowed

its benefits from the top of PA stacks... and as if to underline that, Atco splashed out on another ritzy video for the new single... 'Moneytalks'!

Filmed during November at The Spectrum in Philadelphia it had more of a 'live' angle this time, the only gimmick being the Angus 'dollar-bill' trick. Once again it bore the classy stamp of director David Mallet, but for once the impact was lost in Europe, and the single only got as far as No.36 in the UK charts.

Worse news came at the beginning of the New Year, when three teenage fans were crushed to death during a show at the Salt Palace in Salt Lake City on January 18. Completely blameless, the band were nevertheless devastated by the news. It was the first major incident of that kind at a rock concert since 1979, when 11 people had been killed in the crush to get into a Who gig in Cincinnati. Ironically, AC/DC had opened the show that night.

But the show goes on and by March 20 AC/DC were starting their European tour in Helsinki, unveiling the biggest show they'd ever taken on the road. The new single was 'Are You Ready?', and of course it was accompanied by yet another ambitious video, filmed at Bray Studios near Maidenhead in Kent during March and built around a prison set, with the usual hundreds of extras as headbanging convicts, branded with the AC/DC logo shaved into the back of their heads.

Two collections of the band's promo videos were made available for the first time as well: 'Who Made Who', featuring

footage from 1980-1986, and 'Clipped', which included all of the promos from 'Blow Up Your Video' and 'The Razor's Edge'. With 'The Razor's Edge' entering the UK charts at No.4, clocking up over 200,000 sales in the UK alone (it eventually made No.2 in the US and even outsold 'Back In Black' in some territories), no chance to capitalise on the band's popularity was going to be missed.

The British leg of the tour began at Wembley Arena on April 15, and the author caught up with them on their third night at the old venue. It still rates it one of their best shows to date.

A few of the highlights? Chris Slade's drum kit rising through the stage on a hydraulic platform as he counted in 'Thunderstruck' at the very beginning; Angus doing the same at the beginning of 'Highway To Hell', which also featured a monstrous blow-up Angus effigy complete with glowing eyes and forked tail; thousands of fake dollar bills showering down on the audience during 'Moneytalks'; Hell's Bell lowered down over the centre of the arena this time around, with the tolling sound reproduced on tape; Angus disappearing off stage during 'Let There Be Rock', and appearing seconds later on a platform high above the mixing desk in the centre of the arena; another inflatable the size of a pregnant blue whale, and twice as ugly, springing out from behind the backline for 'Whole Lotta Rosie'; and finally, twin tank turrets extending menacingly out over the first few rows for the blasting finish of 'For Those About To Rock...'.

The glitzy spectacle of this show was a million miles away from the AC/DC that arrived in the UK in 1976. At times it

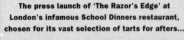

The press launch of 'The Razor's Edge' at London's infamous School Dinners restaurant, chosen for its vast selection of tarts for afters...

'The Razor's Edge' goes gold.

was difficult to believe that Malcolm and Angus would have allowed things to go so far, such was their vehement aversion to razzmatazz in the grotty, snotty Seventies. But if AC/DC were abandoning early principles to the march of rock spectacle, then they made sure most other things stayed the way they always had been: the music, the attitude, the greasy hair, the faded T-shirts, the tatty jeans... and, most frightening of all, the unbridled energy of Angus. At 36 he still broke into a sweat after the first number, still threw himself to the floor in a mock fit, and still ran relentlessly around the set like a First Former – at one point sliding down one of the side ramps on his bare back, the act of a man in a blind frenzy which left a skid mark of sweat on the ramp and a nasty burn on his back.

After Europe AC/DC returned to America in May for the third leg of the world tour, crossing paths with the author again at the beginning of June in Los Angeles. Despite one or two alterations to the presentation necessitated by the outdoor venue – Irvine Meadows in Orange County – the show was pretty much the same as the UK version, and as such just as impressive. Two huge screens above the stage were an added bonus for those furthest away, and Angus's excursions on this occasion took him half way up the steep terracing of the arena, much to the amazement of those standing right next to him!

With support band LA Guns in tow, the 'Razor...' tour blazed on through the summer in America, switching into Monster mode (along with Metallica – or 'Metal Alex' as they became known – Mötley Crüe, Queensrÿche and The Black Crowes) for the start of the longest and furthest reaching European festival circuit since the Monsters Of Rock concept had been conceived: 20 concerts in 18 European cities, finishing at a special free concert on the semi-abandoned Tushino airfield on the ouskirts of Moscow on September 28, incredibly AC/DC's first ever visit to Russia. The schedule itself was fairly flexible, especially as political events in Eastern Europe were creating potentially volatile situations wherever they went. Fortunately, careful negotiation ensured the safest route across the continent, although at the hastily arranged climax in Moscow there were reports of riots, rapes and even a number of fatalities.

When the dust had settled, these reports turned out to have been an exaggeration. Rolling Stone's correspondent, the noted Soviet journalist Artemy Troitsky, saw bleeding fans, security guards clubbing fans and empty glass bottles raining down on police lines. "No-one was killed and about 500,000 people had what they may call fun," reported Troitsky. "But fifty-three people – including sixteen policeman and soldiers – were taken to the hospital. More than 100 were slightly injured and received medical aid on the airfield."

The organisers of the Moscow concert could have learned some lessons from

other European Monsters of Rock promoters, and banned beer and soft drinks in glass bottles, improved security generally and searched fans for offensive weapons at the gates. "Heavy metal is enormously popular in the USSR," wrote Troitsky. "If you count the rock-orientated street graffiti in the USSR, The Beatles and Depeche Mode will probably win but AC/DC will definitely come in third."

The fact that the Moscow show went ahead at all was a tribute to all those involved behind the scenes. There were enormous complications in getting all the equipment from Barcelona to Moscow in the three days that were available (in the end all the gear was air-freighted over in two specially-chartered Russian air-force planes), and worse problems still in how to cater for and control a 500,000 crowd. It made Donington 1991 seem like afternoon tea at the vicarage.

And, appropriately, it's in Moscow that our story ends. As AC/DC flew back to Australia to dance along the razor's edge once again, paying their respects to the birthplace of the whole phenomenon one more time, miles of tape recorded in Russia was being sorted through in preparation for a live album and video due to be released in the first quarter of 1992.

A fitting epitaph or a new introduction to AC/DC? Whatever it turns out to be, it is comforting to know that while even the crusty old face of the Soviet Union is slowly changing as we hurtle towards the 21st Century, the music of AC/DC at least will never change.

Chapter XI

Discography

UK 7" SINGLES

**IT'S A LONG WAY TO THE TOP
(IF YOU WANNA ROCK 'N' ROLL)/
CAN I SIT NEXT TO YOU GIRL?** (4/76)
Atlantic K 10745

JAILBREAK/FLING THING
(8/76 re-issued 3/80)
Atlantic K 10805

HIGH VOLTAGE/LIVE WIRE (10/76)
Atlantic K 10860

**DIRTY DEEDS DONE DIRT CHEAP/
BIG BALLS/THE JACK** (1/77)
Atlantic K 10899

LET THERE BE ROCK/PROBLEM CHILD
(9/77)
Atlantic K 11018

GIRLS GOT RHYTHM/GET IT HOT (11/79)
Atlantic K 11406

**TOUCH TOO MUCH/LIVEWIRE (Live)/
SHOT DOWN IN FLAMES (Live)** (1/80)
Atlantic K 11435

ROCK 'N' ROLL DAMNATION/SIN CITY
(5/78 re-issued 3/80)
Atlantic K 11142

**WHOLE LOTTA ROSIE (Live)/
HELL AIN'T A BAD PLACE TO BE (Live)**
(10/78 re-issued 3/80)
Atlantic K 11207

**TOUCH TOO MUCH/LIVEWIRE (Live)/
SHOT DOWN IN FLAMES (Live)** (1/80)
Atlantic K 11435

HIGH VOLTAGE (Live)/LIVE WIRE (6/80)
Atlantic HM1

**DIRTY DEEDS DONE DIRT CHEAP/
BIG BALLS/THE JACK** (6/80 re-issue)
Atlantic HM2

**IT'S A LONG WAY TO THE TOP
(IF YOU WANNA ROCK 'N' ROLL)/
CAN I SIT NEXT TO YOU GIRL**
(6/80 re-issue)
Atlantic HM3

**WHOLE LOTTA ROSIE (Live)/
HELL AIN'T A BAD PLACE TO BE (Live)**
(6/80 re-issue)
Atlantic HM 4

**YOU SHOOK ME ALL NIGHT LONG/
HAVE A DRINK ON ME** (8/80)
Atlantic K 11600

**ROCK AND ROLL AIN'T NOISE
POLLUTION/HELLS BELLS** (11/80)
Atlantic K 11630

LET'S GET IT UP/BACK IN BLACK (Live)
(1/82)
Atlantic K 11706

**FOR THOSE ABOUT TO ROCK
(WE SALUTE YOU)/
LET THERE BE ROCK (Live)** (4/82)
Atlantic K 11721

GUNS FOR HIRE/LANDSLIDE (10/83)
Atlantic A 9774

**NERVOUS SHAKEDOWN/
ROCK AND ROLL AIN'T NOISE POLLUTION**
(7/84: also issued as shaped picture disc)
Atlantic A 9651

DANGER/BACK IN BUSINESS
(7/85; also issued with poster sleeve and
as shaped picture disc)
Atlantic A 9532

SHAKE YOUR FOUNDATIONS/STAND UP
(1/86; also issued as shaped picture disc)
Atlantic A 9474

WHO MADE WHO/GUNS FOR HIRE (Live)
(5/86; also issued as shaped picture disc)
Atlantic A 9425

**YOU SHOOK ME ALL NIGHT LONG/
SHE'S GOT BALLS (Live)** (8/86; also
issued in gatefold sleeve and picture disc)
Atlantic A 9377

HEAT SEEKER/GO ZONE (12/87)
Atlantic A 9136

**THAT'S THE WAY I WANNA ROCK 'N'
ROLL/KISSIN' DYNAMITE** (3/88)
Atlantic A 9098

THUNDERSTRUCK/FIRE YOUR GUNS
(9/90)
Atlantic B 8907

**MONEY TALKS/
MISTRESS FOR CHRISTMAS** (11/90)
Atco B 8886

**ARE YOU READY/
GOT YOU BY THE BALLS** (4/91; also
available with patch and in satchel pack)
Atco B 8830

UK 7" EPs

**GIRLS GOT RHYTHM/
IF YOU WANT BLOOD, YOU'VE GOT IT/
HELL AIN'T A BAD PLACE TO BE (Live)/
ROCK 'N' ROLL DAMNATION** (11/79)
Atlantic K 11406E

UK CASSETTE
SINGLES

**NERVOUS SHAKEDOWN/
ROCK AND ROLL AIN'T NOISE
POLLUTION (Live)/SIN CITY (Live)/
THIS HOUSE OF FIRE (Live)** (7/84)
Atlantic A 9631C

THUNDERSTRUCK/FIRE YOUR GUNS
(9/90)
ATCO B 8907C

**MONEY TALKS/
MISTRESS FOR CHRISTMAS** (11/90)
ATCO B 8886C

**ARE YOU READY/
GOT YOU BY THE BALLS** (4/91)
ATCO B 8830

UK 10" SINGLES

ROCK 'N' ROLL DAMNATION/SIN CITY
(5/78)
Atlantic K 11142T

**WHOLE LOTTA ROSIE (Live)/HELL AIN'T
A BAD PLACE TO BE (Live)** (10/78)
Atlantic K 11207T

**ROCK AND ROLL AIN'T NOISE
POLLUTION/ HELLS BELLS** (11/80)
Atlantic K 11630T

**LET'S GET IT UP/TNT (Live)/
BACK IN BLACK (Live)** (1/82)
Atlantic K 11706T

**FOR THOSE ABOUT TO ROCK
(WE SALUTE YOU)/LET THERE BE ROCK
(Extended Live)** (4/82)
Atlantic K 11721T

**NERVOUS SHAKEDOWN/
ROCK AND ROLL AIN'T NOISE POLLUTION
(Live)/ SIN CITY (Live)/
THIS HOUSE IS ON FIRE (Live)** (7/84)
Atlantic A 9651T

DANGER/BACK IN BUSINESS (7/85)
Atlantic A 9532T

**SHAKE YOUR FOUNDATIONS/
STAND UP/JAILBREAK (Live)** (1/86)
Atlantic A 9474T

WHO MADE WHO/GUNS FOR HIRE (Live)
(5/86; also available with cut-out
poster sleeve)
Atlantic A 9425T

**YOU SHOOK ME ALL NIGHT LONG/
SHE'S GOT BALLS (Extended Live)/
YOU SHOOK ME ALL NIGHT LONG (Live)**
(8/86)
Atlantic A 9377T

HEAT SEEKER/GO ZONE/SNAKE HIGH
(12/87; gatefold sleeve)
Atlantic A 9136T

**THAT'S THE WAY I WANNA
ROCK 'N' ROLL/KISSIN' DYNAMITE**
(3/88; also available as picture disc)
Atlantic A 9098T

**THUNDERSTRUCK/FIRE YOUR GUNS/
DT/CHASE THE ACE** (9/90)
ATCO B 8907T

**MONEY TALKS/MISTRESS FOR
CHRISTMAS/BORROWED TIME**
(11/90; also available as picture disc and
with poster sleeve)
ATCO B 8886T

**ARE YOU READY/GOT YOU BY THE
BALLS/RAZORS EDGE** (4/91)
ATCO B 8830T

UK CD SINGLES

**THAT'S THE WAY I WANNA
ROCK 'N' ROLL/KISSIN DYNAMITE/
SHOOT TO THRILL (Live)/WHOLE LOTTA
ROSIE (Live)** (3/88)
Atlantic A 9098 CD

**THUNDERSTRUCK /FIRE YOUR GUNS/
DT/CHASE THE ACE** (9/90)
Atlantic B 8907 CD

**MONEY TALKS/MISTRESS FOR
CHRISTMAS/BORROWED TIME** (11/90)
ATCO B 8886 CD

**ARE YOU READY/GOT YOU BY THE
BALLS/THE RAZORS EDGE** (4/91)
ATCO B 8830 CD

UK LPs

HIGH VOLTAGE (5/76)
Atlantic K 50257

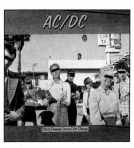

DIRTY DEEDS DONE DIRT CHEAP (12/76)
Atlantic K 50323

LET THERE BE ROCK (12/77)
Atlantic K 50366

POWERAGE (4/78)
Atlantic K 50483

IF YOU WANT BLOOD, YOU'VE GOT IT
(10/78)
Atlantic K 50532

HIGHWAY TO HELL (7/79)
Atlantic K 50628

BACK IN BLACK (7/80)
Atlantic K 50735

**FOR THOSE ABOUT TO ROCK
(WE SALUTE YOU)** (11/81)
Atlantic K 50851

FLICK OF THE SWITCH (8/83)
Atlantic 780 100 1

FLY ON THE WALL (7/85)
Atlantic 781 263 1

**WHO MADE WHO
(ORIGINAL SOUNDTRACK)** (5/86)
Atlantic WX 57

BOX SET 1 (9/87, six LPs plus 12" single)
Atlantic AC/DC 1

BOX SET 2 (11/87, five LPs plus poster)
Atlantic AC/DC 2

BLOW UP YOUR VIDEO (2/88)
Atlantic WX 144

THE RAZORS EDGE (9/90)
ATCO WX 364

AUSTRALIAN-ONLY LPs

HIGH VOLTAGE (1974)
Albert APLP 009

TNT (1975)
Albert APLP 016

DIRTY DEEDS DONE DIRT CHEAP (9/76)
Albert APLP020 EMI

**BOOGIE, BALLS & BLUES VOL 1:
OZ HARD ROCK OF THE 70s**
(1987; includes Australian-only single,
"Baby Please Don't Go", and 1977 live
recording of "Dirty Deeds Done Dirt Cheap")
Raven RVLP 30

BON SCOTT PRE AC/DC RECORDINGS: UK RELEASES

**BON SCOTT WITH THE VALENTINES:
THE EARLY YEARS**
(1988, issued on CD in 1991; includes
nine tracks by The Valentines, comprising
four singles plus previously unreleased
"Sooky Sooky")
C5 C5 520

BON SCOTT: THE EARLY YEARS 1967-72
(1988; includes 15 cuts by The Valentines,
plus seven by Fraternity and Bon Scott
interview)
See for Miles CD 247

AC/DC BOOTLEGS

LIVE '76 Men At Work/5512.2
CD

ELECTRIC SHOCK WL-9
Double LP, recorded in London 1/76 and
3/77, plus Rockville, Md. 10/79

LIVE '76
Recorded in London & Reading, plus Marc
Bolan TV show 28/8/75

PAVILLION Great Dane 9116
CD, recorded in Paris 1976

LIVE AT CLEVELAND AGORE '77
Observation 001
CD

LIVE '77 Men At Work 5013
CD, recorded in London, Offenbach,
Newcastle & San Francisco

LIVE FROM THE ATLANTIC STUDIOS
Recorded at Atlantic Studios, New York
7/12/77

110/220 Impossible Recordworks 1-31
Recorded at Atlantic Studios, New York
7/12/77

LIVE '78 Men At Work 4515
CD, recorded in Boston, Nijmegan &
Glasgow

AGAINST THE CURRENT
CD, recorded 10/9/78 Veterans Memorial
Auditorium, Columbus, Ohio

ELECTRO SHOCK THERAPY Pyramid 066
CD, recorded in Holland '78 and
America '79

FROM DOWN UNDER Metal Memory 9001
CD, recorded at Hammersmith Odeon 9/79

SHOT DOWN IN FLAMES Stoned Records
Recorded Hammersmith Odeon, 1979

LIVE '79 Men At Work 5515
CD, recorded in Paris 9/12/78 & Twoson,
Md. 16/10/79

LIVING IN THE HELL Flashback 152
CD, recorded Twoson, Md. 16/10/79

TROPICAL PRISON Men At Work 5516.2
CD, Hammersmith Odeon 1979

BON'S LAST OUI OUI Drivile Records
DCP600 Recorded in Paris 12/9/79

HIGHWAY TO HELL Iron Cock Records
CD, recorded in 1979

B.S. WE LOVE YOU Oh Boy 2-9094
Double CD, recorded in 1976-80

BAD BOY BOOGIE Discurious 104
CD

BON PLEASE DON'T GO
Golden Stars 1003
CD, recorded Newcastle 1980

BACK IN BLACK TOUR '80
Raven Records 010
CD, recorded in Brussels

MONSTERS OF ROCK VOL. 1
Buy Or Die 210
CD, recorded 1981

MONSTERS OF ROCK VOL. 2
Buy Or Die 211
CD, recorded 1981

ON THE HIGHWAY TO LA
Raven Records 010
CD, recorded at LA Forum in 2/82

LIVE IN THE USA Good Karma
CD, recorded 1983

THUNDERSTRUCK PART 1
Raven Records 011
CD, recorded in Charlotte 16/2/91

THUNDERSTRUCK PART 2
Raven Records 012
CD, as above

DIRTY DEEDS AT IRVINE MEADOWS
Not Guilty 10891
CD, recorded in LA 8/6/91

FIRE YOUR GUNS Deep Records 003
Double CD, recorded in Detroit 1991

ONLY THE STRONG SURVIVE
MGR 2051/52 Double CD, recorded in
Basel, Switzerland, 25/8/91